THE LAND OF COTTON

The Land of Cotton

Culture, Landscape, and the Fabric of Southern History

James C. Giesen

THE UNIVERSITY OF GEORGIA PRESS

ATHENS

Athens, Georgia 30602
www.ugapress.org

Set in Sans and Arno Pro by Westchester Publishing Services

Printed digitally

EU Authorized Representative
Easy Access System Europe—Mustamäe tee 50, 10621 Tallinn, Estonia,
gpsr.requests@easproject.com

Library of Congress Cataloging-in-Publication Data
Names: Giesen, James C. author
Title: The land of cotton : culture, landscape, and the fabric of Southern history / James C. Giesen.
Other titles: Environmental history and the American South
Description: Athens : The University of Georgia Press, 2026. | Series: Environmental history and the American South | Includes bibliographical references and index.
Identifiers: LCCN 2026009850 | ISBN 9780820377582 paperback | ISBN 9780820377575 hardback | ISBN 9780820377599 epub | ISBN 9780820377605 pdf
Subjects: LCSH: Cotton growing—Southern States—History | Cotton growing—South Carolina—Piedmont—History | Cotton growing—Mississippi—Delta (Region)—History | Cotton growing—Environmental aspects—Southern States | Cotton growing—Social aspects—Southern States | Cotton growing—Economic aspects—Southern States | Cotton growing—Political aspects—Southern States | Collective memory—Southern States
Classification: LCC HD9077.S9 G54 2026 | DDC 338.1/73510975--dc23/eng/20260422
LC record available at https://lccn.loc.gov/2026009850

CONTENTS

ILLUSTRATIONS

Figures

Maps

Table

FOREWORD

We might imagine there is little new to be said about cotton. Thousands of books and articles expound on the subject. It seems that cotton is not so much a crop as a gravitational force, drawing every story back to that pale, tufted fiber.

Yet *The Land of Cotton* proves that we still have more to learn. In this deeply researched and genuinely enjoyable book, James C. Giesen argues that the interplay between the ideological construction of cotton and the environmental context of the plant's production shaped policy, identity, and memory across the South for more than a century and a half. Taking readers from eroded hillsides and lavish parades to crumbling Big Houses and quiet museums, this book shows how Southerners projected competing beliefs onto cotton, meanings that often belied or outlived material realities. "The land of cotton" was a place as much imagined as it was cultivated.

Giesen takes us to two legendary Southern locations: Rose Hill Plantation in Union County, South Carolina, and the Yazoo-Mississippi Delta and its de facto capital, Memphis, Tennessee. He shows us how the stories Southerners told about cotton helped obscure the real problems of the region and its physical landscape—those caused by political divisions, strained race relations, or severe soil erosion—while elsewhere, the environmental demands of the crop's production pushed back against those same efforts.

At Rose Hill in South Carolina's Piedmont, Governor William Henry Gist imagined a future where cotton would bind the region into a single, sovereign identity. But this vision, rooted in the domination of enslaved people as well as ecological denial, was undone by the very land he misread and the people he misjudged. After emancipation, African Americans built new political and economic lives but in soils worn thin by monoculture, geology, and time. Erosion carved deep gullies into the hills, and the environmental cost of cotton became impossible to ignore. In the twentieth century, as pine forests reclaimed the fields, cotton's physical presence vanished, but its mythology was reborn. Rose Hill became a monument to a curated memory, one that celebrated Confederate ideals and ignored the scars left behind.

Farther west, in the Yazoo-Mississippi Delta, cotton's story unfolded on a grander, more industrial scale. The Delta's rich, tangled ecosystem was flattened into a grid of fields, and nearby Memphis became King Cotton's capital. As economic uncertainty set in during the early twentieth century, white elites staged the Cotton Carnival to transform city streets into a plantation fantasy. African Americans, excluded from this spectacle, responded with their own celebration, the Cotton Makers' Jubilee, asserting their place in the region's cultural and economic life. Even as these parallel festivals celebrated cotton's material power, the nature of the crop's production was shifting. Machines replaced hands, and thousands of African Americans left the region. In their absence, white Mississippians reimagined the Delta as a tourist destination, selling blues music and retrofitted sharecropper cabins to visitors seeking communion with a romanticized past.

The Land of Cotton not only offers a fresh perspective on Southern identity but also makes a compelling claim that cultural meaning cannot be separated from its physical context—its environment, its place. In many ways, this work builds on Giesen's award-winning first book, *Boll Weevil Blues* (University of Chicago Press, 2011), which demonstrated that it was the symbolic power of the boll weevil and the contested meanings surrounding it—rather than its physical destruction—that profoundly reshaped the early twentieth-century South. *The Land of Cotton* continues to challenge environmental and Southern historians alike to move beyond the binary frameworks that treat nature and human activity as separate or oppositional. Natural change is often culturally mediated.

Giesen's conclusions will resonate with anyone who has lived in, traveled through, or studied the South, especially those still reckoning with the legacies of its past. For me, that reckoning is personal. Reading *The Land of Cotton* helped me better understand the forces shaping my own Tennessee hometown, a place built on tobacco. Drive the road to my childhood home and you'll pass the spectral traces of nineteenth-century tobacco kings' plantations tucked among modern subdivisions. Shop the main street and you can buy candles to evoke the scent of smoking tobacco barns. Ask anyone, and they'll tell you it's a tobacco town, even if all the growers are gone.

So, to me, Giesen's work is a reminder that landscapes carry stories, even when the crops are gone, and that memory, like soil, is always shifting beneath our feet.

Erin Stewart Mauldin
Coeditor, Environmental History and the American South

THE LAND OF COTTON

Introduction

ON TOUR IN 1972, Elvis Presley started performing three folk songs pushed together into one odd medley he called "An American Trilogy." The Mississippian's signature croon opened the number, resonating loudly over faint acoustic guitar and rising percussion.

> Oh, I wish I was in the land of cotton
> Old times there are not forgotten.

It was the opening stanza from "Dixie," which, long before Elvis brought it back, had been probably the most famous song in the United States. Written by an Ohioan sitting in a hotel in New York City in 1859, and first played in antebellum Southern minstrel shows, it is not an exaggeration to say that it was sung for a century by nearly every white Southerner, whether at a political rally, a football game, or a school assembly.

Elvis slow-rolled those opening lines, but the band built a crescendo of syrupy strings and piano behind him, as Presley promised to "take my stand, to live and die in Dixie." His backup singers repeated the lines and Presley joined them.

> For Dixie Land, that's where I was born
> Early, Lord, one frosty morn
> Look away, look away, look away Dixie Land.[1]

That opening line, a wistful lament on being outside the South, defines the region by the plant that made the place particular: *the land of cotton*. The lyric gets right to the heart of the issues of cotton, culture, and landscape that form the core of this book. The land of cotton was both a literal place and a figurative one, where narratives about the plant and the realms it inhabited were mutually dependent and, as Elvis reminds us, never forgotten.

That mutual dependence—between cotton's material reality and the stories told about it—can be found all over the cultural and agricultural landscapes of the American South. Just as Elvis used "Dixie" and cotton to evoke a time and a place for his audience, Southerners had long let cotton fields and fibers evoke powerful ideas.

When I began teaching at Mississippi's land grant university in 2006, I wasn't listening to much Elvis, but I was surrounded by the cultural afterlives of cotton. One of the first things I noticed was that hundreds of students wore T-shirts emblazoned with the Seal of Cotton, Cotton Incorporated's official logo. (See figure 1.) I recognized the icon because it was on the tag of my towels, but I also knew it as the visual for a decades-old "Fabric of Our Lives" ad campaign. The shirts came in a seemingly endless combination of colors, mixes like maroon and white meant to evoke the school's sports jerseys, or the green and yellow of a John Deere tractor. No matter the combination, each had the stylized blooming cotton boll image front and center.

The shirts were so popular that I began keeping a rough count. One semester in 2014, during my three-hundred-student U.S. history survey course, I recorded more than 150 appearances of the Seal of Cotton, whether on T-shirts or hats. That's an average of five cotton logos per lecture. Outside the classroom, the pattern continued. A walk through campus parking lots revealed the same icon on front license plates and bumper stickers, plastered across hundreds of student and staff vehicles.[2]

This book began with a question: Why were so many people—college students and thousands of others around Mississippi and the South—proudly displaying a modern, stylized image of a cotton boll on their bodies? I was suspicious. Cotton, after all, was a central factor in human suffering and environmental degradation in the very region where our university sat. How could it now be a symbol of pride? Was the T-shirt, like "Dixie," meant to evoke nostalgia for an era when King Cotton ruled Mississippi? Or was the logo a proxy for something else, a Confederate flag by another name, sanitized for the twenty-first century?

There were plenty of incidents of racial intimidation that involved cotton. In 2010, for instance, two white University of Missouri students were arrested after littering cotton balls outside the Black Cultural Center on campus during Black History Month. It was common throughout the early 2000s to see small stands of cotton growing in the yards of all-white fraternities at the

FIG. 1. License plates like this bug-splattered example appeared on thousands of trucks and cars around the South, especially in the early 2000s. This image is used for scholarly purposes, with no implication of endorsement by or affiliation with Cotton Incorporated. Photo by James C. Giesen, 2025.

University of Georgia. There could be no doubt that cotton, in some cases, was serving as a message of racist cultural power.[3]

But was that the case for the people on my campus? The logo itself was part of the National Cotton Council's marketing of the plant as a soft and cuddly fiber that people touched every day. It was entirely possible that my students were just embracing that version of cotton as consumers. Alternatively, maybe they were farmers. Many of those enrolled in my class were from rural parts of the South, and perhaps they were simply proud of their local industry or celebrating the labor that their families had done to produce the crop.

I also knew of black celebrations of the plant. Julius Tillery, a fifth-generation cotton farmer in North Carolina with an economics degree from Chapel Hill, ran Black Cotton, a company that sold ornamental plants and had a large social media presence that detailed his work as a farmer. Rather than associate it with the historical pain of his community, Tillery "wanted to give cotton a different value." Not only did he sell cotton-centric jewelry, art, and home decor via mail order, in 2022 he made a deal with international shoe and clothing brand Vans to market a "Black Acres Cotton Stalk T-shirt," which presented the crop in a very different way than my students' Cotton Incorporated shirts. The Vans shirt showed a drawing of a white cotton plant against black fabric woven from the plants on his farm. Hidden in the image of the plant's stalk are the words "Cotton is our culture."[4] These examples uncovered what I thought was a complicated set of questions about the meaning of the commodity.

The crop's cultural significance could be found in lots of places beyond T-shirts. Sites across the South, like museums and restored plantations, offered celebrations of the plant. Markers in a mill village or at the birthplace of a famous musician or writer told brief cotton stories. In addition to print and television ads, the plant was all over the virtual landscape. Internet and magazine fashion spreads showed models in fancy dresses standing in cotton fields holding baskets of bolls. Instagram feeds served up wedding photos taken amid blooming cotton plants at harvest time and images of newborns lying in piles of freshly picked bolls.

There were less obvious locations for cotton's cultural legacy as well. As a historian of the South's environmental and agricultural past—and as someone who has spent most of his life in cotton-producing states—I learned to see traces of the crop in places that most passersby might overlook. Rusted gins at rural crossroads, old cotton mills repurposed as lofts or offices, and eroded fields now shaded by pine forests all marked landscapes shaped by cotton, even if they were never preserved or interpreted as historic sites. The crop persisted in symbolic form in all of these places, on bodies, in media, and across the built environment. But while cotton's cultural presence was thriving, its actual footprint in Southern agriculture had shrunk. The white fiber's status on the street—and online—had grown wildly disproportionate to its role on the farm.

As Seal of Cotton license plates and T-shirts had become more and more popular in Southern society, fewer and fewer farmers were planting the crop in Southern soil. In 2008, about the time I first noticed the branding phenomena, there were only 845 cotton farms left in Mississippi, on which growers managed the second-smallest cotton crop in the state since 1875. (Nationwide, cotton acreage for 2009 was the lowest *ever* recorded to that point.) That year, farmers in the Magnolia State made more money from eight different individual crops than cotton, and not just corn, cattle, and catfish. *Hay* meant more to the agricultural economy that year than the crop that thousands of people were celebrating on their clothes and social media feeds.[5] By the early 2010s, throughout the entire South, King Cotton had long since given up its crown, yet there were no soybean T-shirts or hay license plates. This agricultural reality made it clear that, perhaps ironically or perhaps intentionally, contemporary stories about cotton were about something other than contemporary cotton.

The popularity of Seal of Cotton T-shirts—set against the steep decline in the number of people who actually farmed cotton—revealed a deeper tension between landscape, culture, and history. Cotton's meanings seemed far from settled. Some Southerners saw the fiber as an emblem of racism and exploitation; others embraced it as a symbol of heritage, identity, or nostalgia. Explaining how and why cotton came to embody such different and powerful meanings, how those meanings shifted over time, and how they shaped and were shaped by the region's environmental landscapes is the task of *The Land of Cotton*.

THIS BOOK IS ABOUT fields of white cotton that stretched out in arrow-straight rows all the way to the horizon, and what those fields meant to the people who lived in and around them. It is also about blood-red erosion gullies carved across the face of a hillside that used to be a cotton farm, and what those scars on the land meant to the people who helped make them and to those who marveled at them. It is also about parade floats, pulled by African American men, that carried white Carnival queens through urban streets lined with segregated crowds. Readers will encounter cotton ideologies bound to white supremacy, black pride, and nostalgic agrarianism, belief systems that Southerners both took from and projected onto landscapes, parades, and television ads. Together, this book is about how cotton changed the South, how Southerners fought over its meaning in agricultural and ideological ways, and what the Sturm und Drang of these battles meant for the people of the region and the land on which they lived.

The Land of Cotton argues that the plant's power in the American South was never purely agricultural, economic, or symbolic. Cotton was all of these and more. It was a material force that shaped landscapes and labor systems, and a cultural symbol whose meanings shifted to meet the needs of different times and communities. By tracing cotton's presence and absence—in fields, in factories, in memories, and in myths—this book shows how agriculture and culture intertwined to create, mask, and reimagine Southern identities. Understanding cotton's evolving role reveals how environmental change, historical memory, and political ideology worked together to shape the South's past—and continues to influence how the region understands itself today.

The ten chapters that follow travel over 150 years to chart the dueling influences of landscape and culture. My goal was not to uncover every artifact of cotton or to discuss every place where it is has been grown. I aim instead to highlight places and moments when landscape and culture connected in ways historians and Southerners in general have not always appreciated. Instead of trying to trace the seemingly endless expressions of the plant in American and Southern culture, I ground these often-ethereal concepts in two specific places over long periods of time. Place mattered to cotton's story. The local details of geology, weather, topography, slavery regimes, laws and customs, political power, constraints on human freedom, and the aesthetics of built and natural spaces all dictated how cotton's ideologies played out. Rooting this history in these places is the best way to understand the relationship of the plant and culture in a way that makes sense (and in a book that ends).

Part 1 of *The Land of Cotton* focuses on Rose Hill Plantation in Union County, South Carolina, from the eve of the Civil War to the twenty-first century. It follows its first owner, the state's secessionist governor William Henry Gist, as he and his fire-eating colleagues pushed the idea that the diverse environments of the South could be united under the banner of "the Cotton States," and he endorsed the notion that white Southerners were powerless subjects of "King Cotton." These political arguments were aimed at protecting the institution of slavery and were based on his conception of the South's agricultural productivity. A bedrock of his thinking was that the work of enslaved people could make cotton bloom almost anywhere and in perpetuity. Not only did this prove to be a horrifying human, political, and social mistake, it was a profound environmental miscalculation. He understood the future of the South in cotton's terms. What he did not understand was the degree to which enslaved laborers, working in the material conditions of the surprisingly diversified operations of his Piedmont plantation, used many natural, agricultural, and social tools to carve out lives within the system of bondage.

The years after the Civil War reveal the degree to which the work of the enslaved had been keeping Gist's cotton operation going. Newly freed African Americans quickly built structures of political power in Upstate South Carolina. Laboring as tenants on former cotton plantations was one way they attempted to protect their freedom. However, geology, and an international appetite for more and more cotton, quickly hastened soil erosion and gullying. The results were devastating for black farmers in Union County and for the hillside farms themselves. An influential white writer who visited Rose Hill in the 1930s ignored these environmental factors and crafted a backward-looking narrative about cotton and race. He blamed the crumbling mansion and the farmland's terrible condition on African Americans and emancipation itself, failing to grasp the roles of geology and market forces.

In the middle of the twentieth century, however, cotton's landscape and culture around Rose Hill again changed radically. As pine forests covered the old gullies, the ideology of cotton—the plant itself long gone from Rose Hill and the surrounding area—found a rebirth. When local white developers rebuilt Gist's former plantation, they were guided by Confederate nostalgia and contemporary politics rather than any compulsion to tell an accurate story about slavery or erosion. The mansion became a tourist site and later a state park that celebrated Governor Gist and the plant that he mistakenly believed held the South together. Twenty-first-century battles of historical memory have again changed and been influenced by the landscape of the modern Piedmont.

After a bridge that allows for some grand-scale comparisons between different parts of the cotton South, part 2 of this book moves west and back in time, to the Yazoo-Mississippi Delta and its de facto capital of Memphis, Tennessee. The remaking of the Delta in the years after the Civil War—from a rich, biodiverse subtropical landscape of cane, mud, and bears, to a flat, nearly treeless industrialized cotton dystopia—not only had a profound effect on the people of the alluvial region, it gave Memphis its economic livelihood. When the Great Depression threatened that connection, powerful white Memphians organized a weeklong cotton celebration, the Cotton Carnival. Every summer for nearly fifty years, parades wound through city streets that had been remade to look like a cotton plantation, with stacked bales of the fleece on corners and an archway of cotton bales spanning a downtown avenue. African American business and cultural leaders resented the segregated event, which intentionally diminished the black role in the agricultural and industrial life of the crop. Rather than distance themselves from cotton's racist rhetoric, however, African Americans organized their own cotton-centric celebration, the Cotton Makers' Jubilee. Both events ran in parallel for decades, and played out the social, racial, and political divisions in terms of the crop that both events put on a very public pedestal.

While Memphians tried to hold onto the plant's cachet, down in the Delta the material reality of cotton farming changed radically in only a few decades.

Technology and the civil rights movement altered the relationship between landowners, labor, and the crop itself. Machines began performing the work done for generations by human hands. This new landscape—with more cotton per acre yet with far fewer people—had tangible effects on the culture of white and black Mississippians. Thousands of African Americans in Mississippi found they were no longer needed to work the rows, and many no longer sought to be part of cotton's new economy or its cultural celebrations. Thousands left their houses amid the fields and the tiny towns that once thrived with gins and plantation stores.

This new landscape, with more machines and fewer people, worked like the pine trees covering the gullies of South Carolina. It changed the role of cotton in Delta culture. Industry leaders launched a marketing campaign specifically designed to separate the fiber from its sordid past, a rebranding effort that was now much easier thanks to mechanization. At the same time, white Mississippians made efforts to attract tourists to cotton's landscapes, selling the Delta as a blues mecca where one could commune with the places the music was born. In the late twentieth century, visitors from across the world flocked to the cotton fields, staying in sharecropper cabins retrofitted with electricity, air-conditioning, and Wi-Fi. Many visited Cottonlandia, part theme park, part living history museum with African Americans "playing" enslaved farmers tending a patch of cotton.[6]

The juxtaposition of the book's two parts—the Piedmont and the Delta—reveals how specific material realities of the land shaped cotton's culture and cultivation. Environmental differences helped determine not just how cotton was grown but how it was mythologized and remembered. As those landscapes changed—abandoned fields giving way to forests, machines doing the work of men and women—new cultural uses for cotton emerged. Yet even as these changes on the land occurred, the cultural meaning of cotton often obscured those same material transformations. Shaped by the reciprocal forces of environment and culture, Southern people created—both on the ground and in their imaginations—a land of cotton.

ONE GOAL OF THIS BOOK is to use cotton's history in these two places to reposition how we understand the relationship between culture and landscape. That may seem like a grand ambition, but it stands on the shoulders of decades of work in Southern, environmental, and agricultural history—fields that have explored aspects of this relationship from different angles. In terms of cotton itself, historians of capitalism, slavery, and the South have written excellent books that mostly concentrate on the crop as an economic or agricultural force. They have traced cotton's role in shaping global capitalism, American expansion, and the lives of enslaved and free people; they have deepened our understanding of labor, production, markets, and state power.[7] Few books, however, have examined cotton's place in culture, beyond occasional references folded into broader accounts of Southern identity.[8] In both cases, these books often lack a sense of the physical world of the plant, and the soil, labor, and technology that made cotton possible.[9]

The field that has been most interested in—or perhaps obsessed with—the interaction of nature and culture is environmental history. Its early focus on the American West and wilderness, however, made agriculture a poor fit. In the mid-1990s, environmental historians pivoted away from what separated humans and the natural world toward what entangled them. The concept of hybridity—most clearly explained and critiqued by Paul S. Sutter—emerged as a way to understand how nature and culture were intertwined, and it gave agriculture a clearer place within environmental history.[10]

Nowhere did the early wilderness framing of environmental history fit less comfortably than in the American South. The region's landscapes have long been shaped by intensive labor, racial hierarchy, and agricultural extraction, topics that Southern historians had covered with interest for more than a century before environmental historians turned up. Too often, however, this older scholarship treated the environment as either deterministic or a canvas that humans drew their history upon. Since the early 2000s, there has been an explosion of work on Southern environments by scholars who have done a great deal to expand our understanding of the region as a whole. Many put farming at the center of the South's environmental history. From lowcountry rice fields to upland cotton farms to coastal pine forests, these authors demonstrated how the natural world, human labor, ecological knowledge, and racial power operated together. In doing so, they helped make the South a site of innovation in environmental history and expanded the field's scope beyond wild places. Yet even in this region—perhaps especially here—the cultural meanings people made from their environments remain only partially explored.[11]

Yet another historiographical turn has emerged to position culture more firmly in the physical world. New Materialism, a newish theory best articulated by Timothy LeCain, argues that scholars have too severely separated the ideas, meanings, and imaginations that form human culture from the ecological, microbial, corporeal world where humans actually live. LeCain sees the material environment not only as a limiting force but also as a creative one "that sparks and nurtures human (and nonhuman) thoughts, beliefs, cultures, and actions."[12] Phenomena as seemingly ethereal as justice and freedom, "the very things that have made us human," should be understood as "products of the material things we partner with," LeCain argues.[13]

In a provocative *Agricultural History* roundtable about New Materialism's implications, several scholars offer caution about the field's framing. One skeptic is the Southern environmental historian Mark D. Hersey, who presents New Materialism as old wine in new casks. Arguing that environmental historians made *basically* the same argument decades ago, he writes, "Materialists old and new will warn against the dangers of cultural determinism (which are no less real than those of environmental determinism) and agree that the best environmental history (and agricultural history) melds the ideal and the material, even if it denies the separateness of the categories."[14] At the end of the day, Hersey convincingly argues, theoretical pontification about the connections and disconnections of culture, nature, and humans means less than how historians actually craft and tell histories of change over time. It's about the storytelling. Analytical and convincing histories are hard to write even with concrete categories. "The difficulties of narrating stories elide distinctions between nature and culture. It is much easier to reject their separateness as a philosophical proposition than it is to narrate a way that avoids recapitulating those ontological categories in one way or another."[15]

The Land of Cotton takes on this challenge. There is plenty of New Materialism in this book, as well as agricultural, environmental, and regional approaches. But, to paraphrase Hersey, the devil is in the narrative. What follows is a history of cotton in two places that demonstrates the deep entanglement and reciprocal influence of its culture and material conditions. It demonstrates how the very physical properties of cotton and the ecological context in which it grew—or where it was no longer farmed at all—shaped what people thought was possible, desirable, or even imaginable. In turn, it reveals how ideas about cotton, identity, race, and politics had tangible effects on the hills, fields, and forests of the South. My hope is that it offers not just a new perspective on the region's signature crop but a new way of thinking about how culture and landscape coproduce meaning in history.

PART ONE

Rose Hill Plantation and the South Carolina Piedmont

CHAPTER ONE

King Making

ON THE EVE OF THE Civil War, Rose Hill Plantation in Union County, South Carolina, was the literal seat of political and agricultural power in the southern Piedmont. From a small wooden desk in a second-floor study in 1860, a month before the presidential election, the plantation's owner, Governor William Henry Gist, wrote a letter to his fellow Southern governors that put secession into motion. The setting and the power of his message—that South Carolina would leave the Union if Republican Abraham Lincoln was elected president—were inextricably linked.

Writing at that second-floor desk gave him a view overlooking the fields spread out to the east of his house. He could likely see from that window enslaved African American women and men at work alongside horses, mules, and oxen; outside of his view were acres and acres of corn, oats, wheat, sweet potatoes, and Irish potatoes. There were pigs roaming the woods, sheep looking for fresh grass. Gist knew that enslaved people might at that moment be milking cows, churning butter, or cooking his supper. From his privileged vantage point, the fifty-three-year-old planter could, of course, also see acres of waist-high cotton plants, bolls full, nearly ready to open.

How Gist understood the scene out his window undergirded his ideas about political power, the fortunes of an independent Southern nation, slavery, white supremacy, humans' dominion over the natural world, and international affairs. Along with a few dozen other white, wealthy planters and politicians, Gist had put into motion an idea about cotton—the linchpin of the Southern economy, the so-called King of the South—that led thirteen states and nine million Southern people to the brink of war. These political leaders imbued the flowering white crop with so much power that it sat at the heart of their pleas for secession. But while this rhetoric was critical to the region's political march toward nationhood, it vastly overstated both cotton's role in the economy and its material place in the fields of the South. Crucially to their cause and fate, these leaders' cotton ideology also underplayed the role of 3.5 million enslaved people who were keeping the region's agro-environment productive.

Gist's letter and its replies attest to the place of the crop at the heart of leaders' ideas about a Southern nation. He reached out to his fellow governors to make it clear exactly where South Carolina stood on the question of a new president. Sectional debates had roiled the United States for decades, and Gist was prepared to draw the Palmetto State's line in the soil. Though Lincoln and his party had not campaigned to end slavery, they opposed the extension of the institution into western territories. Southern slaveholders, however, were bent on expanding the cotton-and-slave system into new regions. Gist and his cohort understood that if Americans voted to put the young Republican from Illinois in the White House, it was a direct threat to Southerners' right to own slaves. Should Lincoln win, Gist promised his fellow governors that South Carolina would lead the South's secession. At his Rose Hill desk, he sealed the confidential letters and gave them to his tellingly named nephew, States Rights Gist, to deliver to capitals across the South.

Cotton sat at the center of Gist's letter and the replies he received. It was the "almost certainty" of Lincoln's election, Gist wrote, that impelled him to reach out to the leaders of "Southern, and more especially the Cotton States," so that their actions following Lincoln's inauguration might be in "concert." Florida Governor Madison S. Perry, a cotton planter himself, replied promising that his state was "ready to wheel into line with the gallant Palmetto State, or any other Cotton State . . . looking to the vindication and maintenance of the rights, interest, honor, and safety of the South." Perry promised Florida would follow any "Cotton State which may secede." The governor of North Carolina, who had become a lawyer after growing up on a cotton plantation, worried about "a fatal blow to the institution of negro slavery" if Lincoln was elected. The Louisiana executive—owner of three cotton plantations—was more apprehensive about secession, citing what he saw as a rift between Southerners in cotton states who were more dependent on slaves and those living in border states. While the threat to slavery was the foundation of Gist's letter and the replies, the governors' consistent identification as planters and evocation of the "Cotton States" moniker reveals their understanding of both the Republican menace and the promise of a Confederate nation.[1]

That moment, when Gist looked over his bustling farm and wrote this message about secession, embodies a telling disconnect between the attempt to unify Southern interests under the "Cotton States" banner and the environmental reality of the South. It is an understatement to say that in 1860, the agro-ecological worlds of each of the Southern states were quite different, not to mention the social, cultural, and political traditions, ideologies, and mores in each place. This chapter explains the rise of the Cotton States rhetoric and juxtaposes it with a picture of the South's agricultural reality. The dissonance between elites' *ideas* about the Southern environment and its reality in dirt and wind and humanity had life-and-death repercussions.

GIST'S UNDERSTANDING of the Southern landscape's productivity, and the ability of slave labor to maintain it, was based on a long environmental and human history. In the years before upland cotton arrived in the South Carolina Piedmont, it was a frontier land of scattered indigenous tribes, self-sustaining white farmers, and isolation. As Timothy Silver details, from 1500 to 1800, white settlers transformed the South Atlantic, chopping away much of the forests, reducing the animal populations through hunting and destruction of habitat, and bringing unforeseeable and irreversible changes to the natural world. The appearance of white settlers continued the disruption of the southeastern forests that native farmers had started centuries earlier. When British settlers arrived to carve out a life in the backwoods, Native American tribes, including the Catawba, Congaree, Cherokee, and Saluda, suffered most from the new arrivals' disruption of game and the influx of disease. Hundreds of thousands of native men and women died.[2]

Around the time of the American Revolution, white settlers turned to farming and brought slaves to the South Carolina Piedmont to do more work clearing fields and planting indigo and other crops that they then shipped to the coast for sale in commercial markets.[3] But two movements at the end of that century pulled the region into closer contact with not only the South Carolina and Georgia cities along the Atlantic Coast but also the economy of the entire globe. Eli Whitney's improvement of the cotton gin in 1793 and the immense rise in demand for the fiber from the industrial mills of England brought Southern farmers across the region into a growing international commodity network. No place saw the impact more quickly or dramatically than the parts of South Carolina and Georgia that lay inland from the major coastal cities.[4]

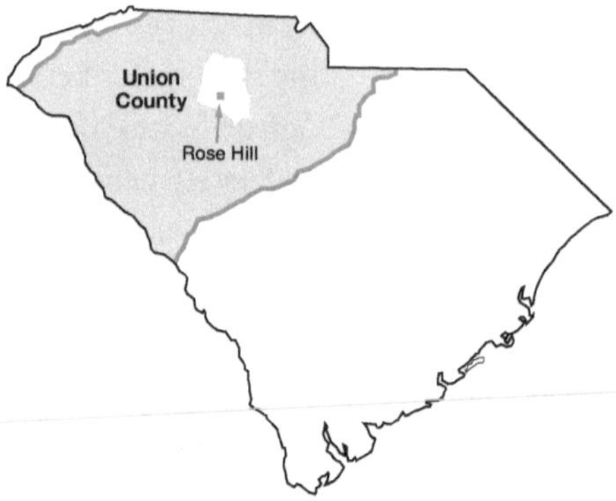

MAP 1. The South Carolina Piedmont (shaded area) with locations of Union County and Rose Hill. Map by Jeff Scalia.

The southern Piedmont is a six-hundred-mile stretch of land that runs from Virginia to Alabama, roughly parallel to the coast of the Atlantic Ocean, sandwiched between the Appalachian mountain range on its west and the coastal plain on its east. While geologists and geographers classify it as a plateau, the hills of the Piedmont rise and fall with varying severity as one moves closer to the mountains. In the "upper Piedmont," as Silver notes, elevation can reach two thousand feet above sea level, while the highest points of the "lower Piedmont," that area closest to the coastal plain, rise only a couple hundred feet. Overall, the region embodies a significant drop in elevation from the foothills to the coastal plain.[5]

The prospect of farming in the hinterlands was limited by these environmental conditions. Early settlers brought cattle, which roamed freely, feeding on the flora of the wooded hills and the grasses of the natural clearings. When these white landowners wanted to grow cash crops for the market, it meant working—or putting slaves to work—to clear fields. As Silver explains, this was not only a major task but also one with serious environmental consequences. "Clearing a field on a piedmont slope produced conditions not encountered in the more level coastal plain," he wrote. "In any setting—especially the topographically diverse English South—the natural environment within which humans work is at least as important as the cultural and economic background out of which they come."[6] The environmental impact made by the first few generations of agriculturists in the Piedmont had drastic implications not only for the people living there but for the world trade of cotton, and ideas about the plant, for at least a century.

While enslaved people had raised long-staple Sea Island cotton on coastal lowcountry plantations for generations before Whitney's gin, that variety thrived only because temperate coastal summers stretched longer into the spring and fall than in the rest of the South. Sea Island cotton had no chance even a hundred miles inland on the cooler, hillier lands of the coastal plain and Piedmont. Southerners' dreams of growing enough cotton inland to make the plant an export commodity relied on a different plant entirely: short-staple cotton. This type could grow well in the shorter seasons of the Piedmont, but its seeds were fused to its fiber. Before 1800, separating the sticky pods from the cotton threads by hand was too time- and labor-consuming to make the crop profitable. Whitney's refinement of the cotton gin changed that calculation, suddenly making short-staple or "upcountry" cotton *the* crop choice for former subsistence farmers and enterprising planters.[7]

The technology made the Piedmont a natural place for cotton's expansion. The rolling hills around Rose Hill benefited from navigable inland waterways that reached the coast, and proximity to coastal cities like Charleston and Savannah unlocked the Piedmont's agricultural potential. Short-staple cotton opened up a vast market network to these frontier farms, which quickly became ensnared in a global system of commodities, capital, and the trade in human beings. Wealthy lowcountry planters began buying up larger and larger tracts of land in the Upcountry, and slavery and cotton followed.[8] While the arrival of the cotton gin and newly connected market and transportation networks explain the demand side of the white fiber's story, the production side is one of enslaved labor and very specific environmental conditions.

The soil that Gist owned and his slaves worked was old, acidic, and lean. Compared to the younger, richer, and deeper topsoil of the South's Black Belt or the Yazoo-Mississippi Delta, the Piedmont's thin layer of earth was fragile and relatively unforgiving. These Ultisols—the scientific name for the soils that made up most upcountry South Carolina farms—formed millions of years before the forests were cleared. Rocks and minerals weathered beneath the surface, and tree litter, plant decomposition, and other deposits from the atmosphere settled on the ground, combining into the substance under farmers' feet. At the moment Native Americans and white settlers burned the trees to clear land for farming, the soils began losing minerals, first through the fires themselves and later from exposure to rain and erosion.[9] This geological backstory was crucial to cotton's fate, even if few upland farmers understand its intricacies. By the time William Henry Gist arrived in the South

Carolina Piedmont in the early nineteenth century, with cotton fever raging through the countryside, the land had already undergone that major transformation.

Despite its importance to their operations, the soil mattered less to these pioneering enslavers as the adaptable qualities of *Gossypium hirsutum*, upland cotton. The plant needed a long, warm growing season to mature, and it was much hardier than its long-staple cousin. Big and small farmers alike found these inland Piedmont lands an ideal place to grow the plant because it appeared to thrive in newly cleared "fresh" soil.[10] So they planted it. Over the course of the first half of the nineteenth century, planters, enslaved people, and overseers grew acres and acres of the plant and experimented with soil treatment, planting, thinning, and harvesting.[11]

The Gist family was one of the first to take advantage of the newly cleared soils of Union County. William Henry was born in Charleston in 1807, in the parlance of the time, "illegitimately." His mother and father were never married. He was raised by his mother, Mary Boyden, until his father, Francis Fincher Gist, died in 1819. Then Nathaniel Gist, William Henry's uncle, petitioned to become the boy's guardian. Nathaniel raised his nephew until he went off to college, which turned out to be a brief detour. Gist revolted against South Carolina College's compulsory board policy—the university had begun requiring students to eat on campus to protect them from the local tavern scene—and he joined a boycott of campus dining. In 1827 the college expelled Gist and forty of his classmates over their "mess hall rebellion."[12]

In the short five years following his exit from the university, Gist had an incredibly eventful life. He had already inherited from his father a great deal, including a small fortune in bank shares, thousands of acres of land, and twenty-three human beings. Through a series of land grants and purchases, he expanded his upcountry footprint while quickly making a name for himself among the planter elite. His reputation came not just from his budding slave-built operation but from a series of events that brought him regional fame: Gist fought at least one duel, during which he *probably* killed a man named Samuel Fair; he married eighteen-year-old Louisa Bowen, who died after giving birth to a daughter; he witnessed his brother-in-law execute a man (for which Gist was charged as an accessory to murder); and the still-young man married again, to Mary Elizabeth Rice, who would eventually bear twelve children.[13]

During the 1830s Gist also oversaw construction of Rose Hill. His role was mostly directing free and enslaved craftspeople to build the mansion and to move the earth and flora around it into a productive agricultural landscape. The house embodied the nature around it, as bricks were made from the clay of the surrounding hills and the wood milled from nearby hardwood stands. According to the National Register of Historic Places, the house was finished in 1832, when Gist was still only twenty-five years old. But it was only the beginning. Over the course of the 1830s and 1840s, he amassed more land, more human property, and more power. He expanded his landholdings from fifteen hundred acres to more than three thousand and built onto the mansion house.[14]

GIST'S RISE TO POWER and prominence overlapped with the explosion of cotton growing in the Piedmont and its spread across the South. To hear Gist and his cohort tell it in 1860, cotton had become the central feature of the Southern landscape *and* the cornerstone of its economy. They bound together these factors as if to create the image of "the Cotton South" as a singular region blanketed in blooming white bolls. Yet how much of the crop was planted, where it grew within the South, and the commodity's economic importance were actually three different factors that were crucial to both the creation and fate of the Confederacy.

Maps tell part of the story of cotton's spread. (See maps 2 and 3.) In the 1830s, as Gist was expanding his upcountry operation, other planters, yeomen farmers, and, against their will, hundreds of thousands of enslaved men, women, and children moved west, cleared new land for farms, and planted more and more cotton. By 1858 the center of agricultural production had moved dramatically west. The maps bear that out. Yet, as the eye is drawn to the black dots representing cotton bales produced, we should also consider all of the white space in the eleven states that would become the Confederacy and consider how much of the actual area had nothing to do with production of the crop. Gist's Piedmont was certainly no longer as densely planted in the fiber as it had been decades earlier. On the eve of war, the Alabama Black Belt and Mississippi Delta had become centers of cotton agriculture, but parts of Texas and Louisiana had also become significant suppliers for the world market. North Carolina, Arkansas, Tennessee, and Florida could point to areas of the state where cotton farming was important. It appeared to many, inside and outside the South, that cotton on the land was an organizing principal for a new nation.

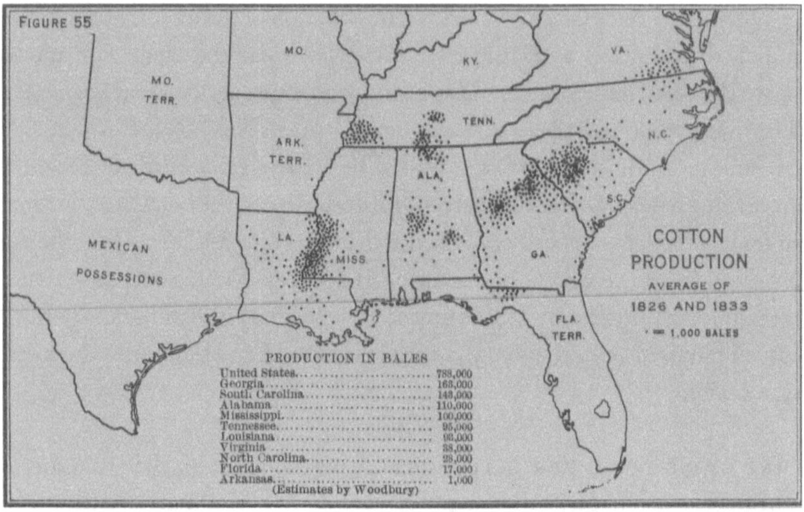

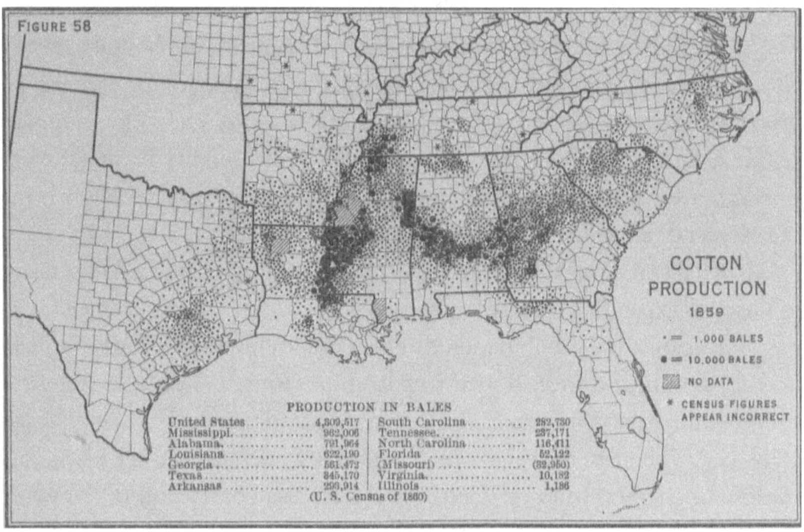

MAPS 2 AND 3. Movement and intensification of cotton production from 1826 to 1859. *Atlas of American Agriculture*, part V, section A, *Cotton* (Washington, D.C.: U.S. Department of Agriculture, 1919).

Yet, as slavery and its signature crop expanded their footprints, and region-wide people talked of a "Cotton South," there remained significant environmental and cultural differences within each place. Soil type and quality, weather, topography, pests, and a host of other nonhuman factors made cotton growing in one area of the South—or even within a single county—vastly different from another. The expansive plantations around Natchez, Mississippi, bore little resemblance to the small farms of central Tennessee. The living and working conditions of the millions of enslaved men, women, and children varied dramatically as well. These differences, as would soon become clear, played an important role in how locals understood what was possible on Southern land and in a Southern nation.

Maps of crop production are not the only way to discover the agricultural differences across the "Cotton States." The state-level agricultural censuses reveal just how little of the Southern landscape farmers actually planted in cotton. In 1860 Gist's South Carolina, for instance, was roughly 20.5 million acres in size, with a remarkable 13 million acres classified as farmland. However, less than 14 percent of that farmland was considered "improved," which according to the Census Bureau's definition meant land currently under cultivation in a row crop like cotton, or a permanent meadow or orchard. This meant that only 8 percent of the land area in the Palmetto State was actively farmed, and only a fraction of that grew cotton.[15]

Although in their letters to Gist the governors of Florida and Mississippi claimed to represent "Cotton States," their lands were similarly mixed-use. Florida was 1.8 times bigger than South Carolina in land size but had less than a quarter of South Carolina's farmland. Mississippi, on the other hand, was 50 percent larger than Gist's home state, with more farm acreage and a much higher rate of farmland in active cultivation. The physical landscapes of the cotton-rich areas of these states—like the Mississippi Delta, the Florida Panhandle, and the South Carolina Piedmont—were all cotton-producing, but a visitor riding horseback through the fields in each area would find little in common among them.

The place of cotton within each Southern state further muddies the picture of a region reigned by the crop. Specific cotton acreage numbers are not available for 1860, but the census did record the number of four-hundred-pound cotton bales produced within each state. It is possible, then, to see how many acres of farmland accounted for each bale, which provides a basic snapshot of each state's devotion to cotton. As table 1 shows, Virginia and

TABLE 1. Farmland and Cotton Production of Southern States, 1860

	Acres improved, in farms	Acres unimproved, in farms	Percentage (%) of total farmland that was improved	Ginned 400-lb cotton bales produced	Acres of farmland per bale
Alabama	6,385,724	12,718,821	33.43	980,955	19.5
Arkansas	1,983,313	7,590,393	20.72	367,333	26.1
Florida	654,213	2,266,015	22.40	65,153	44.8
Georgia	8,062,758	18,587,732	30.25	701,840	38.0
Louisiana	2,707,108	6,591,468	29.11	777,738	12.0
Mississippi	5,065,755	10,773,929	31.98	1,202,507	13.2
North Carolina	6,517,284	17,245,685	27.43	145,514	163.3
South Carolina	1,572,060	11,623,859	11.91	353,412	37.3
Tennessee	6,795,337	13,873,828	32.88	296,464	69.7
Texas	2,650,781	22,693,247	10.46	431,463	58.7
Virginia	11,437,821	19,679,215	36.76	12,727	2,445.0

Agriculture of the United States in 1860: Compiled from the Original Returns of the Eighth Census (Washington, D.C.: Government Printing Office, 1864).

North Carolina each had a relatively large amount of land in farms, but those areas grew very little cotton. Louisiana and Mississippi farmers, on the other hand, devoted a larger percentage of the available land to the crop. Yet this calculation of acres of farmland per bale of cotton produced is a rough measure and cannot account for the specific productivity of any given area within a state. The overall point is that, even in the most cotton-productive states, there was a lot happening on the landscape that was not cotton.[16]

Planters who moved into the Mississippi Valley and points west encountered soil conditions vastly different from those in the Carolinas, Virginia, or Georgia. The remoteness and political infancy of these territories and states also created new challenges for their cotton operations. Enslaved people developed new forms of resistance and distinct cultures that reflected both environmental and social realities. Given these tangible differences in cotton farms and plantations, it is no wonder that white leaders, intent on protecting slavery, emphasized the crop's unifying importance. Agricultural and environmental forces shaped Southern life and the region's economy, but the political class sought to obscure these variations. The rhetoric of the

"Cotton South" was compelling precisely because it concealed such on-the-ground complexities. The idea of a region unified by a single crop was no accident—it was a deliberate political creation.

THIS INSISTENCE THAT the plant was a regional unifier saw its most powerful rhetorical expression in the phrase "King Cotton." The term seems to have originated from a Northerner, David Christy, who was an agent of the Ohio branch of the American Colonization Society. Christy first published his pamphlet *Cotton Is King* in 1855, though it became so popular among pro-slavery Americans that he had it reprinted several times leading up to the Civil War. The book's thirty-five-word subtitle hinted at the tract's true purpose, to employ the crop's power in the world economy to defend Southern slaveholding. The mostly unknown Ohioan could not have predicted the degree to which this message would resonate among anti-abolitionists across the country.[17]

Christy's argument boiled down to the idea that cotton was so important to the world economy—the livelihoods of so many various people across the globe depended on the fiber—that no individual slave or free laborer, no farmer, planter, or ginner, no mill hand, politician, or consumer, had any power against it. It was a ruler, a king. "It is shown that King Cotton sits entrenched in a position impregnable to all the forces marshaled against him; and that he not only successfully resists the assaults of his enemies, but makes them contributors to the support of his throne." Cotton was not a benevolent ruler; he called the monarch an "incubus" that we "could not shake off . . . if we would."[18]

Although this "King Cotton" argument swept across the South among fire-eating defenders of slavery, Christy's true target was not Southern slavery per se but the presence of free African Americans in the United States. He was a colonizationist, after all, part of a group that purchased land in Liberia that they called "Ohio in Africa," with the intent of paying for the export of the state's black population.[19] Christy argued that Revolution-era abolitionists in the Northeast had failed to promote "industry, intelligence, and morality among the free blacks," so that by the 1850s, black Northerners "persevered in their evil habits."

This was not simply a problem with race, Christy argued, but a symptom of cotton's despotism. Shortly after the movement to abolish slavery took hold in Northern states and the Northwest Territories, cotton production spread throughout the South. As Christy explained, Vermont abolished slavery the year before the invention of the gin, a machine that became "an unparalleled impulse given to the cultivation of cotton." By the time New York followed suit, Christy explains, "exports of cotton to England had reached 9,500,000 lbs." With "each movement for freedom," he argued, cotton expanded, creating a "counter-movement to stimulate slavery [in the South and] the manufacture of cotton goods" in the North.[20]

In Christy's telling, the spread of the crop, along with the failure of white Northerners to improve the "moral character" of African Americans, meant that by 1855 there could be no persuasive argument for emancipation *anywhere.*[21] "The whole African race, freedmen as well as slaves," Christy wrote, was "an intolerable burden." The only answer, now that cotton was central to the world's economic order, was the continuation of enslavement in the South and the forced export of free African Americans to Africa. "Emigration to Liberia," Christy's group promised, "is not only a certain means of securing to the colored man all the social and political rights which he so ardently longs to possess, [but also] . . . all that happiness which wealth can bestow." It is telling that this promise of riches relied on "the soil of Liberia," which "is so fertile." These forcibly emigrated women and men would not only harvest the "native exportable products" but also earn their fortunes growing and exporting "coffee and cotton, throughout the world."[22]

Despite his own interest in colonization, Christy's description of the absolute power of the cotton crop was what Southern leaders like Gist took to heart. Perhaps the loudest voice to proclaim the supremacy of cotton's power in the South and the world was Gist's confidante, U.S. senator and former South Carolina governor James Henry Hammond. As early as 1845, Hammond wrote to English abolitionist Thomas Clarkson in a widely published letter that argued simply if slavery fell, so too would the entire world's economy. Cotton was the only domino that mattered in his scenario. "I do not undervalue the importance of other articles of commerce," he wrote, "but no calamity could befall the world at all comparable to the sudden loss of two millions of bales of cotton annually." The end of slavery, he promised, would be the end of cotton production, and the effects would be felt everywhere. "From the deserts of Africa to the Siberian wilds—from Greenland to the Chinese Wall, there is not a spot of earth but would feel the sensation."[23]

The importance of the crop to the global machinery of finance, agriculture, and manufacturing, Hammond believed, made it, and by extension the whole South, untouchable. Employing Christy's now-famous term in a speech on the Senate floor in 1858, Hammond claimed that cotton possessed power beyond mere value, as staggering as that value was. To threaten the plant, he told abolitionists everywhere, would be to challenge absolute power. "Would any sane nation make war on cotton?" he asked.

> Without firing a gun, without drawing a sword, should they make war on us we could bring the whole world to our feet. The South is perfectly competent to go on, one, two, or three years without planting a seed of cotton. I believe that if she was to plant but half her cotton, for three years to come, it would be an immense advantage to her.... What would happen if no cotton was furnished for three years? I will not stop to depict what every one can imagine, but this is certain: England would topple headlong and carry the whole civilized world with her, save the South. No, you dare not make war on cotton. No power on earth dares to make war upon it. Cotton *is* king.[24]

Hammond's description of the imperious power of the plant struck a chord in the antebellum slavery debates and took hold in the consciousness of Southern cotton planters across the region.[25] His rhetoric took Christy's phrase to a new level.

Hammond enshrined cotton as king because it made slavery a servant of the plant. His logic was simple. The crop demanded the labor of slaves, and the entire world depended on the crop. Therefore, the economies of New York and London were fixed not only to the fields of the South Carolina hills and Mississippi bottomlands but also to the black women and men working there. Going to war to end slavery, he exhorted Northern senators, would be going to war against themselves. "The South have sustained you, in great measure," he told his Yankee colleagues. The money created by slave labor in Southern cotton fields "keep[s] your machinery together and in motion."[26]

Though the thrust of this argument was about cotton's economic linkage to the fate of the world's fiscal health, Hammond showed his hand by pivoting to a defense of slavery. He contrasted the white laborers in English mills and Northern factories with the women and men who lived in bondage among the cotton plantations of the South. Mill workers were free in name only, he argued. "Why, you meet more beggars in one day, in any single street of the city of New York, than you would meet in a lifetime in the whole

South." The enslaved, he countered, "are happy, content, unaspiring, and utterly incapable, from intellectual weakness ever to give us any trouble by their aspirations."[27]

Hammond's arguments were captured, reprinted, and spread throughout the world, but they especially took hold among those defenders of cotton and slavery in the South. His judgment of the moral and intellectual weaknesses of the enslaved held sway, even as the details of his rape of an enslaved woman and her thirteen-year-old daughter, and his molestation of four of his nieces, became public. It did little to damage his political reputation or change his views on slavery and cotton.[28]

Throughout the decades leading up to the Civil War, defenders of slavery continued to use cotton as their most potent shield against abolitionism. It became the cornerstone of practical economic defenses of slavery. Eschewing the moral and political grounds on which some abolitionists, most notably Harriet Beecher Stowe, attacked the institution, cotton-centric defenses were pragmatic, even logistical, in tone and content.[29]

These arguments persuaded more than planters. Gist may have read an 1852 upcountry South Carolina newspaper article reprinting a Charles Dickens essay where the English writer warned that abolishing slavery would doom cotton and trigger global economic collapse. Abolition would make industrial London even more, well, Dickensian: "The lives of nearly two millions of our countrymen are dependent upon the cotton crops of America. . . . Should any dire calamity befall the land of cotton," he wrote, "a thousand merchant ships would rot idly in dock; ten thousand mills would stop their busy looms; two thousand mouths would starve for lack of food to feed them."[30]

These defenses of cotton had begun to take on a cultural life of their own. By design, all of these defenses of slavery that put the blooming white staple at the center of Southern life pushed an image of the rural South that belied reality. Cotton-as-king arguments drastically oversimplified the diversity of farming and environmental conditions of the South. Gist and his compatriots argued for the importance of cotton to the very fabric of who they were as people, and how helpless they were under the rule of the monarch, yet they consistently overstated the crop's place on the land. It was a rhetorical sleight of hand: By making this agricultural product the ruler of the entire South, the fate of the region and of the slavery system was determined not by human decision or labor but by a crop. It flattened the natural environment of the region into simply "cotton plantations" and stripped any force of economics, politics, or even humanity of its agency.

Gist wrote his 1860 letter as a cotton farmer about the "Cotton States." Replies came from men who focused on the crop's role in their own lives and states. These arguments were not only made by Gist and his fellow planters but were also told in the music, fiction, and products that fused cotton with the South in the American imagination. While this rhetoric worked in the realm of speeches, pamphlets, and campaigns, enslaved men and women were literally making and keeping the South's agro-ecosystem intact. As the next chapter demonstrates, the South had become the land of cotton despite what was actually on the land.

CHAPTER TWO

Enslaved Labor in a Fragile Cotton Ecosystem

WILLIAM HENRY GIST sat at the center of efforts to make the diverse environments of the secession states into a single "Cotton South." Along with James Henry Hammond, David Christy, and the secessionists in positions of power, Gist had built a rhetoric of cotton that shrouded differences among Southern states. The unifying language around the single crop elided the South's disparate environments. It attempted to make the coast and the mountains, the alluvial deltas and the balding hillsides, the dense pine forests and the urban streets, one single place. It also, crucially, ordered Southern planters' expectations and understandings of the future productivity of Southern farms. It morphed their sense of the capability of the landscape to grow enough cotton for the plant to earn its place at the center of their civilization.

No single force was more important to this environmental calculation than the work of enslaved women and men. The "Cotton South" notion, for all the political and cultural work that it did, was most important because, while it foregrounded the work of picking cotton, it also shrouded the labor that people did to keep these ever-changing agro-environments functioning. In fact, as Gist was trumpeting the power of the plant to protect slavery and the South, cotton growing in the Piedmont had become harder and increasingly dependent on environmental management done by the enslaved. And it was management. While many people oversimplify the work of enslaved people to walking through the fields at harvest time, bent over, filling sacks with the bolls they ripped from the tall cotton stalks, the actual labor that men and women did was far more skilled, year-round, and diverse than these flat images portray.

Increasingly over the nineteenth century, the labor of enslaved people focused not on the cotton itself but on keeping the entire plantation agricultural system functioning. On places like Gist's own Rose Hill, slavery seemed to most as the only method of labor that could stem erosion and declining soil fertility. It was a bulwark against environmental decline. The rhetoric, then, was crucial. Organizing Southern culture with King Cotton at the center allowed enslavers like Gist to unify a region around protecting slavery, and in the process to reduce the agro-environmental diversity of the entire South to a singular, if mythical, cotton world.

The South Carolina governor was hardly alone in thinking that what made his state and the entire region the peak of American civilization was the social order created by cotton and slavery. White Southern leaders had spent decades defending human bondage by wrapping the idea in agricultural and environmental ethics. Secession, to be sure, was predicated on a belief in the cultural and economic value of the institution of slavery and the white supremacy that undergirded the system. But it was also built on the perception that the environmental sustainability of plantation agriculture was only possible with slave labor. Leaders in Mississippi, for instance, saw slavery's role in perpetuating their cotton kingdoms in radically different ways than South Carolina slaveholders. Gist's belief in white supremacy was as strident as his faith that the environment around Rose Hill would be able to produce marketable farm goods for the foreseeable future, as long as he held people in bondage to do the work. Despite each Southern leader's own varied understanding of farming's potential, for Gist, Southern independence was married to this optimistic view of the *sustainability* of his cotton plantation.[1]

To audiences of fellow white men within the region, throughout the United States, and across Europe and the Caribbean, this Cotton South idea suggested that the crop, slavery, export markets, low tariffs, and patriarchy—the whole of this plantation society—was going to live on in perpetuity as long as abolitionists and the federal government let it. They tied slavery's future to cotton's, which implicated the soil, weather, rain, and the entire organic machine. To men like Gist, however, the point where environmental sustainability left off and political or social stability began just did not matter. They were one and the same; the cotton plant made it so.

NATURE, HOWEVER, MATTERED. Very real environmental differences existed across the South and became exacerbated in the mid-nineteenth century. In the rich, newly cleared, and fertile lands of the old Southwest, for instance, Southern leaders' vision of cotton's sustainability seemed realistic, as long as slavery continued. But the soil erosion and declining fertility of places like Union County, South Carolina, would make cotton's future far less certain. By the 1850s the permanence of cotton agriculture, not to mention just how central the crop was to the agriculture and economy of the Piedmont, was very much in question.

As early as the 1840s, newspapers recorded the decline. Articles discussing strategies for liming or manuring soils to rebuild nutrients were common, and some even pointed to the appearance of erosion's most serious symptom: gullies.[2] The most famous Southern agricultural reformer, Edmund Ruffin, had been blasting Southern farmers for wasting soil nutrients since the early nineteenth century. From the pages of books, in his newspaper *The Farmer's Register*, and on the lecture circuit, the Virginian decried the state of farming, and by extension Southern farmers themselves. "The recuperative powers of nature," he wrote mid-century, were the only forces working to "repair the waste of fertility caused by the destructive industry of man."[3]

Not only did he bring attention to agricultural lands failing, he researched ways to stop it. Ruffin fixated on soil improvement through the application of manure, marl, and guano to add much-needed nutrients back into the suffering ground. His books, especially *An Essay on Calcareous Manures*, published in 1852, caught the attention of some Southern farmers and many Northerners, who read them as evidence of the damage that slavery was inflicting on Southern soils.[4] Scholars too have been enchanted by Ruffin, particularly his midlife pivot from planter and self-taught soil scientist to fire-eating secessionist and ardent defender of slavery. His writing and life story are a telling window into how land use and slavery meshed. Ruffin's friendship with Hammond also suggests that the connections the Virginian made between perceived African American inferiority and soil health reached the minds of regional leaders.[5] The degree to which Southern landholders actually put Ruffin's advice to use has remained a contested question in the historiography.

For decades, scholars have put soil at the center of debates about the coming of the Civil War. In the 1920s Avery Craven argued that Southern tobacco and cotton farmers simply mined the soil, extracting as much fertility every season as they could. Farmers wore out their fields with crops year after year, drawing out nutrients and then moving to "newer" lands to the west. In the 1970s and 1980s, pushed first by Eugene Genovese and adapted by Gavin Wright, historians argued that planters had so much capital tied up in human property that they protected that investment to the detriment of land and machinery. Large slaveholders were "laborlords," Wright put it, not landlords. The evidence is that enslaved workers, when not working in the cotton fields, might cut down trees to clear "fresh" land for cotton, but owners and overseers rarely had those men and women collecting marl and manure, or building terraces, or digging drainage ditches, all work that soil experts at the time recommended in order to save the precious nutrients.[6] Likewise, it was easier to leave the Piedmont and move the enslaved people to a new plantation to the southwest than to work harder to eke out profits on the thin Carolina soils.

This concept of "shifting cultivation" has rarely been about land use, but rather politics.[7] As Paul S. Sutter argued, "Shifting cultivation was a political problem, then, which helps explain why many of the region's most important agricultural reformers were also prominent defenders of slavery and guardians of regional political power."[8] Much of the scholarship that used this idea was based on a rudimentary understanding of soil ecology, but it led to the argument that, as a whole, Southern white men sought territorial expansion and protection for slavery because they needed more and healthier dirt in which to plant cotton. To this day the common view in the historiography of slavery and the secession crisis is that worn-out soils forced the slaveholder elite to push for territorial expansion, and the extension of slavery, into new areas of the West and Caribbean. Southern leaders, the common sentiment argues, envisioned a Confederacy that would reignite the external slave trade and expand the institution to lands that had not been worn out by two centuries of farming.[9]

This thinking has recently come into question, and evidence from Rose Hill suggests that shifting cultivation across long distances was hardly the norm. Instead, many planters moved crops around within their own plantations with some success. (Sutter, the foremost historian of Southern soils, calls the question of shifting cultivation's impact on the region "thorny.")[10] Thousands of cotton farmers, as many as 60 percent region wide, did relocate during the 1850s, suggesting that in addition to simple population pressures, many sons raised on farms were leaving bad conditions in search of better.[11] But in Union County, the overall population *increased* from 1840 to 1860, and the number of cotton bales produced rose nearly 400 percent.[12] Environmental historians, geographers, and soil scientists have found evidence that within the restrained confines of a single plantation, shifting cultivation could be a sustainable practice.[13] Farmers directed laborers to clear new lands contiguous to fields already in use, then let the old fields lie fallow. After a decade or two, they returned to the lands, some of which resembled more forest than field. They directed their enslaved laborers to clear the trees and plant crops. Many visiting Northerners looked at the seemingly haphazard and destructive treatment of farming land—the aesthetically unpleasing look of fallow fields and hacked-up forests—and saw only ignorance and inefficiency.[14] But it certainly worked in many places, at least for a time. As Sutter explains, the result may not have looked good, but "it may have worked reasonably well as a method of managing soil fertility within a given property or area."[15]

Though historians have gone back and forth on the extent and exact nature of shifting cultivation, much of this debate has ignored or diminished the most crucial aspect of shifting cultivation: the role of enslaved labor. Some of this scholarship treated labor as transportable to any land where a master directed them to work; other scholarship simply downplayed the labor of the enslaved.[16] Notable exceptions, like books by Diane Glave and Erin Stewart Mauldin, detail the ways that enforced labor literally held together landscapes that would otherwise have declined more quickly.[17] Yes, planters may have resisted spending money on land improvements and machinery, but they did direct enslaved people to make real, material changes to the farmland throughout the year, season after season. The point is that two kinds of cotton farmers emerged: Those who picked up and left, and those committed to using slave labor to make their plantations sustainable. Region-wide Southern agriculture was extensive, but within the "older" sections it was intensive, and increasingly reliant on slave labor to preserve the fragile agro-ecosystem.

GIST'S ROSE HILL is a prime example of the intensive plantation held together by the work of enslaved people. The governor needed only to gaze from the second floor of Rose Hill to understand how that labor was keeping his operation productive. A view from his veranda would take in a patchwork of forest and field, of good soil and bad, of hills and flats. Everywhere he looked, whether onto the stands of cotton and corn, a pasture with grazing cattle, the sloping banks of the Tyger River, or the woods where pigs and people roamed, he saw living and nonliving things working to produce life, either stringy cotton fibers eventually bound for sale in markets around the world, or grains and produce that would nourish the people and animals who worked at Gist's determination to make more of that fleecy white crop. What he saw was a diversified landscape at work.

While the cotton plant was the lever that radically changed the Upcountry's environment, it did not dominate the farm landscape. Plantations and small farms made up the agricultural areas of the South Carolina Piedmont, but much of the land was not planted in anything. Despite the "Cotton is King" rhetoric that suggested antebellum Southerners grew cotton from the field's edge up to their mansion doors with little care for any other kind of agriculture, and that farmland made up the vast majority of rural space, for the decades leading up to the Civil War the plant was hardly a monocrop, even on the most productive plantations. Upcountry cotton production was not possible without a panoply of other crops and animals and the slave labor that supported these ancillary industries. Even on smaller operations, the cash crop was dependent on the self-sufficiency of the entire farm.[18]

In his study of three upcountry counties that surround Gist's Union County, historian Lacy Ford found that in 1849 most farms—all that were larger than a mere twenty-five acres—were producing enough foodstuffs to be self-sufficient. This meant that farmers were raising enough food for the enslaved people, the free people, and the animals on their land.[19] The most productive cotton farmers had the space to grow corn, oats, and hay, and to raise pigs, cows, and chickens. Ford cites William Henry Gist's uncle Francis, the man who raised William Henry, as an example of a well-diversified planter who improved his fortune quickly. Within the older Gist's first ten years in Union, he increased his landholdings from three hundred acres to more than a thousand, bought thirty-three additional human laborers, and had property worth more than $25,000. But those statistics belie the material reality of Piedmont farms large and small. In 1839 alone, Union County farmers harvested 1.6 million pounds of seed cotton, but also raised more than three-quarters of a million bushels of corn and twenty-four thousand bushels of potatoes, and sheared nearly eight thousand pounds of wool.[20] As historian Lewis Gray and many others have recounted, as a region, the cotton South produced enough food to sustain itself and, as a whole, grew more corn than cotton in the prewar nineteenth century.[21]

The specifics from Union County bear this out. For decades leading up to secession, enslaved workers had brought nature under their control in the name of diversified agriculture. Cotton was not the only crop that mattered. As a whole, the county's cotton production in 1860 was worth $761,952, only a little more than half the total value of agricultural output, which the census bureau estimated was $1.37 million. Plenty of other crops and farm products never made it to market, but of those that did, monetarily cotton was only 56 percent of the county's total farm output.[22] These value numbers are hardly the only way to measure cotton's importance. The 650 acres Gist devoted to cotton comprised only about 16 percent of his overall land, which, along with enslaved labor, produced 218 four-hundred-pound bales of ginned cotton in 1850. Cotton, while surely the soul of his worldview and his dominant economic interest, made up only a fraction of the land's and labor's work.[23]

This diversified approach to farming was written all over the Rose Hill landscape. If Gist could stand on the porch and see all of his holdings at once, he would have taken in much more than cotton fields. The numbers are striking. In 1850 alone, Rose Hill's enslaved people produced 7,000 bushels of corn, 600 bushels of wheat, and 2,000 bushels of oats, along with hundreds of pounds of Irish potatoes, sweet potatoes, and barley. His dairy operation churned one thousand pounds of butter. His slaves slaughtered livestock worth $1,725.[24] His view might also take in many of the plantation's structures. These buildings housed the enslaved people and the overseer, as well as a number of barns needed to take care of the farm's many animals, including ten horses, twenty-nine mules, and six oxen. Fenced pastures also held sixty milk cows, one hundred other bovines, and, when they were not roaming at large in the woods, two hundred pigs. It was one of the largest such operations in the county; the census valued the land at $34,000 plus another $5,100 for the livestock and $1,000 in farm implements. Off the Rose Hill property, Gist held interests in sawmills and gristmills as well.[25]

These impressive figures suggest a productive and diversified agricultural operation, but what is perhaps most interesting about the landscape were the areas that, to the untrained eye, were not doing much at all. In 1850, of the more than 4,000 acres that comprised Rose Hill, 2,300 were what the census called "unimproved," meaning that they were not being cultivated when the census taker visited. Much of that unimproved land was wooded, some of which likely lined the Tyger River and Fair Forest Creek. (Pigs and other animals roamed freely and were certainly "using" the lots that appeared to census takers as unimproved.) The 1850 census reported a similar breakdown of land among Gist's neighbors. Union Countians held 162,787 improved acres of farms in the county and many more—235,363 to be precise—of unimproved farmland.[26] Despite the rhetoric of southern leaders about the "Cotton States" and the "Cotton South," the varied agro-environment of Rose Hill is evidence that these terms are hardly descriptive. Even calling something a "cotton plantation" only told half (or in Gist's case, 16 percent) of the story.

THIS BREAKDOWN OF ACREAGE and crop yield reveals the lie at the heart of Southern leaders' rhetoric, but it is only a crude way of understanding what was actually happening at Rose Hill or other Piedmont plantations. It flattens the work of enslaved people and the environment itself to a simple calculation of land cover and market production. And it leaves out the deeper ecological foundation that lies at the heart of ideologies of slavery and cotton. There is a lot Gist did not know about the lives of his enslaved laborers, but one thing he did understand was how much work they were doing to hold together his plantation. The evidence of terracing and ditching—still visible on the landscape today—suggests that Gist was both aware of the problem of erosion and that he believed it could be slowed or halted. By the eve of the war, Gist was practicing this kind of shifting fallow to stay one step ahead of soil decline, what Steven Stoll called "emigrating while staying in place."[27]

Gist's diversified operation, hardly a monocrop cotton farm, was made possible by enslaved women and men growing diverse crops, raising animals, mending terraces, and carving ditches. On thousands of Southern farms, like those of Gist, slave labor held together the fragile Southern agro-environment of the antebellum years. Letting fields lie fallow, manuring, fertilizing, clearing new lands, building terraces and digging irrigation trenches were only a few of the major earth-moving projects that Gist could put the enslaved to work doing when they weren't milking cows or chopping weeds. Gist was not one of Wright's "laborlords," more concerned about maximizing their financial interest in slave property than with making improvements to the land they also owned. Evidence from Rose Hill suggests instead that he understood control over labor and control over land as one and the same, or put another way, that a healthy slave system meant a healthy land.[28]

But keeping the plantation sustainable was labor intensive. Planters directed enslaved men and women to do the work, and thus slaveholders understood the sustainability of their plantations as fused to the work of their human property. Slave labor could keep the land productive, but moreover the women and men working in bondage came to understand the agro-environment of places like Rose Hill to a far greater degree than most enslavers.

In 1860 Rose Hill was the home to 178 enslaved people and 10 white people: Gist, his wife, seven children, and an overseer.[29] Gist had about doubled his enslaved property every decade, owning 62 slaves in 1840 and 139 by 1850. The government's slave schedules reduced these people to the kind of work they performed: a cook, four blacksmiths, four carpenters, five seamstresses, a brickmason, four house servants, and 120 field workers.[30] To put those numbers in context, there were 676 slaveholders in Union County who held in bondage nearly 11,000 men, women, and children. But the great majority of the county's slaveholders owned fewer than fifteen slaves. Only six people owned more than one hundred slaves, and none owned more than two hundred, meaning Gist was one of the largest enslavers in the county. The average Union County slaveholder held sixteen enslaved people. Gist held eleven times as many.

That we know the names and ages of the ten white people who lived on Rose Hill in 1860 but scant details about the African-descended human beings held against their will as property reveals a great deal about how power on (and over) a plantation landscape worked. For Gist, controlling land and people was a singular effort, and as a result, environmental history has brought a great deal to historians' understandings of the institution of slavery.[31] Slaves like those on Gist's plantation worked in a very specific agro-environmental context. As pioneering Southern environmental historian Mart A. Stewart argues, it is impossible to understand slave labor and the environment in which slaves worked separately. Hence the life, health, and humanity of enslaved people, and in fact the whole slavery system, was dependent on the environment, and in turn this inhumane labor system shaped the dirt, briars, and fibers of the cotton plantation environment.[32] Perhaps no incident underscores the tight connection between slaves and their landscape as the story of Gist's slave Jack (he had no codified last name at the time, though census records suggest he took his owner's surname following emancipation).

It was at some point in the 1850s—it's hard to say exactly—when Jack ran away from Rose Hill. The ambiguity is important, for it is impossible to separate the details of his escape from the conditions of its telling. In the 1930s Mary Smith, a former slave on the Gist plantation, sat down with Caldwell

Sims of the Works Progress Administration, a New Deal agency for which a small part of its mission was to record "everyday" histories, including personal memories of former slaves. According to Smith, she was born into bondage on Gist's plantation in 1853. It was seventy-two years after the end of the Civil War when Smith recalled a number of stories about life as a girl, the most striking of which is that of Jack's flight.

Smith remembered that the day that Jack ran away from Rose Hill he went straight for "the forest," most likely those wooded unimproved lands that lined the property's waterway borders. Jack made his way to Fair Forest Creek and followed it off the Gist plantation onto land owned by someone named Jackson. He stopped at a spot in sight of what was then known as Harris Bridge, which carried Sardis Road (State Road 44-16 today) north toward the county seat, Unionville.[33]

Near the banks of Fair Forest Creek, Jack found a spot with enough seclusion to protect himself, yet with a view of the road. He dug a cave, probably carving out the head of a ditch that ran into the creek. He most likely would have found the sandy subsoil exposed at water's edge easy to remove by hand, without a tool.[34] Over the coming days he amassed a stock of corn, "two middles of meat," and living animals: two geese, several chickens, and a hog. Smith reported that Jack had stolen most of this, though some rations had come from friends—enslaved people, most likely either back at Rose Hill or on neighboring plantations—whom he had visited during the night. Jack's supply of both live animals and meat not only suggests the porousness of borders between farm and field but is also evidence of both the productivity of Rose Hill's landscape and Jack's resourcefulness and his understanding of the area.[35]

According to Smith, Jack hid out along Fair Forest Creek for *five months*, a surprisingly long time. One night as he crossed the waterway on a log, a man named Anderson, himself enslaved by Gist, spotted him. They talked briefly, but Anderson returned the next day with the Rose Hill overseer. Smith recalled the consequences: "They took all of his things on to the 'big house' and he was whipped and put back in his house and he went to work."[36]

Jack's five months in quasi-freedom in the woods, near the agricultural landscape but not a part of it, and then his forced return to the Rose Hill mansion for violent punishment demonstrates how power radiated out from the house itself, and could be escaped if one moved far enough away, albeit usually only temporarily. But the story also underscores the larger connection between the environment and power, that nature was a decisive factor in bondage, freedom, and how stories about the past are told. As Loren Schweninger and John Hope Franklin have indicated, a runaway slave "lying out" in a nearby river, forest, or swamp was common. Jack's fragmented story reveals how knowledge of the environment is as important a factor as any, and not only for Mary as storyteller but also for Jack as protagonist.[37]

Jack's fate and Gist's personal involvement in the punishment is unclear, but it is certain that the governor had no qualms about the institution of bondage. He was opposed to emancipation under any conditions as well as to the hiring out of enslaved workers. Gist was all-in on white supremacy. He told the state legislature in 1860, "There must be a distinction between the two races, as marked as their different colors and it must be distinctly and universally understood that the white is the governing race, without an exception, and without regard to disparity of intellect, merit or acquirements."[38] In the same message to the legislature, Gist called for a new law carrying the penalty of "punishing summarily and severely, if not with death, any person . . . [who] avows himself an abolitionist."[39]

From his mansion, the literal seat of his power, William Henry Gist retained social, economic, and legal power despite slave resistance. The governor recognized that slavery was the single force that, more than any other, shaped and controlled the natural landscape around the house. Gist understood the fickle nature of cotton production in the Piedmont; he understood the extent to which his operation relied on constant improvements to the land and material fixes to the fields. He saw enslaved people therefore as investments—cultural and political, to be sure, but also economic. Slavery was Gist's only hedge against future environmental decline. His monetary investment in human property, which conservative estimates put at well over $100,000, had very real, tangible implications for the land itself.[40]

In many ways, the degree to which Gist's enslaved laborers succeeded in protecting Rose Hill's agricultural viability was less important than the fact that planters like Gist believed they did. The "King Cotton" and "Cotton States" rhetoric worked to unite the interests of the vast majority of whites, slaveholders or not, in protecting the labor system. Gist did not represent all of these people, but he did understand the fate of the South from a worldview of his specific environmental situation. It stands to reason that fire-eaters in other parts of the South saw expansion as important. But from where Gist sat, the only way forward was slavery on a diversified cotton plantation. Others saw the world through their own places, but they were all united through the rhetoric of cotton, a crop that hardly dominated the Southern landscape to the degree that leaders presented it. South-wide rhetoric tied together a region that was actually very different, but culturally "cotton" could hold it together in a way other identities, even slavery itself, could not.

IN LATE 1860, as replies to his letter to Southern governors began arriving, William Henry Gist set to the business of secession. In November he called for a state convention, to be held in Charleston on December 18. The day before the body met, Gist resigned from the governorship. As the state's congressional representatives had resigned their positions and returned home from Washington, Gist must have felt that an entirely new government should be constituted as a sovereign state after secession. Over three days the convention met in Charleston, where members—buoyed by the responses to Gist's letter and the promises by Southern governors that their states would follow—voted to secede from the United States. The crisis was finally at hand, and the state's leaders were still confident that, while slavery was their cause, their trump card was cotton. As Gist's friend Senator Hammond had said the previous summer, "Come what may, with our surplus productions of Cotton, Rice, Sugar, etc., and our substructure of black slaves, *we are safe*."[41]

Over the next six months, as expected, other cotton states fell in line, and many lay their motivation at the feet of slavery and cotton. One of the recipients of Gist's 1860 letter was Mississippi Governor John Pettus. Like his South Carolina colleague, Pettus was a fire-eating rebel. He had promised Gist that Mississippi would secede after Lincoln's election as long as any one other state went with it. Material and environmental differences between the Palmetto and Magnolia States were many—and are crucial to the narrative of this book—but at this moment both Southern, slaveholding, planter governors agreed that secession was the only sustainable way forward for slavery and cotton. As expected, less than a month after Gist led South Carolina to secession, Mississippi's legislature met to make the same decision.

In early February 1861, only weeks after South Carolina's declaration, a Natchez, Mississippi, newspaper ran two articles that capture the connections of this political and agricultural moment. In abutting columns, the *Free Trader* ran the headlines "The Production of Cotton and Its Importance" and "A Declaration of the Immediate Causes Which Induce and Justify the Secession of the State of Mississippi from the Federal Union." Both made the same point: Cotton controls the fate of the world. The first article promised readers in this plantation-dense section of the state what most white Mississippi already believed: The world was dependent on American cotton, and if war cut supplies to Europe, the world's economy would grind to a halt. "Hundreds of thousands of starving people would be driven to extremities . . . and riot after riot would occur." If France and Great Britain could not retain access to Southern cotton, "a sensation greater than a civil war" would be felt across Europe.[42]

If white Southern readers weren't convinced of cotton's importance with that prediction, they would be swayed by the document next to it, which was a verbatim reprint of Mississippi legislators' explanation for why they had voted to secede. Their actual secession decree was legal and dry, but they knew the eyes of the world were upon them, so they followed it up with a formal, straightforward explanation for their decision to leave the United States:

> Our position is thoroughly identified with the institution of slavery—the greatest material interest of the world. Its labor supplies the product which constitutes by far the largest and most important portions of commerce of the earth. These products are peculiar to the climate verging on the tropical regions, and by an imperious law of nature, none but the black race can bear exposure to the tropical sun. These products have become necessities of the world, and a blow at slavery is a blow at commerce and civilization. That blow has been long aimed at the institution, and was at the point of reaching its consummation. There was no choice left us but submission to the mandates of abolition, or a dissolution of the Union, whose principles had been subverted to work out our ruin.[43]

For readers of the Natchez *Free Trader*, or any American reading along as the Southern states began to secede, the explanations relied baldly on environmental determinism. Mississippi leaders' hands were tied, they argued, because cotton was the *only thing* they could grow to make money, and "the black race" was the only group that could work the fields. Slavery had to be protected, in other words, because the Southern sun was so hot.[44]

For his part, William Henry Gist thought the war would be over swiftly. South Carolinians seceded in December 1860 and fired on Fort Sumter four months later. In May, Gist promised that it would take only two battles to "close the war and our independence will be acknowledged." Relying again on the rhetoric of cotton's importance to the world, he predicted that "Great Britain & France will offer their mediation & the yankees will gladly accept it and make peace."[45] By November, however, Union ships had seized Port Royal off the South Carolina coast and Ship Island off the Mississippi mainland, strangling Southern attempts to move cotton. The blockade limited most large shipments, though some small amounts of cotton slipped through. The Union permanently shut down the Charleston port in 1863. The world's demand for cotton failed to become the savior of the Confederate cause that Southern leaders had promised. At the same time, the war dramatically exposed the gaping distance between cotton's rhetoric and its environmental reality.

The Confederacy's cotton problems were not limited to getting it through the blockade. Inland from the coast on the fields of the region's farms, cotton did not fare any better. Historians have described the crushing effect of the war on the South's cotton production.[46] Mauldin demonstrates how the war exacerbated the fragile agro-ecosystems on the region's already compromised, acidic soils. As enslaved persons seized freedom at various times and locations throughout the war, depending on their own will and Union troop proximity, cotton planters found themselves powerless to protect their land, or to make more of the crop that they had thought was their side's greatest weapon.[47]

As a result, the war changed not only the character of Southern agriculture but also its rhetoric. As Drew Gilpin Faust points out, the conditions of war and specifically the loss of several years' worth of cotton crops led Southerners like Gist to quickly adapt the "excesses of greed that secessionists had identified as peculiarly northern."[48] The former South Carolina governor had a great seat for the changes wrought by war as the Confederacy's chief of construction and manufacture, which meant he made decisions about what to build, when and where to declare martial law, and when to impress enslaved people for work. From this vantage point he must have seen the limitations of his rhetoric about cotton as well as about the preeminent place of virtue in Southern society. Not only did thousands of white Southern men find themselves working as wage laborers across the region for the first time, the reality of fighting the war brought the irony that independence meant Southerners had to embrace the very market system that they had admonished in the North. Faust puts it clearly: "The lure and logic of the free market directly challenged both the political economy and morality of a slave society. Slavery . . . rested . . . on an ideology of paternalistic obligation and authority fundamentally at odds with the notion of a laissez-faire world."[49] In his position as chief of construction and manufacture, Gist fought these purportedly immoral free-market pressures each day. In fact, he faced enough pushback that the Confederacy disbanded Gist's board by late 1862. The former governor returned to Rose Hill and was never formally involved in politics again.[50]

By 1865 Charleston, the city that hosted the secession convention and where the first shots of the conflict had peeled across the bay in 1861, lay in ruins. Cotton bales, which Gist and Hammond had promised would protect the South against occupiers, were now stacked in public squares and set on fire, by either advancing Union troops or Confederates not wanting the valuable crop to fall into Yankee hands. As historian David Blight aptly put it, the cotton bales burning around the Confederate city were "the funeral pyres of a dying civilization."[51]

From anyone's perspective, cotton's world seemed to crumble at once. Enslaved people were now free. Records do not give a clear indication of what happened to Jack and all of the 178 men, women, and children who had been forced to live at Rose Hill. It is unclear when and how they emancipated themselves, though Union troops cut through the middle of the Upcountry as early as 1863. Planters' cash—the Confederate currency itself emblazoned with images of cotton—was worthless. The political system white Southerners had desperately put together was in shambles. With this material loss, the rhetoric of cotton's power dissolved. Hammond and Gist's vision of sustainability became *apparently, unmistakably, visually* untenable. The failure of their cotton rhetoric was revealed in the millions of women and men no longer enslaved, in the industrial and military might of the North, and in the physical and natural world itself. As the following chapter details, the land in the Piedmont became one of the New South generation's clearest pieces of evidence. Slave agriculture had not been sustainable, at the very least, because the political and economic world that it depended on could not live any longer.

Gist and the other plantation men of the Piedmont had believed in the power of this crop. They had constructed an understanding of the antebellum South and an independent Southern nation around the cotton plant and the form of labor that kept it growing. They believed that cultivating, harvesting, ginning, and processing the stringy white fibers ordered society and put them on top. But now the stacked bales of cotton turned to ash in the Charleston streets.

FOLLOWING THE CONFEDERACY'S surrender and dissolution, the former governor swore an oath to the United States, which included a promise to "abide by and faithfully support" emancipation. President Andrew Johnson pardoned Gist in September 1865.[52] Though records are sparse, historians Daniel Bell and Al Hester have shown how, in the final years of his life, Gist saw to the carving up of Rose Hill and his other properties, distributing land to various relatives. The acreage that Gist chose to keep perhaps hints at the environmental conditions around his estate. Whereas in 1860 he held 5,000 acres, 2,000 of which (40 percent) were improved, a decade later he had lost all his enslaved property and held merely 1,500 acres, of which only 10 percent was improved.[53] The breakup of Gist's holdings was in line with much of what was going on across the Piedmont. Former planters no longer had the cash or the labor force to keep their operations together, yet the world market was clamoring for cotton.

On September 30, 1874, the former governor died at Rose Hill.[54] In its obituary the *Anderson Intelligencer* unironically called the secessionist "an incorruptible patriot."[55] Within four years, Gist's widow Mary Elizabeth was overseeing the sale of the house and his estate.[56] The collapse of Gist's cotton kingdom had happened quickly.

The physical world of Rose Hill, however, kept together by the work of enslaved persons before the war, faced a whole different environmental situation after emancipation: the effect of free labor on the land. Cotton was no less important to the people of the world, and the fate of the crop in the absence of slavery was certainly unknown to the black and white people of the Upstate. Gist's "Cotton South" rhetoric had hid the agro-ecological reality from thousands of other Piedmont planters as well as those growing other crops, or not farming at all, across the South. He had argued that slavery and cotton were sustainable, but the 1865 perspective showed they were clearly not. There was no "Cotton South," but that rhetoric, which covered over the stark variety of different environmental landscapes in the region, had been a powerful factor in calls for a civil war.

CHAPTER THREE

Freedom on a Broken Land

On July 20, 1871, Alfred Wright sat down behind a table at a courthouse in Columbia, South Carolina, to face questioning. His inquisitors were part of what was known commonly as the Ku Klux Committee, but officially as the Joint Select Committee to Inquire Into the Condition of Affairs in the Late Insurrectionary States. Congress had established the committee following passage of the Ku Klux Klan Act to investigate violence in the former Confederacy, and it quickly homed in on the South Carolina Piedmont near Rose Hill. Alfred Wright, forty-four years old, had just six years earlier been held in bondage by one of William Henry Gist's sons.[1]

Wright had information about the Klan and recent violence in Union County, information that had forced Wright to leave the plot of land where he sharecropped cotton and peanuts to hide out in Columbia, sixty-five miles away. Wright testified that in the previous few years he had become involved in local Republican politics, "an active person in my principles," as he put it, not only voting and campaigning for candidates but even serving as a delegate to the Union County convention.

Soon Klansmen started to follow and harass him. It came to a head one night in December 1870 when he worked until sunset moving ginned cotton onto wood pallets to keep it out of the rain. When he returned home, he took some food from the house and then hid out in the woods—he had been tipped off not to stay in his house for long periods. At about 9:00 p.m., as he "laid back in the pines," he saw twenty-six masked men ride past him and up to his house. "It was the citizens," he told the committee; "they call them Ku-Klux. . . . They went into my house. They had false-faces, and them that had no false-faces had handkerchiefs with holes cut in them." Wright, "sitting looking at them like a rabbit sits in the bushes," heard them say they "came *from hell* for Wright." When they could not find him, they searched the outbuildings and even pried up the boards of the kitchen floor. They searched the barn, where Wright had put up his peanut crop for winter; they grabbed as much of the harvest as they could, but they never found Wright himself and eventually rode away.[2]

Alfred Wright lived to tell about the Klan's visit and, remarkably, gave the Joint Committee the names of his would-be attackers. He, along with his daughters and wife, knew the voices and statures of the masked men and gave the investigators those identities one by one. More generally, he reported on the chaos and intimidation that seemed to have become the norm in Union County and throughout the Piedmont during Reconstruction. The Klan had taken to posting threats of violence on the courthouse door and even ran stories in the local Union paper warning of coming bloodshed and retribution.[3]

For their part, African American men raised armed militias that attempted to protect new citizens from vigilante attacks. Amid the political and social violence of the area, many African Americans had fled Union altogether, leaving for Arkansas, Mississippi, and Alabama, while others, like Wright, were hiding out in Columbia or Charleston.[4] In fact, Wright was not the only African American in the Upstate with a close connection to the Gist family who testified to the congressional committee that same 1871 day.

Eliza Chalk and her son Alfred Vanlew sat down in Columbia to tell their own story of the Klan's violence, and their charges laid blame much closer to the Gist family. William Henry Gist's son David C. Gist was a founding member of Union's "Slickers," a night-riding precursor to the KKK, and a known leader of the Klan in the county. Chalk recalled in detail two nights in early 1871 when Klansmen broke into the Union County jail in search of African American men who had been involved in a whiskey robbery and shootout on a country road not far from Rose Hill. On January 4, masked white men stormed the jail and murdered two men in custody, though some inmates had managed to escape. Chalk testified that six weeks later, the sheriff and other white leaders knocked on her front door, where they found the escaped men, including Chalk's son Joseph Vanlew. The sheriff, along with members of the Klan, put the group back in jail.

On February 12, a reported "five to seven hundred" Klansmen from all over the Piedmont rode into Union, sealing off the roads in and out of town. According to Alfred, David Gist was "Captain of the company" that broke into the jail and seized the eight black men. Members of Gist's group—perhaps

Gist himself—shot six of the men, and the group hanged two others.[5] It was a dramatic but not isolated incident. Another witness told the investigators that there had been at least eleven murders and hundreds of whippings leading up to the jail seizure.[6]

The committee interrogated Chalk and Vanlew's stories and interviewed scores of other witnesses from Union and surrounding areas. Its investigation uncovered the names of dozens of white South Carolinians in the Klan, but it narrowed in on David Gist as a leader of the racial violence. In fact, the former governor's son received a subpoena to appear in front of the congressional committee, but he ignored it. The Joint Committee reported on December 6, 1871, that David Gist had refused to appear, and the chairperson stood on the floor of the Senate chamber and offered a resolution instructing the sergeant at arms to find Gist and take him into custody.[7] While eventually President Ulysses S. Grant would order federal troops back to the Piedmont to put down Klan activity, there is no evidence that Gist ever faced justice for his role in the Union lynching.

THE CONNECTION BETWEEN DAVID GIST, the cotton-centric world his father imagined, and the political and social lives of his former slaves and their children is far more tangible than historians have described. Only a few years before Wright, Chalk, and Vanlew testified about Klan violence, cotton bales burned in the Charleston streets, the crop having failed to save William Henry Gist's slaveocracy like he thought it would. The end of the Civil War brought dramatic and surprising changes to the former governor's world at Rose Hill. The emancipation of the women and men who had been enslaved there was the immediately important event, and it spurred Gist's children and many of their white compatriots to rise up in armed defense of white supremacy. The African American men and women who had fought for freedom in battle now worked to preserve it at the ballot box, in the houses of government, and by walking the streets as part of an armed militia. But the full history of African Americans' impact on the Upcountry was not limited to the worlds of civil and social rights.

Radical environmental change—massive erosion of the farmland of Union and surrounding Piedmont counties that was hastened by the impact of emancipation itself—not only accompanied the rise, and contestation, of black political and social rights; it exacerbated the racist pushback against them. And while historians have charted each of these things separately, most have missed the connection between the two forces, the interwoven factors of freedpeople's impact on the material world and the environment's own role mitigating full African American freedom. The questions that drove all rural Southern communities year after year—what to grow, where to grow it, who to work it, and what it was worth—were central not just to the agricultural livelihoods of South Carolinians but to their political, economic, and social rights as well.

In the face of this relatively quick and stunning upheaval in the physical world, people reacted in a multitude of ways, from uprooting their lives and leaving the region altogether to simply adapting to new occupations. Many white South Carolinians understood the geophysical changes to their land as evidence of long-held racist beliefs in white supremacy and turned back to antebellum ideas to explain their modern lives. Others went a step farther, attempting to invent, re-create, or celebrate Old South conditions and mores in the face of the new reality on the land outside their windows. Cotton, which became even more central to the Piedmont's agriculture, also re-entrenched itself in the white imagination.

AT THE END of the congressional committee's investigation of racial violence in Reconstruction South Carolina, a grand jury foreman reached a telling conclusion. Once the "supremacy of the law" was reestablished for "both races," he argued, "[we] may again join in the cultivation of the soil, build up our common country, and once more live together in peace and harmony."[8] His vision of peace was the establishment of law so that white and black Southerners could get back to farming. Indeed, the "cultivation of the soil" had been the heart of William Henry Gist's prewar vision for the South, and many Southerners, white and black, looked for the return of productive agriculture as the most important sign of peace. Without a change in who owned the land, however, this vision of peace meant white landowners and black farm laborers.

The pressure on former slaves to return to work in farm fields came not only from the Gists and the former planter elite but also from factors around the world. As Sven Beckert convincingly shows, millers and cotton brokers across the globe were obsessed with the question of how emancipation would alter cotton production.[9] Sir Frederick William Aldolphus Bruce, Britain's minister to Washington, tried to reassure the capitalists in his home country that newly freed women and men of the South could be compelled to return to the fields. "Everywhere measures are being taken to force the Negroes to work, and to teach them that freedom means working for wages instead of masters."[10] But small farmers, including the miniscule number of African Americans who had access to their own land, resisted engaging with risky capital markets when they could produce for themselves and their local community. As Beckert dryly puts it, "agricultural wages were too low and too insecure to entice rural cultivators to give up subsistence production, as much greater risks were not balanced by the possibility of higher rewards."[11] And in fact, many laborers sought work in a host of industrial jobs from fertilizer plants to mines and turpentine camps before they would agree to work as farmhands.[12] In Union, some white leaders complained of African American idleness and worse. In 1866 the local newspaper editor charged that "straggling, idle roguish free negroes . . . are pulling the green corn, pundering [*sic*] the orchards, breaking into corn cribs and smoke houses and demoralizing those negroes who are disposed to do their duty."[13]

Beckert's global power brokers and local former enslavers alike not only missed the multitude ways that African Americans were free to engage or not engage in the agricultural economy; they also failed to understand the important environmental realities for a return to cotton production on Southern soils. Extracting more cotton from the land might positively affect production in the short term, but it had decidedly negative outcomes in the longer term, at least in the hilly, erodible soils around Rose Hill. Erosion had been a reality in the Piedmont for more than a generation, but the amplification of cotton planting during Reconstruction, as well as the new methods of farming demanded by a tenant system, would be more than the Piedmont soils could bear.[14]

For black South Carolinians, who by the end of Reconstruction had no voting rights and limited property rights, and faced the specter of violence whenever they stepped out of the narrow space allowed by Jim Crow rules, farming was one of very few options. Tenant farmers, white and black, did not own their land, so they earned a share of the cotton crop that they produced, or paid rent in bales of cotton at the end of the year. With credit tight, the economy—Southern, national, and global—depended on cotton production. Banks only loaned money to landowners who promised to grow the most viable cash crop. This economic pressure to plant more cotton had marked and immediate environmental effects on the land as well as on those who labored upon it.

The fields of hay and wheat and the grazing pigs and cows that Governor Gist could see from his window before the war were replaced by tenant-run farm plots planted end to end in cotton. Trapped in a cycle of debt that depended on producing cotton on rented land, many African Americans and poor whites were crushed by a New South political and economic system that had little space for improvement of their lives.[15] For the African American men and women who worked the lands around Rose Hill, freedom had come at a very complicated cost.

The human ramifications of this nexus of tenancy and cotton are easily visible in the broad statistics of the long postwar period and tell a devastating story. Agricultural output of South Carolina from 1860 to 1870 fell by half, measured in financial terms.[16] The cash value of Union County farms fell by 83 percent.[17] The numbers are stark and bear an important historiographical point. In addition to its exacting human cost, the tenant system undoubtedly had a negative effect on the health of the Piedmont soils, even as cotton production temporarily rose. As one study of the Upcountry puts it, "Uncertain land tenure in the most marginal lands likely proved a lethal combination for soils."[18]

As figure 2 demonstrates, in the last decades of the nineteenth century farmers planted more cotton on more land and production increased. This was cotton's last gasp, as growers put more and more land into cotton, acres that in previous decades may been planted in nitrogen-fixing crops or left to fallow. They also bought expensive fertilizers, which increased yields. Higher production, however, drove down prices, and even in the bumper years, few Union County farmers got rich. After 1890 the number of bales plummeted, in large part because two decades' worth of increased cotton acreage on already sensitive, marginal lands had hastened erosion.

How this played out in a place like Rose Hill is an important and often overlooked detail of the Reconstruction and Jim Crow periods. White landowners—increasingly absent from the land that their families and overseers had once watched very carefully—assigned tenants the poorest areas with the greatest danger of erosion. This part of the landscape, which during Gist's day might have been left to fallow, was now all cotton, all the time.[19] Tenants had little say in what land they were assigned, what they grew on it, and how they went about it. In the parlance of economists, they were being reasonable actors by maximizing their economic chances given narrow choices.

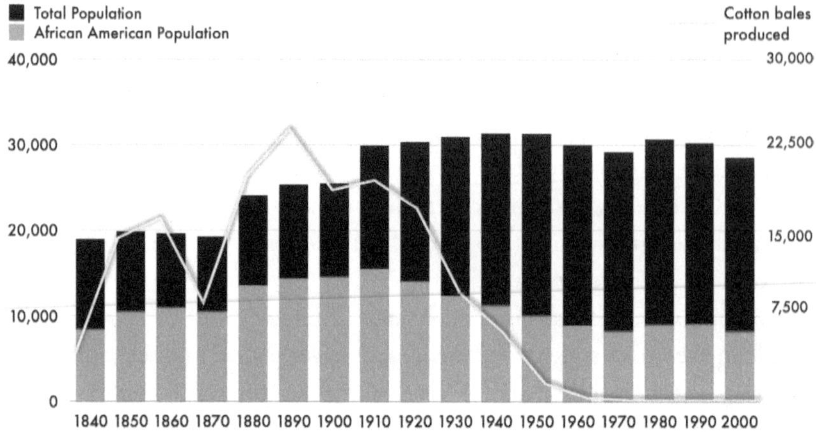

FIG. 2. African American population, total population, and cotton bale production, Union County, South Carolina, 1840–2000. From Population and Agricultural Censuses, 1840–2000.

By 1870 farmers grew more cotton than ever before, and the number kept rising decade after decade, peaking around the turn of the twentieth century.[20] But all of this new cotton did not mean wealth. As Erin Stewart Mauldin points out, for newly freed African American farmers in the 1870s, "long-term economic independence" was now dependent on heavy investments in "fertilizers, improved implements, and other inputs that were often out of reach."[21] For most, agriculture was the only foothold on freedom that emancipated people had, yet it was one of the most important factors in their oppression.

Gist's diversified landscape had been replaced with true monocrop agriculture, and the land and people suffered. But the connection between these events confused contemporary onlookers. Many saw erosion as the fault of lazy, ignorant farmers. As early as 1887, an article in the *Union Times* argued that "a soil would never get exhausted if managed with skill, but would continue to improve in depth and fertility in proportion to the industry bestowed upon it."[22] In other words, erosion was a sign of the lack of work. Of course, as Mauldin, Paul Sutter, and others have shown, most of the problems of erosion were the result of geology and the timing of either of two human factors: the intensification of farming in certain places or land abandonment in others.[23] The situation around Rose Hill was so bad, in fact, that surveyors identified tens of thousands of acres of a "new soil type," Cecil clay loam, that was actually just a lower-horizon soil uncovered by human-induced erosion.[24]

In other words, it wasn't new soil at all; it was just soil that was usually much deeper below the surface. Massive erosion of topsoil had uncovered it.

In 1909 the *Yorkville Enquirer*, a semiweekly newspaper published about forty miles northwest of Rose Hill, ran an article from the forester W. W. Ashe titled "The Waste from Soil Erosion in the South." Ashe saw the problem of erosion not only in five million acres of farmland "now idle" but also that most farmers did not have a reason to put in place methods to protect topsoil. "The exhausted 'old fields,' eroded, gullied, raw with deep wounds, and red as though stained with carnage, need only the touch of knowledge to become revivified."[25] Farm yields were down 70 percent from when lands were "fresh and new," Ashe wrote. He didn't only blame "poor cultural methods"; rather, he pointed to "the heavy rainfall, the physical characteristics of the region, the broken topography and the close-textured soils, and in some measure also the economic conditions." His take was prescient. "Ten million dollars a year will not replace it in the hillside soils whence it came and where it is so badly needed." Ashe recommended landowners stop farming altogether and to plant trees to cover up the bare soils.

By the 1910s it was clear that the area around Rose Hill was some of the most heavily gullied and eroded in the entire Southeast.[26] In 1913 the Clemson College Experiment Station wrote a bulletin, reprinted in several newspapers, called "How Farms Lose Fertility."[27] Addressing what was an obvious concern for readers across the Palmetto State, the article explained that "while it is usual to refer to the effects of erosion as a loss of fertility, its seriousness warrants . . . stronger language." Soils were not being "worn out" but rather "washed away." Organic matter was not being used up by cotton or any other crops; rather, it was being carried away by rain. The authors pleaded with farmers to take care of what topsoil was left, to enact the kind of terracing and drainage efforts that Gist had overseen before the war. But it was clear in the early twentieth century that the problem of erosion was already endemic to the upstate.

A year later the U.S. Department of Agriculture released a soil survey of Union County that had a resigned, even defeated tone. Conditions were bad and getting worse: "The one crop system under which cotton is grown successively year after year and indifference in the preparation and tillage of the soil are largely responsible for the run-down condition of most of the land in the county." The survey was not simply a government document circulated among experts; the Union newspaper printed a short summary so that local farmers could not avoid its findings. It reported on the county's magnificent erosion, an "impaired physical condition," and it listed *nine* crops that it suggested would do better on county farms than cotton. It called for heavier investment in hogs and both dairy and beef cattle. The Cecil clay loam, the authors warned, was good cotton soil *only* with "careful management," given it was "largely an erosion type." The findings would not have surprised anyone who traveled the roads of the county and saw the steep gullies, the red cliffs exposed by the stark absence of the soil.[28]

Farmers understood what the soil surveyors argued and what the chart above bears out. From the end of the Civil War until 1890, the number of acres of cotton, the population of black farmers, and, crucially, cotton yields had increased. African Americans moved to the region to fill landowners' needs for tenants. But by the time the USDA issued its soil warning in 1914, cotton no longer flourished on any but the best Union soils, lands that were rarely those worked by the poorest tenants. The erosion of marginal lands also quickened, and in dramatic fashion erosion became increasingly visible on the landscape.

It is no surprise that black Union Countians began to leave. As banks foreclosed on landowners who could no longer pay their liens or their taxes, more and more tenants were evicted, or they simply could not eke out another year's crop given the requirement to grow cotton and the difficulty of planting it on these marginal lands. The African American population in the county peaked in 1910 and then dropped consistently and dramatically after. The white population continued to climb, though most people now lived in Unionville and not on farms. By 1930 farmers planted half as much acreage in cotton as they had just four decades prior.

The visuals of this land in quick decline, with the bright red clay exposed in dramatic scenes for anyone passing near Rose Hill, became an important aspect of locals' rethinking of both what was possible there and what had come before. To observers seeing the land degrade so quickly in the six decades after the war, environmental decline was a sign of more than just rain, hilly land, and cotton. For the region's white elite, emancipation and African American "mismanagement" became stand-ins for these human and natural processes that had actually created erosion. The growing chorus around erosion and decreased soil fertility from white farmers, politicians, and reformers was "This isn't *our* fault." It was emancipation, the weather, or Northern credit systems that made cotton crops harder and harder to coax from the increasingly jagged hillsides. Despite soil surveys and Clemson extension bulletins, farmers and the men and women who supported their industry increased their talk of Piedmont soils "wearing out," of losing fertility to a century of cotton growing. And they laid blame squarely at the feet of black sharecroppers. This narrative not only excused the failures of white landowners but also reinforced a racialized vision of agricultural decline, one that masked the deeper realities of geology, economic exploitation, and the long arc of environmental degradation.

DECLINING COTTON PRODUCTION, the black exodus from the rural South, and the stark visual reminders of erosion put to the test white Southerners' ideas about cotton. It threatened their understanding of the plant's history, its role in the Civil War and in black freedom, and its central place as an organizing culture for the region. But as cotton slipped from relevance in the late nineteenth and early twentieth centuries, Lost Cause apologists constructed new narratives that put the fiber at the center of antebellum "glory." This narrative was for the most part a story about an Old South past, but it had important implications for both the people of the New South and the region's fields, soil, and trees. The rhetoric of cotton, which was so central to Gist's understanding of the world, was reborn as a worldview that saw the plant's heyday as the pinnacle of the Southern past. This was not a new narrative made up out of thin air. The retelling relied on the visual, social, and economic evidence that was all over former cotton plantations. Racist theories and an unwillingness to engage in environmental realities undergirded this historical rewriting.

At the center of this new framing of Southern history was Mildred Rutherford. Born in Athens, Georgia, in 1851, Rutherford emerged after the war as a leader of the United Daughters of the Confederacy, the leading organization for Lost Cause efforts.[29] Throughout the early twentieth century Rutherford traveled the South dressed as an antebellum plantation mistress, complete with hoop skirt, to give talks about Southern history. Her talks and pamphlets that she wrote paid particular attention to plantation life and slavery. But from her postwar vantage point, at the moment when cotton was eroding the hilly fields around Athens (and the rest of the Piedmont), Rutherford was a leading voice in a curiously timed celebration of the plant.

In "King Cotton: The True History of Cotton and the Cotton Gin," a pamphlet she self-published in 1922, Rutherford recasts the Southern plantation as a site of harmony between slaveholders and the enslaved. Of course, like all Lost Cause rhetoric, Rutherford's said more about the New South than the Old. At the heart of this new telling was cotton itself. "It was the profits from the cotton crop that aroused jealousy in the hearts of the abolitionists, so that they fought to the bitter end every effort on the part of the South to secure additional territory, fearing an increase in the slave states."[30] She claimed that the slave states only wanted to secure western territory "to establish a home for the gradually emancipated slaves."

Since the end of the Civil War, she wrote, things had changed. "The kindly relationship" between owner and enslaved was broken by the aggression of abolitionists. As a result of emancipation, things had gotten much worse for the now-free African American, she claimed. The only savior of the emancipated person's condition was cotton itself. "The cotton crop needs the negro and the negro needs the cotton crop," she wrote. Perhaps fearing the loss of black labor in Southern fields, she decried attempts by Northerners to recruit African Americans out of the South, "to make the negro discontented in his Southern home." "The negroes cannot live in the cold climate," she comforted Southern white readers, "and die rapidly from change of surroundings."[31] If African Americans stayed, she promised, there was a great life available in the cotton fields. "The negroes have bought their homes through cotton—with their earnings they first buy a little piece of land to raise cotton. The cotton requires cultivation, so that he hires himself out while the cotton is growing and thus make the money to support his family. Every member of the family becomes a money earner for the younger child is taught to pick cotton."[32] This idea that free black Southerners sold cotton for cash, used that money to buy productive farmland, and then raised more cotton while hiring themselves out to other farmers was pure invention on Rutherford's part, but reality did not matter. The fantastical narrative not only gained traction among her contemporaries but also became a key part of the Lost Cause histories that educated generations of white and black schoolchildren.[33]

Historians have shown that Lost Cause reinterpretations of history were responses to a perceived threat of African American political power and social equality, but the story of the Southern Piedmont suggests that, alongside race, the environment and cotton were also central to Lost Cause rhetoric. Writers like Rutherford flattened the reality of the antebellum cotton plantation. They made it out to be genteel, peaceful, and prolific. The New South's erosion, abandoned lands, and tenancy served as all the evidence white

Southerners needed to affirm the supremacy of their fictionalized antebellum visions.

Perhaps no writer captured this connection of race, the environment, and Lost Cause rhetoric better than Edward T. H. Shaffer, who made his insights in the very spot that Gist had made his. Like Rutherford, South Carolinian Shaffer was a writer steeped in these Lost Cause narratives about cotton and race, the Civil War and Reconstruction, and the effect of emancipation on the Southern soils.

Shaffer had been raised on a lowcountry plantation in the years following Reconstruction, and by the Great Depression had become an increasingly well-known essayist. From the pages of *The Atlantic Monthly*, he penned relatively straightforward Lost Cause reports from the South, often portraying himself as a sort of translator of "the real South" for Northern readers. For instance, in Shaffer's 1923 article "The Negro Migration—A New South," he linked the "agricultural crisis" of the region with the "Negro exodus." Citing reports of forty thousand African American farmers leaving Georgia in a year and another fifty thousand from South Carolina, Shaffer bid good riddance to emigrating African Americans, not only out of spite but for very specific environmental reasons. In the antebellum and immediate postwar decade, "So long as Cotton was king and needed vast armies of untrained, unskilled privates to maintain his rule in the fields," Shaffer explained, the black population was necessary. Cotton regions "have always teemed with an overwhelming mass of Negro labor." But now, the "sand lands, divided up into small patches, requiring the annual stimulation of high-priced fertilizer," could no longer produce enough cotton to make the effort financially worthwhile. With the "cotton-growing industry prostrate," Shaffer concluded, the South "is definitely entering upon a new phase in which the Negro, as the South visualizes him, can play almost no part." Shaffer saw the threat of black outmigration differently than Rutherford, who was trying to convince African Americans to stay in the South. Shaffer promised his readers that soon the "old system of cotton-growing" would be "as dead as indigo culture," and that the more black Southerners who moved north, the more room there would be for "a beneficial influx of white immigration."[34]

One reader who took issue with Shaffer's characterization of African American migration was the publicity director of the National Association for the Advancement of Colored People (NAACP), Herbert Seligmann. In a letter to the editors of *The Atlantic Monthly*, he took particular issue with

Shaffer's characterization that it was only the cotton-growing coastal regions from which black Southerners emigrated. Shaffer had argued that African Americans working on large cotton plantations after emancipation were "content to jog along in a shiftless, servile status but a step removed from actual bondage," but Seligmann pointed out that it was not simply declining cotton crops that suddenly made this group want to leave the South. "The thousands coming north because their children are denied education, themselves denied justice in the courts, decent treatment in public places, safety of life and property from the mob, could, and do, tell a different story."[35] It was an argument that, while certainly backed by the accounts of migrants themselves, found no quarter among white Lost Cause apologists like Shaffer. For the next two decades, Shaffer spent a great deal of time trying to link the modern rural landscapes of the 1920s and 1930s South to his nostalgic and fictionalized account of the "glory days" of the Old South.

In 1936 Shaffer arrived at Rose Hill and made the condition of the plantation house and surrounding landscape a central organizing framework for his connections between cotton, history, and contemporary society. His visit reveals the extent to which the environmental collapse of the Piedmont was as much a human story as an ecological one, and how much that landscape affected the narrative of the New South that Shaffer told. Shaffer combined the Lost Cause's ideological perspective on cotton with a pseudoscientific understanding of the environment.

What is particularly interesting is how Shaffer understood the Piedmont's ecological decline as a function of black freedom. Shaffer read the landscape not in terms of what was possible agriculturally or environmentally, but rather in terms of what had been lost with the end of slavery and how emancipation itself was written onto the fields and gullies surrounding Rose Hill. Whereas in 1865 William Henry Gist's optimism about the future of the Southern slaveocracy was imprinted on the land and mansion, to Shaffer the clearest evidence of the *failure* of Gist's Confederate vision was the material evidence of that very same house and land. Shaffer's understanding of Rose Hill was a pessimistic one, a reflection on what he saw as the collapse of Piedmont civilization and a warning about the future for the local people and their environment.[36]

Building on his *Atlantic Monthly* essays, in the mid-1930s Shaffer began working on a book about North and South Carolina's remaining grand antebellum mansions and their gardens. Published by the University of North

Carolina Press in 1937, *Carolina Gardens: The History, Romance and Tradition of Many Gardens of Two States Through More Than Two Centuries* is a journey not just over land but seemingly through time, describing Shaffer's travels on the highways and backroads of the Carolinas as he searched for the region's most famous gardens.

For Shaffer, these outdoor spaces were living historical sources for understanding the antebellum South, a time and place that he believed was the peak of American society. "No finer culture has existed in America than that agrarian civilization that from 1660 until 1860 found its most perfect expression in the two Carolinas," he wrote. When the crop spread inland from the coast, "cotton became enormously profitable; and the fields of Carolina were whitened with summer snow."[37] For Shaffer, white pioneer families like the Gists, who carved out these farms from the primeval forest and settled the hills with their cotton and slave labor, were the progenitors of a great civilization because, as he put it, they were a "land conscious race."[38] Cotton transformed the South, he argued, creating a supreme culture. By the 1930s, the most important evidence left were the "stately dwellings," some of which, "overlooked by Sherman, survive to attest the culture, wealth, and artistic taste of plantation masters in the final, or cotton, period."[39]

In *Carolina Gardens* Shaffer meanders across North and South Carolina, attempting to tie the well-kept mansions that he visited with what he understood as a failed New South. For two hundred pages he describes colonial and antebellum homes of both states, and the camellias and live oaks that survived in their gardens. Then, in the final quarter of the book, Shaffer's writing becomes more pointed. As he stood in the garden at a house called Cross Keys, a large brick residence located at an important Upstate crossroads in Union County, just eight miles west of Rose Hill, he made striking observations about what had changed in the land and culture of the South. Shaffer underscores the importance of Cross Keys by noting that Confederate President Jefferson Davis (purportedly) dined there during his failed escape from Union forces near the end of the Civil War. Shaffer described his own meeting with the distinguished white owners of Cross Keys, direct descendants of the antebellum family that had hosted the Confederate leader. Shaffer commented extensively on the house, its well-kept furnishings, and its meticulous garden.[40] As he left the grounds, he stopped by "a clump of gardenia bushes," turned back to admire "the solid old house with its protecting grove of cedars," and wondered if "ever my garden quest would again bring such rich rewards." The sanguine remark, and his high spirits leaving Cross Keys in search of "The House of Gist," were perhaps merely a narrative device, a setup for the disappointment he would find down the road at Rose Hill.

As he traversed "many confusing forks and cross-roads," Shaffer noted the transition from the neat and historic landscape of Cross Keys to a different world entirely, if not a different time. "I passed some scattered Negro cabins," he wrote, "then entered an uninhabited region of cut-over hills." Within two sentences, Shaffer had radically changed his tone. While not entirely contradictory, his observation of "Negro cabins" and his judgment of the land as "uninhabitable" hints at the writer's linking of the landscape and black poverty. Yet his observations out his car window were hardly exaggerated. Photographers who visited Union County at roughly the same time of Shaffer's visit captured images of the dramatic erosion. (See figures 3 and 4.) His use of "uninhabitable" seems fair, but the language that he begins to use to describe nature's covering, even choking the remnants of Old South society reveal, and project, the melding of his cultural and landscape ideas.[41]

Shaffer drove on, through "weary monotonous miles of scanty second growth pines spotting eroded hills and silt filled bottomlands." In a foreboding passage, he wrote of his first sign of the Gists' long history in the area, the family graveyard. "In a patch of scrub pines near the road," the writer made out three tall marble towers. He stopped and climbed out of his car, walking toward the gravestones through a "rust-eaten" gate, "tearing my way through briers and chinquapin bushes." He read the monument and stood there, while narrating for the reader a brief, Lost Cause–inspired history of William Henry Gist's leadership in the state's secession. Graveside, Shaffer described Gist's governorship as "South Carolina's moment of glory." Yet he could not stop himself from linking the scene with the environmental collapse around him. The graveyard was overgrown with pines and scrubby bush, yet the author found "euonymus, English ivy, mimosa, the last man-planted things to wage the losing struggle against rank forest bushes and the roots of trees that rend the wall." The symmetry of his description of Gist's Confederate leadership—and loss—and the trees pushing in to choke the non-native plants and destroy the antebellum stone enclosure foreshadowed his opinion of Rose Hill itself. This understanding of the landscape, Shaffer's pitting of *new* nature crowding out an older, more ordered nature, had only just begun.[42]

A few miles down the road Shaffer stopped, this time struck by another monument to the Old South, "a sudden grove of timber," which he found

FIGS. 3 AND 4. Photographs show the dramatic gullying and soil erosion in southern Union County around the time of Shaffer's visit to Rose Hill. For perspective on the size, note the person standing on the gully rim in Figure 4. Coweeta Hydrological Laboratory Archive, Coweeta, North Carolina.

"stately" and "magnificent." He understood the old growth hardwood plot as a sign that the Gist mansion must be near. Rather than the short-leaf pines that had crowded in on the eroded lands he had seen driving, these were "poplars, hickorys, red and white and chestnut oaks." He left his car—"deep gullies and sharp stones" made him doubt that an automobile had ever traversed the path—and made his way toward the stand of trees. Finally, the "leaf-strewn and vine-grown" walkway led him to a small clearing where he could see ahead of him "a dark line of magnolias and beyond them the façade of a tall, melancholy vested mansion."[43]

The house was far from the freshly painted grand abode of Gist's time, but Shaffer's descriptions of how nature was retaking the slave-made structure are revealing. The mansion's once-stuccoed walls were now "weathered buff and green." In places, the stucco had "fallen away in great scars exposing the blood-red brick, all so splotched with mosses and lichens that it seemed a dream castle of the woods that would vanish should one attempt to enter it." The rose plot had gone wild. Shaffer imagined what it once had been but determined that the "tangle" he saw made it the "most melancholy garden that I found in all my Carolina journey."[44] "I shoved my way through dense masses of long untrimmed tree boxwood," he wrote, and made his way toward the back door of the "macabre ruin." There, he found "desolation more horrible." "The high, double verandas with Corinthian columns and carved pediment tottered at crazy angles as though in the throes of an earthquake," he wrote. It was a house "once stately," but now "contorted in a frenzied, drunken dance of death."[45]

He walked inside and found a cool central hallway but heard noise in the drawing room. Shaffer made his way to the second floor, describing the condition of the house in terms of the nature he saw indoors. The "large mullioned end windows were shattered, and wasps buzzed in and out." An old wooden secretary's drawers sat opened, "filled with red clay tubes of the 'dirt dauber's' industry." He made his way onto the west-facing balcony and took in the view. From this vantage point, Shaffer returned to his analogy between the lost war and the lost gardens of the Old South. He portrays a battle waged between the remnants of cultivated nature and the wild forests and even the people of this New South. He labeled as "valiant" the occasional "slim tendril of ivy" or periwinkle that burst through the decaying garden. Shaffer did not like what he saw or smelled, "an odor of strange compounds—the keen breath of boxwood, rotting leaves in the enclosing forest, and the aroma of cooking food and boiling clothes in the drawing-room."[46]

FIG. 5. Photograph of Rose Hill taken around the time Shaffer visited. South Caroliniana Library, University of South Carolina.

FIG. 6. Photograph of Rose Hill taken around the time Shaffer visited. South Caroliniana Library, University of South Carolina.

FIG. 7. The only image of Rose Hill that Shaffer included in *Carolina Gardens* showcased what he saw as the wild encroachment of plants covering the antebellum, manicured, civilized garden. Shaffer, *Carolina Gardens*, image between pp. 252 and 253.

What Shaffer saw around him was the collapse of the Old South imprinted on both the landscape and the building itself. Rose Hill, rapidly decaying and open to the elements, was being swallowed up by the "enclosing forest." For Shaffer, the relic of Rose Hill, its house and its garden, was the symbol for Old South civilization, and the creeping forest representative of its New South ruin.[47] Shaffer's biggest disappointment, it seems, was that he could still see the remnants of Gist's time. At other plantation sites, especially in the Lowcountry, Shaffer took satisfaction in the fact that nothing was left, that nature had reclaimed all signs of human presence. And yet here at Rose Hill not only could he still make out the pattern of the boxwoods in the garden and the intricate woodwork of the mantel, there was still a very human presence in the house.

When he first entered, he had heard a noise coming from a first-floor parlor. There he found "a group of sullen Negro women washing clothes, their dinner cooking in an iron pot beneath the blackened but exquisitely carved mantel." Laundry was hung on a line running through the large space, "like some monster cobwebs, defiling the lovely room."

"Who lives here?" he asked.

"Us does," Shaffer described as the women's answer, making some effort to record, exaggerate, or make up the women's dialect.

"Is this the old Governor Gist house?"

"Might be, dat what some white folks call 'um."

Shaffer recorded the terse exchange in terms similar to those describing creeping pines or unkempt flowers. Their presence created cobwebs of laundry, like the insects' detritus left in the furniture, or the lichens living on the stucco. He gave the women a quarter, which "secured a welcome a bit more gracious" and left the room.[48]

It is hard to exactly identify the two African American women whom Shaffer encountered in the Rose Hill kitchen. Sally Mae Jeter Vinson was born on Rose Hill in 1923 and lived there until she was about fourteen, which means the women Shaffer met may have been her family. Vinson did not live in the mansion, but in a house "right down the hill from the mansion up there" where her parents had moved during Reconstruction after they were married. Mary Gist Harry, a descendant of the governor, was "head of all that land down there," Vinson recalled. Vinson's parents were almost certainly sharecroppers, working various parts of the broken-up Gist plantation wherever there were fields still flat enough to till. In her late nineties, Vinson still remembered the names of a couple of the fields, including "down in the flat," which was a field near Fair Forest Creek.[49] By the time Shaffer visited in the mid-1930s, there were few fields still flat enough and with enough topsoil to make a crop.

The exchange, set amid environmental collapse and social upheaval, is loaded with meaning. For the women dealing with a white interlocutor who walked into their space uninvited, Shaffer was yet another indication of white power over their lives. The seven decades since emancipation had brought their community a kind of freedom, but the pressure to farm cotton on small parcels had hastened the erosion that had begun in the early nineteenth century. As farming became harder and harder, so many African Americans left the region. Those who stayed faced hardships of every stripe: economic, social, and environmental. A generation earlier, Alfred Wright, Eliza Chalk, and Alfred Vanlew had risked everything to testify about the failures of the Reconstruction government to protect their communities against the violence of William Henry Gist's son. And six decades later, Shaffer appeared claiming that the collapse of the landscape was the fault of emancipation itself. The interregnum between emancipation and the Great Depression had seen decline in most areas of black life in the upper Piedmont.

For Shaffer, the Civil War, black freedom, and cotton's decline had torn up the land, left a once-grand house in ruins, and struck a death blow to what he saw as the pinnacle of American civilization, the Old South. His observations about the Depression-era Piedmont echoed those of writers like Rutherford, who had flattened the complexity of the antebellum plantation into a nostalgic fiction. Shaffer reinforced the Lost Cause's vision of a golden age undone. But if Rutherford romanticized cotton's past, Shaffer fixated on its disappearance. As he left Rose Hill, he took one last look at its "tall bluff façade, the brick wall and iron fence enclosing the raised acre." With fields eroded into gullies, the house nearly swallowed by the forest, and African Americans living inside, Shaffer saw not just a fading landmark but the unraveling of an entire social and economic order. His writings reveal how Lost Cause rhetoric did not simply mourn the fall of the South—it also rested on the ruins of cotton itself, turning its decline into evidence of a world that, in their eyes, could never be restored.[50]

CHAPTER FOUR

Planting the Lost Cause

AT THE END of his mid-1930s visit to the gullied cotton lands around Rose Hill, Edward T. H. Shaffer admitted that he thought the land, the house, and the entire Piedmont cotton society was at its end. It was the final moments of a white-dominated civilization marked by honor, white supremacy, and rows of cotton. The plantation's heyday, he argued, was the antebellum South, when the flowering white crop and slavery ordered the Carolina landscape. The only evidence that Shaffer needed was visual. The deep red gullies along his drive, the African American women living in the mansion, and the absence of cotton on the land *shook* the Southern apologist.

Shaffer, however, was ignorant of the history that mattered there. He understood little of life before the war, Gist himself, or the diversification of the farm's agricultural operations. Crucially, given his romantic view of the pre–Civil War South, he did not understand the labor that the enslaved workforce had done to keep the fragile agro-ecosystem functioning. He misunderstood Reconstruction as well. The soil science and geology at work under the feet of tenant farmers pushed them to put every available inch of land into production. These pressures on tenants to grow cotton and use more fertilizer, year after year, hastened the decline of the fragile geology with disastrous results. Shaffer witnessed the outcome: a visually arresting and bleak place marked by holes in the earth and lots of poverty. He seems oblivious to the efforts of black Union Countians to organize and protect their political and civil rights, as well. Shaffer did not write about the white-on-black violence or political chicanery that local African Americans fought against. He compared black outmigration to the flight of birds.

Shaffer, raised in the Lowcountry and educated in segregated schools, had imbibed the Lost Cause story of cotton, which taught him that the crop reigned over the South as nothing but a beneficial ruler for all that it touched. He wrote Rose Hill's visual and environmental decline into that story, published his book, and influenced readers across the region and beyond. His writings reified the white narrative that had already become canon.

While Shaffer described the time of his visit as the nadir of Rose Hill, the 1930s was actually a decade of both incredible ecological renaissance and social movement. Within a single generation, the continued exodus of the black population and a second wave of transformative ecological change remade Union County to be whiter and greener. With a smaller rural African American population and a new forest springing from the worn red clay, a green canopy covered the monumental gullies. The result was a region with a newfound fertility not for cotton but for the Lost Cause history of the crop. Ironically, in this new forest land where few African Americans still lived and where pines were covering the old fields, cotton's story found a new lease on life.

This chapter tells the intertwined history of these two rebirths, that of pine forests and of the Lost Cause narrative within Rose Hill mansion itself. These two events were linked; the latter could not have happened without the former. White locals' efforts to rebuild and reclaim the house were successful because of the trees' facility for covering over the embarrassing erosion gullies, the visible signs of cotton's damage. At the heart of these dual processes was the old plant itself.

WHILE THE GULLIES of the Piedmont offered the clearest visual evidence of the region's decline, environmentally they were but one part of a complex ecosystem in flux. Since the end of the nineteenth century, geologists and federal agents had been paying close attention to parts of southern Union County. But the pine ascendance and the history of scientists trying to better understand what natural forces were at work picked up speed in the immediate years following Shaffer's visit. Beyond the gullying itself, the clearest evidence of the cotton land's decline was the work of local tax collectors and bankers who saw a wave of property abandonment during the Depression. Thousands of landholders, unable to grow a cash crop or coax tenants onto the land to make something grow, built debts they couldn't pay. Eviction notices piled up. Many packed up and left without a word to their debtors. This environmental and economic problem soon became a political issue.

In 1911 Congress passed the Weeks Act, which allowed the federal government to purchase abandoned lands, parcel by parcel, to piece together national forests.[1] The idea was not vast stretches of contiguous lands all protected by the Forest Service but rather patchwork collections of abandoned lands where, the government agents decided, crops could not be produced and people should not live. In 1933 the National Forest Reservation Commission turned its attention to severely eroded areas around Rose Hill. It bought up what local historian Allan D. Charles called "essentially worthless" Union County land that had been "cottoned-out."[2]

A year later, the Civilian Conservation Corps (CCC) arrived with dozens of young men in tow. The CCC was in the process of transforming America's natural world. Across the United States, the organization's laborers put their fingerprints on at least 118 million acres; they built a million miles of fence and planted a billion trees.[3] In Union County they established a camp in the heart of the cottoned-out land, very near the husk of Rose Hill, at the plantation house of a Gist relative down the road. They called it Camp Jefferson Davis.[4] From there, the CCC cadets took on a massive operation digging drainage ditches, building fire breaks, filling in gullies, and planting thousands of pine seedlings. It was arduous work, performed mostly by young men drawn from cities across the state and the Southeast.

In 1936 President Franklin Roosevelt signed an order that created the Sumter National Forest out of the network of abandoned and marginal lands the federal government had purchased in the Upstate. The USFS kept adding lands as more old farms washed out and owners and debt collectors were willing to sell. The government built a massive holding. Federally owned forest eventually comprised more than 60 percent of all land area in Union County. In 1939 the Forest Service added the former Gist estate itself, owned at the time by a distant heir of the governor, to its holdings. Records indicate that the house was crumbling and the lands unproductive. The deed noted that three tenants were still living on the property, possibly the same women whom Shaffer had encountered.[5]

Though proponents of land-buying programs thought of it as an opportunity to improve the lives of rural people and the land, what they would have called "conservation," functionally the program shut down the social and agricultural viability of these areas. This was about people, not just soil erosion. Federal forest officials and other New Dealers concluded that former cotton fields like in southern Union County were simply "slums of the country." As historian Al Hester has pointed out, many locals lived without clean water, sanitary privies, or safe housing. Malnutrition was rampant. And to top it off, since so many landowners had abandoned their farms, the county suffered a loss of tax revenue and therefore could not afford social programs to help out rural residents, even if those with the political power in Unionville or Columbia had been inclined to help.[6] Taking the land out of production by allowing it to return to forest meant closing down the few opportunities for agriculture that had existed. It was a kind of rural gentrification, pushing policies that made life harder for poor rural people and easier for trees and deer.

Many, if not most, local Union Countians were ready to give up their land, but that decision was based on a number of environmental and social factors. As Michael R. Coughlan, Donald R. Nelson, and their coauthors demonstrate, abandonment and reforestation were already rampant by the time the USFS started knocking on farmhouse doors offering to buy land, which is "likely" why locals had such "buy-in." By studying the degree of the former cotton land's slope—the steepest hillsides indicate the highest rates of erosion and the worst land to farm—alongside the land deeds, these anthropologists discovered that the Forest Service bought up the worst acreage first. This was abandoned land where loblolly and shortleaf pine saplings and other young trees were already growing.[7]

The authors also found that the land purchased first was likely to have been worked by sharecroppers and fixed-rent tenants more so than farms operated by owners.[8] It makes sense. Owners farmed the best land themselves and arranged for sharecroppers to farm the worst. This allowed landholders to keep all of the profits on the flat lands and share the risk of farming the eroding hills. The only land left in cotton production—a few thousand acres in total—was flat, well drained, and not for sale.

The pace and drama of this area's transformation can almost not be overstated. In 1933 all of the acres that Coughlan and Nelson studied were privately held; by 1946, *90 percent* of it was owned by the Forest Service.[9] This dramatic change in landownership was both the product of environmental and social change and a further cause. As figure 2 illustrates, cotton production cratered, the African American population dropped, and the federal government became a major landowner all within a short time. Within two decades of the creation of the Sumter National Forest, the most heavily eroded lands were covered by a blanket of pine trees.

This pair of forces, human and environmental, had fundamentally changed the landscape of the South Carolina Piedmont. Gist's diversified, productive slaveocracy had given way to the cotton-scarred gullies and muddy streams that Shaffer witnessed. But then, within only two decades, it had changed again, at least visually. Now a drive through Union County was a trip through a forest thick with pines and a few hardwoods. Cotton's gullies were gone—at least hidden from the visual eye—and deer and other wildlife moved in to roam the former cotton fields. At the same time, a great number of the county's rural residents emigrated to the county seat or on to Greenville, Spartanburg, or Columbia. Many, especially those African Americans with the means and desire, moved to industrial centers in the Midwest and Northeast.

To a casual visitor to Union County in the early 1940s, there were few farms, lots of pines, and, more importantly, no signs of the 150 years of cotton farming that had wrecked the fragile ecosystem of the Carolina Piedmont. It is this new view, this environmental process of covering up the place's history, that allowed a new interpretation of what cotton, slavery, and the Confederacy had meant to the region. Here again, landscape would affect a new brand of cotton culture, even amid the absence of the crop.

IN 1939 THE U.S. senator from South Carolina Ellison D. Smith, known popularly as "Cotton Ed," wrote a letter to Ferdinand Silcox, chief of the USFS. Senator Smith wanted to know about the Forest Service's plans for Rose Hill. He asked that the agency save the dilapidated mansion as a "Historic Shrine" to honor Governor Gist, so that locals could make a "complete restoration and beautification" of the site.[10]

Silcox's response to the prominent South Carolinian was remarkable. The forest chief wrote that honoring the secessionist governor would be a ridiculous use of federal resources. He told the senator that Gist had been a "pompous politician" and an alcoholic. He pointed to "the fortune that Gist amassed from the slave labor." Something had clearly struck a nerve with Silcox, because he went so far as to write a poem as part of his response to "Cotton Ed":

> And yet dear Edd, you still expound
> [Gist's] home is all historic ground,
> And that you want us to restore
> This worthless house and maybe more.[11]

The reply left no doubt as to what the USFS would do about the falling-down mansion.

Locally, however, a push emerged to save the house. With the Forest Service, who owned the property, refusing to act, and the trees slowly but steadily encroaching toward the dilapidated structure, some local Union County residents looked for ways to halt its demise. Eventually, the regional chapter of the Daughters of the American Revolution (DAR) convinced Clyde T. Franks, who apparently had some financial means, to attempt to purchase Rose Hill from the Forest Service. The government refused to let the property go. After all, the agency was in the business of taking land out of production, of putting together as complete a network of forest property as it could, not of encouraging development or supporting tourism. At the beginning of World War II, the government even considered using the deteriorating Rose Hill house as a bombing target to train military airmen. (Today one of the roads winding through the forest near the mansion is Bombing Range Road.) Franks persisted with the Forest Service and finally succeeded in 1943. With the support of the local Fairforest chapter of the DAR, Franks bought the house and 184 acres surrounding it. The plan was to find local and regional support to fix the mansion so that it could host DAR meetings and social functions.[12]

Though most details of the remodeling are gone, over the course of the 1940s Clyde Franks and the DAR rebuilt and restored the mansion and its garden to accentuate Rose Hill's history within the secession movement and the Confederacy. As the forest covered over cotton's effects on the land, Franks seems to have put special focus on the garden that gave the property its name. This went as far as overseeing the planting of a specific kind of rose in supposedly the same place it had been in Gist's time and more tellingly, grooming the boxwoods that sit right outside the house's entrance into an X shape that evoked the Confederate battle flag.[13]

Once the house and grounds were finished, Franks set to overseeing its active interpretation as an antebellum showplace. He hired Louisa Browning, an African American woman, to live in the house and give tours. Soon visiting groups lined up to walk through the Confederate hedges, the rose garden, and the house. In 1948, for instance, Browning greeted the Abbeville Garden Club in a plaid dress, apron, and head wrap. As historian Kevin Michael Allen has written, her appearance was "visually reminiscent of Hattie McDaniel's 'Mammy' in *Gone with the Wind*." A newspaper story about the club's visit referred to Browning only as the "Aunt" who was "dressed in the costume of the South's famous black 'mammy.'"[14]

There were no regular hours for visiting Rose Hill at this time; tourists just drove up, knocked on the door, and paid fifty cents to Browning for a tour.[15] It is impossible to know how many people visited the private historic site, but it generated enough interest that in the late 1950s local businesspeople began lobbying the state government to buy Rose Hill from Franks and make it into a state park, which they believed would encourage more visitors and help with upkeep and broader marketing.[16] Their efforts worked.

On December 20, 1960, the not-so-subtle centennial anniversary of South Carolina's secession from the United States, the Union High School marching band and choir serenaded local politicians, religious leaders, and nearly a thousand visitors for the official dedication ceremony for Rose Hill State Park. Not to be lost in the crowds were men and women dressed in approximations of antebellum clothing to impersonate Governor Gist, his wife, States Rights Gist, and other legendary Confederate men. "For the Glory of God," began the dedication, "and to the Memory of the Southern Confederacy." The new park was given its charge.[17]

By the time of the dedication, the mansion sat amid a dense forest of federally owned pines rather than fields of cotton and enslaved people, but it told a new, clear story of William Henry Gist. A bust of the governor, some furniture owned by his family, and other period pieces filled the rooms, and the gardens and landscaping were meant to evoke the condition of the house in 1860.[18] One writer observed that the mansion, alongside the "old fashioned roses" and "hand-hewn stone steps," "looks today as it did when it was one of the centers of gaiety for the social elite of upper South Carolina."[19]

The restoration of the house meant the rebuilding of Gist's reputation as well. A 1977 history of Union County called Rose Hill "the cradle of Southern Secession" and noted that the mansion "shows strength as possessed by its builder."[20] It was now a destination for anyone who wanted to "see how a country gentleman lived before the War Between the States." Gist's resurrection—from the slaveholding, fire-eating rebel to "country gentleman"—was complete. In the 1960s the state of South Carolina began using Rose Hill in a national advertising campaign. The tourist office encouraged readers of *Women's Day* to visit the Palmetto State's historic sites, where they could "recall plantation days from the piazza at Rose Hill." There seemed to be no irony, given the cotton land's replacement with forest, in the advertisement's tagline: "Unwind in South Carolina's *unchanging* beauty."[21]

A VISITOR WHO FOLLOWED the South Carolina tourism board's call to visit Rose Hill to "recall plantation days" could walk up the ornate, curved staircase and step through the same room where Gist had written his letter to other Southern governors and where Shaffer had looked out over the weed-infested garden. This was a privileged view, in every sense of the word.

The governor had looked out on an enslaved labor force working night and day to keep his soils intact and his cotton growing. His vision of the Confederacy, which made cotton a unifying force for Southern leaders from disparate environments, was based on ideas of supremacy over both land and people. From the same perch, Shaffer blamed the gullies and abandoned fields on emancipation and the failure of Gist's Confederate vision.

The tourists who climbed the stairs to the same spot in the second half of the twentieth century had to rely on their imaginations to know what was going on in the dirt and pine litter below, but the cultural and historical story was spelled out for them in the furniture, the signage, the rose garden, and the walls of the mansion itself. The Lost Cause celebration of Gist and his way of life anchored the presentation of Rose Hill, and the federally controlled pine forest made it hard for the casual visitor to learn the environmental history of cotton or slavery.

What was buried was the history of black labor on that land. These views from the Rose Hill second-floor gallery intentionally foregrounded white elite understandings of time and space. The park's rebirth as an antebellum cotton farm with no cotton, nor any clear signs of the crop's impact, set aside all alternative understandings of the place. Just as Gist's vision of a unified Cotton South brought together his thinking about the environment and white supremacy, Rose Hill's rebirth as a Lost Cause space excluded African American history at the same time that it venerated Gist's treatment of people and the land. And while the re-created house excluded the African American story from the mansion, the landscape outside its walls did as well.

As was the case for Shaffer decades earlier, the view from Rose Hill State Park was about what a tourist could not see. Nothing about the state park spoke to the plight of the property's black residents. For decades after the park's rebirth, there was no sign explaining Ku Klux Klan violence, or the ways that black South Carolinians seized the weapons of freedom the moment they had access to them. Nothing spelled out the local story of

Republican Party politics, or the fact that Governor Gist's former slaves had organized militias to protect their community from Gist's son.

These stories were not recorded in the land either, though certainly the natural features around the mansion were telling a version of black history. The pines hid the story of African Americans' access to land after emancipation. The gullies—still there and still deep—told the story of the world's appetite for cotton pushing sharecroppers to make fragile soil produce nothing but cotton. But without an interpretation of that land, or even a footpath that a tourist might take away from the house to see the erosion, it was not a story that a visitor could have easily engaged.

And who were the visitors coming to Rose Hill State Park anyway? By 1974, there were only thirty-three African American farmers in all of Union County, less than 10 percent of farm operators overall, and likely none of them was growing any cotton.[22] (There were only 140 acres of cotton being grown by anyone in the entire county.) By 2000, African Americans comprised only 28 percent of the county population, and most lived in the towns rather than among the rural pines. The more the black presence in the county shrank, the more white political and economic leaders recited the Lost Cause story: This was a glorious place before the war, a land of cotton, wealth, and enslaved labor. Emancipation, they insisted, had ruined both the land and the economy of the Piedmont. And so, with cotton long gone and the landscape transformed, the myth itself became the county's most enduring crop—preserved in the stories told at Rose Hill, in the work of the DAR, and in the tourist brochures that cast the past in sepia tones. In the end, the pines covered more than just the eroded soil; they buried histories that no one in power wanted to remember.

CHAPTER FIVE

The Limits of Reconciliation and Recovery

AT THE DAWN of the twenty-first century, a driver who wanted to retrace Edward T. H. Shaffer's trip from Cross Keys to the Gist mansion would have found much similar to the writer's trek during the Great Depression. The traveler would have bounced over the same hilly roads alongside some of the worst gullying in the United States, the same scars on the land that horrified Shaffer decades earlier. But in 2000, unlike in Shaffer's time, no one riding along the road would have noticed the erosion. Rather than seeing the cuts in the land from the windows of a car, travelers mainly would have seen trees. Most of the land along the roads in rural Union County was federal, owned and managed by the U.S. Forest Service. The Sumter National Forest, not eroded cotton fields, dominated the landscape. Shaffer had seen the erosion and been wistful about the "loss" of cotton's heyday; few visitors seven decades later would have such strong emotions. Most would not understand what they were *not* seeing.

A tourist in 2000 would likely also miss the small, poorly marked Gist graveyard about a mile from the entrance to Rose Hill. Shaffer had complained that it was overgrown in his day, and by the turn of the twenty-first century it was only slightly cleaned up. A knee-high brick wall along the sides and back, which failed to keep away either natural or human interference, crumbled in places. At some point in the seventy years between Shaffer's visit and the early twenty-first century, the Union County Historical Foundation and a local couple who owned a monument company had placed a stone marking the site. "Ancestral Cemetery of the Gist Family," it read. "Among those buried here are the secession governor of South Carolina." The stone also made sure any visitor who stumbled upon the graveyard would not miss the house. "Rose Hill the Gist Mansion is located one mile east of here," it noted.[1]

FIG. 8. Rose Hill seen from the side, as a visitor would encounter the mansion walking from the parking lot, 2014. The flagpole flies the Confederate battle flag and the South Carolina secessionist banner. Photograph by Everett Leigh.

Following the stone's directions, a car would pull into the driveway of Rose Hill past signs identifying it as a state park, through the gates, and along the path until the house came into view. At this point, the State of South Carolina's interpretation of the site's history began, but the vines and trees had already begun offering history lessons for the miles leading to the house. A car would pull into the parking lot that sat a few dozen feet south of the house, down a small hill, on a flat area. The gravel lot was at some point part of the house grounds; it could have been a vegetable garden, or held a slave cabin or carriage barn. Exiting the car, a visitor would almost certainly look up toward the imposing side of the mansion and take in the first sign of the state's continued Lost Cause interpretation. Standing prominently next to the house was a flagpole, which at least for some considerable time in the early 2000s flew the South Carolina secessionist flag underneath the more familiar Stars and Bars of the Confederate battle flag. It was clear, before the visitor could read any signage or walk through the grounds, that this was a site celebrating the Confederacy. (If tourists timed their visit on a particular weekend each year, they would encounter Civil War reenactors.)[2]

In many ways, Rose Hill at the turn of the twenty-first century was a Lost Cause monument like any other. It fit squarely into historians' understanding of the ways that white Southerners built spaces to celebrate a false history of the Old South and the Confederacy in the service of contemporary purposes, most often the perpetration of white supremacy. Since Rose Hill State Park had opened, on the very centennial of the state's secession, it centered its interpretation on William Henry Gist and his vision of the world. The state park service designed the property so that, from the moment you drove up the path to the house, the experience was about visiting a place frozen in 1861.

Despite the claim on a 1999 map that Rose Hill "shows how plantation families lived in the 1800's," it was hard for visitors to understand the lives of anyone who lived there except the Gist family.[3] There were hundreds of other people living on the property at the time being depicted, but one had to work very hard to see any signs of them. There were no restored spaces that enslaved people had worked beyond the ornamental garden and the interior of the house, and both of those areas were interpreted from white perspectives. There was no explanation of how African Americans lived and worked to keep Gist's cotton plantation going.

On the other hand, despite this classic Lost Cause interpretation, there were many ways in which, by 2000, a visitor's interaction with the history told by the governor's house was nothing like that at other neo-Confederate spaces. Its physical situation in the landscape set it apart from other Lost Cause settings in important ways. Whereas most of the well-known Southern icons like statues and obelisks often sat next to symbols of state power like a county courthouse, or in urban settings where Jim Crow was to be most strictly enforced, Rose Hill was far removed from those places. A visitor had to seek out this manufactured site of Lost Cause memory, not interact with it on the way to the post office or at a restored battlefield.[4]

Likewise, Gist's mansion was unlike the more famous restored plantations of South Carolina's Lowcountry or Louisiana's River Road district. Rose Hill was relatively remote from other sites; it did not appear on driving guides for Confederate historic sites or on lists of must-see mansion homes. It was not a day trip destination for those visiting Charleston or New Orleans.[5]

Most crucially to its representation of the Southern past, however, was Rose Hill's situation in the midst of a national forest. Amid the Sumter, in a sparsely populated county where no cotton was grown, the mansion allowed for a vision of a cotton plantation without any signs of what that history had actually meant for the people living there or the land they worked. With no attempt to re-create the site's agricultural history or its ecological legacy, the park's planners were directing visitors to the story of the Gists, not of the enslaved or the cotton lands they maintained.

There is a significant body of literature from scholars in a range of disciplines that speaks to how the way one moves through a historical space, like a museum or historic site, can enforce an interpretation about the past. Relatively little of this scholarship, however, shows how landscape change around or in a site dynamically alters cultural understandings of that place.[6] A rare example is Ashley Carse's convincing demonstration of how in the Panama Canal Zone, the United States was free to rewrite local histories with an imperialist bent *only after* the Americans had radically altered the environment and kicked out the local population.[7] Rose Hill also falls under Kenneth Foote's notion of an "obliterated landscape," meaning one that a person or community self-consciously "not just cleansed but scoured." Foote's most powerful example is the former house of mass murderer and necrophiliac Edward Gein. His Plainfield, Wisconsin, home was burned by arsonists after Gein was jailed, but the site remained both an eyesore and an attraction for vandals until the property owner planted 160 acres of pine trees on and around the site. The trees made all the difference. They covered the site of Gein's crimes and people stopped associating the place with what happened there.[8]

The trees at Rose Hill also obfuscated the terror of that site's past. Cotton's presence on the landscape had always dominated people's understandings of the place. In 1861, when Governor Gist looked out his windows onto the fields below, or when the enslaved man Jack, who had escaped bondage and hid out in the woods for months, took in the mansion after being captured by an overseer and returned to the house, or when Edward Shaffer visited in the 1930s, each articulated an understanding of Rose Hill's power and stature through the lens of cotton. A visitor to the state park in 2000, however, would see a building freed from the plant's presence. The forest directed a visitor's "way of looking" toward the history of the house separated from the land around it.[9]

Seeing, the actual sensory experience of observing a cotton plantation but not seeing any cotton, was determined by both the state—literally here the South Carolina State Parks Department—and the environment, the trees covering the gullied land. As a result, the King Cotton myth, created by Gist and his colleagues to perpetuate slavery and retold in the form of the state park, was nearly unimpeachable without any signs of the crop's or slavery's effects. The house told Gist's story, and his alone, and the pines hid any other narrative from view. As humanities scholar Jennifer Price once pointed out in a discussion of landscapes, "Myths have a way of making metaphors real."[10] The cotton-was-king metaphor helped tell the Lost Cause myth because there was no attempt at a complete accounting of the crop's place in history. With no rebuilt slave cabins or on-site discussion of the violence of the labor system that propped up cotton's sustainability, no visible fields where enslaved women and men worked, King Cotton seemed alive and well.

In many ways, Rose Hill at the turn of the twenty-first century was an example of what Paul S. Sutter has called "the ecology of erasure." He finds many examples from across the South of "the ways in which environmental forces have, with much human encouragement, obscured the South's history of human-induced erosion from view." Throughout the region, "it has gotten easier by the year *not* to see the history of erosion in the landscapes of the former plantation South, and thus to forget that history."[11] But Rose Hill's lesson extends Sutter's concept. Not only did the forest cover up erosion, but this environmental force shaped historical interpretation and cultural understanding. In other words, the "erasure" in Sutter's "ecology of erasure" does not only happen on the landscape.

Beyond the mansion itself, there are examples of this erasure. In his massive five-hundred-page history of Union County, historian Allan D. Charles described seemingly every tiny event to have ever happened in the small county. Rich details about pioneering families, church-building, and locals' participation in the Revolution and Civil War fill the tome. There are in-depth explanations of the arrival of cotton farming, and the building of cotton gins and mills. Yet Sumter National Forest—its arrival, management, massive size, and impact on locals—gets *a single page*. There is no discussion of land acquisition, demographic shifts, or even recreation within the Sumter. This was the arrival of a federal agency that bought out Union County farms and ended up owning more than half of the entire area of the county, but it got less coverage than the story of a single Revolutionary War battle. When the forest appears, it seems from reading Charles, history stopped.[12]

ERASURE IS JUST PART of the story. The trees of the Sumter not only hid the former cotton fields and directed one's gaze from the land to the house;

they also told a story of environmental restoration, offering their own environmental recovery narrative. Ecologists, environmentalists, and casual tourists have long associated tree cover with ecological health. For a visitor to the park in 2000, the forest must have, most assumed, "healed" the land.

Rose Hill at the dawn of the twenty-first century is a great place to understand how conceptions of ecological restoration and recovery are socially contingent concepts rooted in the legacy of cotton itself. The Sumter National Forest surrounding the state park had introduced the thick green forest that had hidden the worn-out fields and gullies. And to the untrained eye, trees meant a vibrant, diversified environment. The general sense was (and remains) not only that trees created a blanket over the scarred land, but that the ecology underneath the impressive canopy improved as well.

Historians and the general public have repeated this notion. In his book on the reforestation of the South, Thomas D. Clark wrote, "It was a blessing indeed that the persistent shortleaf and loblolly pines had the capability of withstanding three-quarters of a century in which much of the human population of the South plowed itself almost irredeemably into land exhaustion and agrarian poverty."[13] The idea that pines meant recovery for the cottoned-out South has taken hold. The Wikipedia page for the Sumter National Forest declares that, though once marred by the signs of erosion, "over time, the land has been slowly restored and has become productive again."[14]

Scientists, however, have come to disagree with the common perception of ecological recovery, and they have done so by studying the very lands around Rose Hill that are the site of this erasure. Much of what we know about Southern soil loss and forest regrowth is from the USFS's Calhoun Experimental Forest, created in 1947. The Forest Service had created the Calhoun in part for practical reasons; it was overwhelmed with the task of managing the degradation of old farmland that it had begun purchasing in the 1930s.[15] From their Calhoun lab, which began in 1947, the first team of scientists, led by Louis Metz and Carol Wells, discovered that while the erosion was the most visually dramatic consequence of two hundred years of agriculture, it was hardly the only problem. Metz described the time before white settlement as when "the land was covered with trees, mostly hardwoods, the soils were fertile, and the streams ran clear." Then the first white farmers' crops were "displaced by King Cotton," and "now after 200 years of settlement and erosion we have land with reduced productivity for trees and crops." By the late 1940s, the result was fewer farms and a forest floor that was "hard and feels almost like cement." The land could not absorb water, which meant rainfall frequently flooded the "formerly productive bottomlands . . . and muddied streams." The scientists concentrated on the effect of erosion on water levels within the soil, streamflow after rainfall, and flooding within reforested areas.[16]

While the forest service closed down the Calhoun site in the early 1960s, not only was its data preserved, but several scientists carried on some of the work independently from the USFS. In the twenty-first century, the National Science Foundation funded the experiments' rebirth, in a sense, when it created the Calhoun Critical Zone Observatory. Using historical documents like land deeds and photographs, archived soil samples going back decades, and methods like LiDAR, the team of ecologists, geographers, and environmental anthropologists have put together a detailed picture of exactly what happened in the late 1930s through the end of the twentieth century. The resulting picture speaks to the eagerness of shortleaf pines to grow in disturbed soil as well as the swift pace of forestation.[17]

Since 1987, Daniel D. Richter, a forest ecologist from Duke University, has studied the former cotton lands around Rose Hill. As the author or coauthor of nearly two hundred articles and one book about the environmental changes within the Sumter National Forest, and with millions of dollars in research funding, Richter has come to understand the relationship between historic cotton farming, soil weathering, and forest regeneration better than anyone.

Only a few years after their establishment of the Calhoun Critical Zone Observatory in 2013, Richter and his team had already developed a striking hypothesis: Despite the brilliant green tree cover, the health of the ecosystem around the plantation had not markedly improved since the time of Shaffer's visit. Cotton farming during Gist's time, which accelerated after the Civil War, took a toll on the soil and water in ways that are "hard to unwind" with mere pine trees.[18] In article after article, he and his colleagues have found that the soil, water systems, biogeochemical assets, flora, and fauna have not recovered in the decades since cotton's disappearance from the landscape, and that even the trees' ecological functions like carbon sinking have not been as major as once believed.[19]

The data puts into question the very ideas of ecological recovery and restoration. For decades, the field of restoration ecology, as Richter explained in a 2022 essay, was based on an understanding that there could be a "nature in climax." If humans left an environment alone, the ecosystem would reach a "stable endpoint." Eugene Odum, the ecologist who developed many of these ideas in his study of forests and waterways of the South, described nature as having a "strategy," an invisible hand of sorts, that guided ecosystems toward equilibrium.[20] But as scientists pushed back against Odum's ideas over the course of the second half of the twentieth century, Richter saw plenty of evidence around Rose Hill that there could be no "restoration" even with little human involvement.

Rather than finding the fields and streams inching toward a pinnacle state of nature, Richter described "evolutionary change" that was not headed in a single positive direction. Instead, the succession of the forest covering the eroded fields was "as much mask as repair." Richter explains:

> Viewed from an interstate highway or an airplane window, it is easily seen that much of the Piedmont is impressively reforested and no longer much cultivated. But to understand the dynamics of ecosystem succession following agricultural abandonment, one must walk and read the land with its southern pines and southern oaks, kudzu, and Bermuda grass. Such readings or in fact soundings readily turn up rain-gullied hillslopes under secondary forest canopies and lead to the conclusion that a century of reforestation has both healed and hidden cultivation's severe impacts on the land.[21]

The trees do not, then, simply hide the ecological reality; they obscure the human legacy as well. If one lifts the "green blanket" of vegetative cover, Richter pointed out, "you can still see all the gullies and the slave villages are yet to be uncovered and not only that but the Native American villages up and down the Tyger River are amazingly rich and completely forgotten, almost, yet to be discovered."[22]

The result is that the Piedmont at the dawn of the twentieth century had merely a rhetoric of recovery. The trees and restored Rose Hill mansion told a story of restoration that belied the ecological reality below. When famed philosopher of science Bruno Latour visited the Sumter National Forest with Richter in 2015, he commented on this very point. The human history of the place is the key to understanding the work of scientists, Latour argued. The history at the Calhoun Critical Zone Observatory is "linked to the notion of a plantation . . . which is a certain way of acting on the land." With the plantation's impact—the one hundred years of cotton farming—now hidden from view, it obscures not only how a visitor understands the past but the possibilities of the future as well. "You can't think of a future," Latour remarked, "first because it is a national forest, but also because the land has not recovered. The soil is not there, [it is not] back . . . so this is a dramatic aspect of everything we want to do with the land, yes, but it has been destroyed beyond recovery, if recovery is the right word."[23]

"Recovery" and "restoration" are indeed complicated terms when it comes to Rose Hill and the forests of the Piedmont. Lost Cause interpreters recovered the mansion from its near collapse in the 1930s. And the trees recovered the landscape in the sense that green foliage covered the gullies and erased the scars from a century of cotton farming. But at the turn of the twenty-first century, it was impossible to say that there had been cultural *or* ecological restoration.

IN THE DECADES SINCE 2000, much changed in the ways that Union Countians engaged with their past. New narratives emerged. The historical landscape, both human and environmental, has changed. And crucially, so has the amateur and state-sponsored interpretations of it. Black Union Countians have become crucial stewards of the past in a way that they had not done—or been allowed to do—in the previous 150 years. The result is that the difficult history of slavery, cotton, and civil rights in the miles around Rose Hill has been rewritten in important ways. A suite of efforts led by various local groups and the state park service have worked to claim the county's history.

One such effort has been the formation of the Union County Community Remembrance Project (UCCRP). Its website opens with a black-and-white photograph of the bars of the cell where masked and unmasked white vigilantes pulled twelve African American men from the jail. Members of the mob murdered all but one (and possibly the twelfth, though his fate is not known for certain). The words "Record. Recognize. Remember" lay over the image. The page highlights their organization and accomplishments. "Our vision is to foster ongoing collaborative education, justice, and healing," the site reads, and it is clear that their work has borne fruit.[24]

Three new historical markers in downtown Union explain the 1871 jail raid, as well as provide context for the lynching of African Americans that happened in the years between 1865 and 1934 in the county.[25] Situated around the city, the markers add information about the violence but also serve as a visible presence, a counter to the older Lost Cause stories still told on extant historical markers situated nearby. Two hundred people attended the new markers' unveiling in 2021.[26] The UCCRP has plans to further improve the interpretation of the historic jail building itself.

THE UCCRP HAD important collaborators in this effort. It became a "Remembrance Project" partner of the Montgomery, Alabama–based Equal Justice Initiative (EJI), which has helped communities across the South erect historical markers and tell the stories of historic violence both in Southern towns and at the EJI's Legacy Museum. One of the museum's most powerful displays is the wall of containers holding the soil of the places where lynching occurred. The variety of colors of soil, from brick red through brown and black, fill jars inscribed simply with the name of the location. Union County's own soil sample became part of the wall in 2021. Curtis Hunter, a member of UCCRP and a local tourism official, remarked that "by honoring the soil where lynching victims died, we are acknowledging the history of bloodshed that has seeped into the earth while simultaneously reclaiming it as sacred."[27]

The fact that soil is one of the mediums through which both EJI and the UCCRP tell the history of lynching in Union County is revealing. That dirt—the crucial life-giving layer of earth on which cotton grew and so much human labor, slave and free, was performed—is an important part of how people and institutions in the local community have tried to reimagine their past. Even at Rose Hill, the history of the soil, cotton, and the forest increasingly have become part of the interpretation of the state park.

One of the leaders of the effort to bring environmental history to Rose Hill has been Al Hester, a historian who is historic sites coordinator for the South Carolina State Parks. Hester wrote his public history MA thesis on Rose Hill, and though he oversees sites around the state, he has always kept a close eye on the interpretation at the former Gist home. In addition to spearheading an oral history project to record voices of local people who once lived on or near the former plantation, Hester has worked to make erosion and reforestation central to the human story told as part of the experience of visiting the park. "Places like Providence Canyon in Georgia and Rose Hill in South Carolina," he wrote in 2018, "can serve as reminders that historical abuse of people and land has lasting consequences that can still be felt and seen today."[28] Perhaps the most striking—and most accessible—place where Hester and the Parks Department have linked the human and environmental histories of Rose Hill is an online story map that first appeared in the early 2020s.

Under the title "Rose Hill Plantation: Memorial to a 'Land-Killing Past'?" the site uses striking modern and archival images, including some of the scientific evidence found by Richter and his team, to tell a complex history of the people who have lived at the site for centuries. The text and images together demonstrate the connections between cotton agriculture, the human story, and environmental degradation and rebirth in a local context that remains rare for historical sites.[29]

Even though some of this effort lives only in cyberspace, from a historical interpretation standpoint, walking through the physical landscape of Union County in the 2020s is fundamentally different than it would have been at any point prior. One can't miss the UCCRP's new signs, some of which sit close to the older markers, putting the more-complete historical interpretation in contrast. Still, from a sheer numbers standpoint, the built memory sites are hardly equal. Including the project's new historical markers, there are a total of six in the county that highlight African American history, but there are thirty-five that do not.[30] Though the UCCRP's website claims that historical markers are "just the beginning," their work to add accurate historical voices to the landscape of the county through these signs is certainly an important measure of their success.

However, the other aspects of the built and natural landscape still endorse a different historical memory, or at least make it difficult to understand a fuller picture of the history. The mansion itself still offers its own narrative of the past, even as the park rangers and the state think through more inclusive and accurate signage to tell the Gist story. Work is yet to be done on the actual landscape at Rose Hill, where walking paths out to the gullies, past the locations of former slave and tenant houses, would give the visitor a better sense of what was there within the pine forest.

Hester has written about the ways that rethinking the interpretation of Rose Hill could incorporate a closer reading of its environmental history. He points to the work of the critical zone scientists in the forest around the state park, and he argues that if the ecological health of the land has not been restored by the trees, that fact matters to the interpretation of the mansion and grounds. Incorporating that environmental element and "encouraging dialogue among visitors about these topics could help make the site more relevant," Hester hopes. The result would be to allow tourists to understand Gist, and the histories of slavery, poverty, and cotton farming, in not just a local and regional framework but a global one. The parks coordinator suggests that the best way to do this would be to concentrate on cotton itself, the plant that unites these human and environmental histories as links from Rose Hill to the outside world. A focus on cotton would "encourage visitors to consider labor and environmental concerns . . . issues ranging from damaging fertilizer and pesticide use in the Southeast, to human trafficking and forced labor in cotton-producing countries like Uzbekistan and Cameroon."[31]

AT ROSE HILL and across the South, much has changed in the larger culture of celebrating cotton plantations. As sites continue to wrestle with the degree to which they can and should represent slavery and agriculture, in the larger culture the popularity of plantations as sites for celebrations, not history, seems to be decreasing. Not only have several well-known plantations stopped hosting weddings, but in 2019 the wedding website The Knot and the image-based social media giant Pinterest announced that they would stop promoting plantation wedding images.[32] This has not, of course, put a stop to people celebrating cotton itself or using the fields as a backdrop for baby photos or prom pictures. So while the plantation as a site of celebration has receded, cotton itself remains crucial to the stories that many Southerners are telling about themselves and their history. Indeed, as the lesson of the Yazoo-Mississippi Delta tells, cotton remains a powerful icon, even as the historic built landscapes of agriculture have all but disappeared.

PART TWO

Memphis and the Yazoo-Mississippi Delta

THE RADICAL ENVIRONMENTAL changes of the post–Civil War Piedmont had their mirror image in the Yazoo-Mississippi Delta. As part 2 demonstrates, in the mid-nineteenth century, when the South Carolina Upstate became increasingly gullied and difficult to farm, the alluvial region between the Mississippi, Yazoo, and Tallahatchie Rivers was mostly swamp—a rich, biodiverse ecosystem, but a swamp nonetheless. Over the next century and a half, as cotton disappeared from the lands around Rose Hill, it flourished in the Delta. The second half of this book not only explains these changes to the region's landscapes; it also details the ways that Southerners understood changes in those cotton fields in cultural terms and, in turn, how they reimagined the plant's narrative as the labor and material conditions of the fields transformed.

Figure 9 is a snapshot of these dueling transformations. While cotton rhetoric was so important to Gist and to his heirs, the actual production of the crop in Union County appears in sharp relief when compared with the Mississippi Delta's Coahoma County. In 1870, when Piedmont farmers briefly doubled down on cotton production, Delta landowners and thousands of tenants were quickly transforming that region into the most productive land in the world. Union County farmers would not reach their maximum production for two more decades, but after 1870 they would never come near Coahoma's levels again. Erosion and forests tell the South Carolina story, while the Mississippi one is equally dramatic.

The land to the south of Memphis between the Yazoo and Mississippi Rivers fans out for 225 miles and already by 1870 was understood to be the richest soil in the world. Over the nineteenth century the Delta was remade by three forces: enslaved and later free African American men and women; speculating white farmers; and credit from banks in the North and Europe.

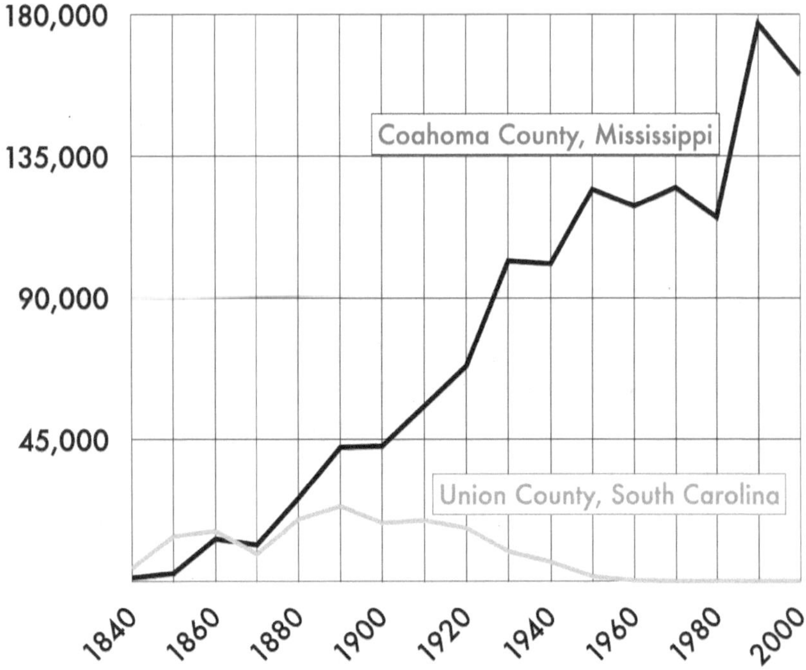

FIG. 9. Cotton bales produced annually, Coahoma County, Mississippi, and Union County, South Carolina, 1840–2000. Agricultural Censuses, 1840–2000.

Together, humans and their money transformed the Delta from a wetland of thick cane, bears, and hardwoods to the world's most productive and rigidly organized farmland.[1]

The Yazoo-Mississippi Delta would never have become synonymous with cotton monoculture, African American oppression, and blues music if not for floods. For millennia, the Mississippi River, which forms its western boundary, and the natural levees along the Tallahatchie and Yazoo Rivers, which form its eastern, spilled over their banks and deposited dirt, bacteria, and minerals in the land between. Descriptions of the results border on the unbelievable. Topsoil, inches deep in most places on earth, was in the Delta measured in "tens of feet," according to John Barry.[2] To Delta writer David Cohn, it was "pure soil endlessly deep, dark, and sweet."[3]

Before that alluvial floodplain could become a cotton wonderland, however, humans, animals, and capital had to chop down the trees, clear the cane, and drain the soil. Over the course of the second half of the nineteenth

MAP 4. The Yazoo-Mississippi Delta. Map by Jeff Scalia.

century, that is precisely what happened. Following the government's forced removal of the Choctaw, Chickasaw, and Cherokee in the 1830s, white land speculators—many of them wealthy enslavers, or at least men with access to enslaved labor and credit—began buying acreage along the rivers and ordering the clearing of trees and the moving of earth by human hands.

Given the Delta's material conditions and the agricultural promise of the soil, it was a frontier unlike any other in America. As historian James C. Cobb has explained, it would be wrong to confuse this pioneering generation of white landowners with the hard-scrap yeomen usually associated with American frontiers. "The Delta," he wrote, "was destined from the beginning to be the domain of substantial planters."[4] Even those with capital and slave labor had no easy task, however, and many landholders failed and sold out to others. By the Civil War only 10 percent of Delta land was cleared for agriculture, and there were still fewer than fifty thousand residents, the majority of whom were enslaved.[5] In 1860 Coahoma County had a population of only 6,606, of which 77 percent were held in bondage. Those men and women produced 13,325 bales of cotton. By contrast, back in William Henry Gist's home county of Union, South Carolina, that same year, the population was double Coahoma's but produced only 16 percent more cotton.[6]

Following the Civil War, Delta landowners found themselves more dependent on Northern credit and facing the specter of building their cotton kingdom without slavery. In response, Mississippi planters, like those around the South, attempted to re-create the labor control they believed to have had under the former system, but the freedpeople of the Delta fought back. The result was a system of tenancy created in tandem between white landowners and African Americans who understood that white Mississippians needed them. Though most of the arrangements fell under the header "sharecropping," the actual terms of the planter-laborer relationship were both dynamic and hyperlocal.

In the Delta of the 1890s and the early twentieth century, the sharecropping system—along with the highly productive environment—did allow for the possibility of limited black economic advancement. Again, a comparison with Union County is revealing. As the previous chapters demonstrate, in the post–Civil War Piedmont, erosion meant that tenants rarely had access to the best lands. On the poor soils around Rose Hill it was nearly impossible for a tenant to profit at the end of the season. And any who somehow managed to earn the money to buy their own plot would not have been able to afford anything but hillsides and worn-out acres prone to gullying. The material conditions of the environment were a major obstacle that South Carolina tenants faced.

The Delta's soil and weather, however, at least made the tenant-to-landowner rise a possibility. A lot had to go right for the laborer, however. If the credit terms with the owner were not too onerous *and* if the weather was good *and* if the merchant, ginner, and landholder were all honest, *and* if none of the Jim Crow constraints on social and economic behavior struck, then an African American tenant could end up with a profit at the end of the season. If they could find a landowner willing to sell a plot, one could become an independent farmer. In fact, black landownership was far more possible in the Delta than in most other parts of the South. Drawn to the legendary soil, thousands of black Southerners also sought the modicum of independence that was sometimes allowed in the Delta's majority-black communities. By the turn of the twentieth century, the region had the highest concentration of African American labor in the nation. And with relatively few white sharecroppers, the bifurcation of black labor and white land ownership had become stark.[7]

Along with the settling of the labor question—although calling it settled is not quite right considering the constant negotiations that went on between tenants and landholders—many changes to the environment of the Delta allowed for greater cotton production. The most important of these were the building of levees, which kept floodwaters out of the fields, and the arrival of the railroads, which could carry cotton to market. Here again, successful planters teamed with Northern capital and the Illinois Central Railroad to subsidize and develop a network of lines sufficient to get the ginned cotton out of the inland plantations.[8] These two developments had finally made possible what Delta planters had always envisioned: a flat, well-drained monocrop landscape with a reliable source of labor, and a network of transportation routes linking their fields to the mills of the world. It was a cotton kingdom.

The statistics bear out just how transformative this environmental work had been. At the start of the 1900s, Delta farmland prices were as much as five times higher than in non–Delta Mississippi counties.[9] Cotton yields, success against the boll weevil, and erosion rates all tilted favorably toward the alluvial region. The average farm was much bigger, and tenancy rates were higher as well, both positive factors for those landowners in power. Most importantly, the region had become the world leader in cotton production. Mill owners from England even eschewed the Nile Delta in favor of Mississippi's for their main supply.[10]

The early twentieth century marks a pivotal moment in Delta history, one that stands out for two key developments with lasting consequences for both the region's culture and environment. First, as Cobb argues, this was a planter's region from the moment of white settlement. The transition from swamp to monocrop agricultural wonderland had been swift, without time for an oppositional class or culture to develop beyond white landowners and black farmers. Second, there was no period of trial and error with industries other than agriculture or with alternative crops to cotton. The result was a "New South plantation kingdom," in Cobb's words, with an overwhelmingly African American population and a class of white planters who thought of themselves as modern versions of the mythic antebellum cotton planters hyped in Lost Cause literature. These men and women believed they had inherited an Old South tradition, yet they had created a modern industrial cotton kingdom with a façade of the *fictionalized* antebellum picture drawn by Mildred Rutherford and her Lost Cause ilk.

There was no doubt that, based on fiction or not, the Yazoo-Mississippi Delta had become a cotton-centric culture like nowhere else in the world. The plant organized the economy, labor, environment, politics, and social lives of the Delta, and locals knew it. Mississippi writer David Cohn filled books chronicling the ways "cotton was more than a crop." People on the streets of Mississippi towns met each other not with "Hello" but with the rhetorical "How's crops?" And as Cohn explained, that "meant only one crop—cotton."

One might reply to the question with "fair to middlin," he explained, an allusion to how cotton fiber was graded, with middling meaning it was just fine. Cohn put cotton at the center of everything in the region. The Delta was "of, by, for cotton."[11] It was "more than a crop. It is a form of mysticism. It is a religion and a way of life. Cotton is omnipresent here as a god is omnipresent. It is as omnipotent as a god is omnipotent, giving life and taking life away."[12] Cotton was both king and god along the Mississippi River floodplain.

This view of the fiber's domination over the region's culture and environment was shared well beyond the Delta. In 1930 *The New York Times* sent Anne O'Hare McCormick, normally a foreign correspondent (and who would later become the first woman to receive the Pulitzer Prize for journalism), to report on cotton's grip on the South. For three full newspaper pages, illustrated with several photographs of cotton fields and tenant farmers, McCormick reveals herself dumbstruck by the fiber's place in Delta society. While she explained the financial and agricultural state of the crop, she wrote mostly of its psychological grip on women and men in farm fields, mills, and town squares. "Cotton is something more than a crop or an industry; it is a dynastic system." King Cotton was "map-maker, trouble-maker, history maker." "You can hang the epic of mankind on a thread of cotton," McCormick explained. "There is something about cotton like the power of poetry."[13]

As Cohn, McCormick, and hundreds of others who wrote (or sang) about the Delta in the early twentieth century came to recognize, what made cotton king was more than a romantic attachment. The region's economy, social life, and natural environment were bound tightly together with the plant. Sharecroppers were paid in cotton. Blues singers sang about it. Banks held some cash, but they watched cotton prices far more closely than bond rates. Natural perils like the boll weevil, floods, and droughts were understood by black and white Mississippians not as threats to human life but almost solely in terms of their potential impact on the crop.[14] The connection of the plant to the Delta was no ethereal, romantic bond. It was as real and tangible as could be.

Take, for instance, Coahoma County. In 1850 this north Delta locale along the Mississippi River, about fifty miles south of Memphis, had a population of 2,780 and produced only 2,430 bales of cotton. By 1930 there were 35,000 black residents and 10,000 white. The rich bottomland and the thousands of hours of labor by men and women with mules and hoes coaxed more than 100,000 bales of cotton from 178,000 acres. For context, Gist's Union County, South Carolina, in 1930 had one-third the population and produced merely 16.5 percent as much cotton. By mid-century, Coahoma was the highest cotton-producing county in the nation.[15]

The ideological order that cotton placed on Delta society—like in Gist and Hammond's South Carolina Piedmont a century earlier—had tangible, material implications for the Delta. If cotton was king, then everything else fell in a natural order according to what the plant and its business needed. Much of what made this language of "king" and "god" both so ubiquitous and revealing is its acceptance. The more cotton that grew, the more people, white and black, understood their fates as tied solely to the crop. What made *it* prosper, most Mississippians believed in the first half of the twentieth century, would make *them* prosper. They thought their unique situation as the center of cotton's world to have been ordained and fixed forever.

But the crop's place was not permanent, nor was the role of the women and men who worked its fields. Some of the clearest evidence of these transformations was on the streets of the Delta's de facto capital, Memphis, Tennessee, rather than on Mississippi farms. As cotton, money, and people moved between the rural Delta and the region's nearest big city, the geography of cotton culture stretched. New spaces—urban, commercial, and symbolic—became arenas where elites and workers alike celebrated, contested, and reinvented the fiber's significance. White Memphians worked to stage cotton as a triumphant symbol of regional pride, but black Memphians also laid claim to the crop's meanings, using it to assert their community's historic and ongoing role in Southern agriculture. The next chapters trace that expanded and contested geography, beginning with the rituals and performances across the landscapes of the "Bluff City."

CHAPTER SIX

Pageantry and Power in Cotton's Metropolis

IN THE EARLY EVENING of May 15, 1956, as the sun set over the Arkansas side of the Mississippi River, a crowd of a hundred thousand people—more than a quarter of the total population of the city of Memphis—met at the foot of Monroe Avenue, where the levee gradually sloped down toward the slow-moving muddy water. The mostly white crowd gathered atop the cobblestone-lined landing facing the river; African Americans peered from segregated clusters along the fringes. People had come from around the city, the Mississippi Delta, and neighboring farm regions for a show, the opening ceremony of the twenty-fifth annual Cotton Carnival. On the first night of what was billed as "The Nation's Party in the Land of Cotton," events left no doubt as to white Memphis's allegiance to both the crop and a good time.[1]

As the people gathered at dusk, the Confederate Quartet played while dancers from a local troupe performed atop a moored scow that served as a stage. A few minutes after 8:00 p.m., the first fireworks erupted in the sky, lighting the rolling waters of the river, where a flotilla of boats from the Memphis Yacht Club signaled the arrival of the main event. Minutes later, the "royal barge" came into view. Towering fifty feet above the river, pulsating with hundreds of electric lights, and with music blaring from a full high school marching band that was seated onboard, the large boat was decorated from stem to stern with white symbols of cotton. As a tug slowly pulled the vessel to the dock along Monroe Street, Eddie Fisher, a nationally popular crooner and television star who had had seventeen top ten songs in the preceding decade, began entertaining the crowd from the levee. After singing a few of his hits, he made his way onto the barge to serenade its prize cargo, the king and queen of the Cotton Carnival.[2]

For five days in May 1956, as it had each spring since 1931, the Bluff City put on a performance to prove cotton's importance to Memphis and the world. In 1956 this meant the arrival of the royal barge, with its concert on the landing, *three* public parades down Main Street, and countless private parties hosted by secret societies in ornate hotel dining rooms and country club halls. It meant the Maid of Cotton Fashion Show and Luncheon, dances for kids and teens, public talks about cotton and the economy, a tennis tournament, art exhibitions, and seemingly countless other events. For those five days, cotton took over the city. Downtown, cars on Second Street drove through a thirty-foot-tall archway made of stacked cotton bales that spread from one sidewalk to the other. Signs attached to the street lamps featured smiling anthropomorphic cotton bolls proclaiming "Hail! King Cotton." Stores along the city's busiest streets put cotton-themed displays in their windows, with everything from uprooted cotton plants to mannequins wearing the latest cotton fabrics.

The king and queen whom Eddie Fisher serenaded on that night in 1956 were no strangers to the elite social scenes of Memphis. King Oscar Carr Jr. was a thirty-two-year-old planter who owned 3,500 acres of prime cotton land south of Clarksdale in the Mississippi Delta. Queen Clare Mallory was the twenty-year-old daughter of a prominent Memphis family. As they made their way from the barge to shore and up the bank toward a fleet of horse-drawn carriages, they were followed by their "royal court," including the Memphis mayor and dozens of others with pseudo-regal titles like "Maid of Cotton." In a short ceremony, city officials presented the king and queen with a key to the city, then African American carriage drivers piloted the royal court ten blocks to Ellis Auditorium for a different kind of royal meeting. The hall—Memphis's biggest indoor venue with a ten-thousand-seat capacity—was festooned with images of the white flowering plant in preparation for the night's concert: Elvis Presley's headlining performance at the Cotton Pickin' Jamboree.

Twenty-one-year-old Elvis was amid a meteoric rise unlike anything in American musical history. A Mississippi native, Presley had lived in Memphis since 1948, but after years of only local fame, he took the stage on opening night of the Cotton Carnival as a household name, not just in the Mid-South but around the world. In the previous few months he had signed a record deal with RCA, appeared on Milton Berle's national television show, and watched "Heartbreak Hotel" reach number one on eight different record charts. Backstage at Ellis Auditorium, King Carr and Queen Mallory met

FIG. 10. Signs on street lamps during the Cotton Carnival parade hailed "King Cotton." Photographic Collection, Memphis and Shelby County Room, Memphis Public Library.

with the singer and posed for pictures before the King of Rock and Roll took the stage.[3]

As for Elvis's performance, it left no doubts of his surging popularity. Paul Molloy wrote in the *Memphis Commercial Appeal* that when Presley appeared the crowd became electric, surged out of its seats, and mobbed the stage. A fourteen-year-old girl was so excited to see the singer she "screamed as if suddenly scalded," and "from the throat of her companion came a weird, guttural whine, like that of a hurt puppy." Elvis, who "rose from guitar-twanging truck driver to bobby-sox idolatry before reaching voting age," proved to Molloy that the young rocker was "plainly a salesman of masculine sex." When he played "Heartbreak Hotel," some in the audience, Molloy wrote, fell to their knees while Elvis "gave them everything, including the erotic bumps and grinds" associated with female performers at strip clubs.[4] According to historian Peter Guralnick, Elvis saw this hometown concert as a chance to prove to Memphians that he hadn't "got the big head."[5] But it was clear that the local boy could no longer walk down the streets safely without being mobbed by fans. After his Cotton Pickin' performance "he was whisked away into the night before the applause had even died down."[6]

Elvis was clearly the new king of rock and roll, but his presence at the Cotton Pickin' Jamboree on opening night of the Cotton Carnival spoke directly to the power of King Cotton. In fact, despite the reaction of teenagers in the crowd, the show was evidence of the Memphis business elite lending the limelight to Elvis, rather than the performer bringing his crowds to the week of cotton events. While music journalists at the time and historians since interpreted Elvis's concert as a major milestone in his career, it was a mere blip on Cotton Carnival's radar that week. Remarkably little in the official records of the festival speak to Elvis's visit. In fact, the local papers spent much more time describing Carr and Mallory, the Carnival king and queen, than Presley. And while the singer certainly ruled over the one night, King Cotton reigned all week. When the final notes of Elvis's closing number "Hound Dog" echoed through the segregated coliseum, out on the streets Memphis had become an urban cotton landscape.

Cotton was no mere excuse for a party. After the Civil War, Memphis had emerged as the capital of the Cotton South, but it was during the Great Depression that Memphians created the Cotton Carnival to draw attention and business to the struggling city. In the first half of the twentieth century, environmental and social changes in the cotton lands surrounding Memphis unsettled the city's cotton elite. Locked into the rhetoric of cotton, the white leadership turned the Carnival's parties and parades into a symbolic language through which they clung to power. Throughout the twentieth century, they used the Carnival to perform cotton's supremacy in both racial and environmental terms, staging public displays of plantation fantasy and economic sovereignty.

As white Memphians made their public paean to the white crop on the streets every spring, black Memphians carved out their own language of power and resistance through the crop with the Cotton Makers' Jubilee. This weeklong event was African Americans' effort to, at first, stake a claim to equality by putting on their own cotton festival, complete with kings, queens, concerts, and parades. It too began in the 1930s, though its politics changed remarkably as the Depression led to World War II, and then the modern civil rights movement. Through those years, the city's population swelled as black farmers were pushed off the farms of the Delta through agricultural mechanization, tighter white control of black life, and the never-ending onslaught of racism and violence. Jubilee organizers and participants, many of whom had firsthand understanding of the language and culture of King Cotton, clung to the crop as a viable means of expression, even as their aims moved from equality, to freedom, to Black Power.

The Cotton Carnival and Cotton Makers' Jubilee lay bare how both white and black Southerners projected onto cotton their wildest dreams and darkest fears. For much of the twentieth century, the crop served as a medium for political, economic, and cultural debates—a scapegoat in times of trouble, a symbol of hope in times of possibility. Yet cotton was never simply a stand-in for white supremacy. The material realities of growing, harvesting, and spinning cotton remained central to Memphians' narratives about themselves. As the environmental and industrial demands of cotton changed, so did the social performances built around it. The assassination of Martin Luther King Jr. in Memphis on April 4, 1968, catalyzed the collapse of both celebrations, at least in their traditional forms. But behind this immediate cause lay deeper forces: Agricultural and environmental changes outside the city had already begun reshaping how cotton could be celebrated, especially as many Memphians sought a more integrated future. The enduring link between cotton, place, and race was possible only because Memphis had long built its identity on the agricultural lands beyond its borders.

LIKE CHICAGO, MEMPHIS ROSE to prominence through its proximity to naturally rich hinterlands and the ability of its people to transport, process, and commodify the products of those places.[7] However, whereas Chicago was "nature's metropolis" because of the breadth of products that arrived on its waterways and rail lines, Memphis could more narrowly be called "cotton's metropolis."[8] While the natural gift of the Delta soil and the human labor that worked it were obviously crucial to the production of cotton, the region could not make money without its connection to international markets. The region was different not because of its remoteness but because of its connections to the world. The rivers whose floods gave the soil its nutrients were also its earliest transportation routes. Flatboats and later steamers moved the cotton from Mississippi river landings to Memphis and New Orleans, but it was the arrival of mainline railroads like the Illinois Central in the late nineteenth century, and the extension of smaller lines, that connected individual plantations and gins to the rail network that truly linked the cotton fields—and the Delta culture—to the world. So too did the telegraph lines that brought Liverpool and Manchester to rural plantation offices. Prices and orders reached dusty storefronts in Delta towns like Clarksdale and Greenville in one direction, while news about the crop and weather made its way to England, where mill owners could decide whether Mississippi, Egypt, or India would supply its machines that year. This economic connection made planters keenly aware of their place in a world market, and few shied away from extending their outward reach to the world.

These connections were the lifeblood of the region's cities. The Delta's largest landholders usually had relatively modest homes among their cotton fields but more stately houses in cities like Greenville, Cleveland, and Vicksburg. The place where cotton's money and power showed off the most, however, was Memphis. Not only did hundreds of white Delta planters keep addresses in the city; their children were raised there, and their social orbit centered there. Mississippians' business connections with the Memphis cotton buyers, shippers, and merchants fused with social lives, to the benefit of both groups. David Cohn's oft-quoted line defining the dimensions of the Yazoo-Mississippi Delta, that it "begins in the lobby of the Peabody Hotel in Memphis and ends on Catfish Row in Vicksburg," is more than a clever geography lesson.[9] Without the business conducted in the fancy hotel lobby, the Delta's cotton would have rotted in Clarksdale warehouses or on Memphis wharves.[10]

For their part, white Memphians had always embraced the city's role as cotton's metropolis. In one decade alone, from 1850 to 1860, there was a 300 percent increase in the value of the crop moving through the city's wharves and depots, and as a result the city's taxable wealth increased 500 percent. In 1858 the mayor cabled to his counterpart in Manchester, England, to advertise its newfound place among in the world market. "The city of Memphis on the shores of the Mississippi, the largest interior depot of cotton in America," he wrote, "sends her greetings to the city of Manchester, the largest manufacturing city of that staple in Great Britain."[11] That pre–Civil War declaration was as much projection as it was an honest claim to the city's situation.

During Reconstruction, white Memphis cotton brokers were cash poor, but their pleas to Northern outlets for more credit went mostly unanswered. The entire Southern cotton business was disorganized. Questions over labor, credit, landownership, transportation, ginning, and marketing hung over the entire rural South. In Memphis, brokers who had before the war built some infrastructure for buying and selling the products of plantations up and down the river had to rebuild warehouses and reconnect to the cotton-producing hinterlands. In 1873 the city's top buyers and sellers reorganized cotton trading. Rather than hurrying from river landing to warehouse to office to discuss fiber quality, confirm shipment arrivals, and debate over price, they moved all of that business to the Memphis Cotton Exchange, a single building with a large trading floor.[12] Telegraph lines and a bank of phone booths kept traders in constant contact with the news of the world, whether swings in prices or credit.

The new operation brought some stability to prices and made Memphis the most reliable and central place in the Mid-South to buy and sell the crop. Soon, it was the biggest spot market for cotton in the world. From their offices on Front Street, one block from the landing where steamboats laden with hundreds of bales of "white gold" moored, cotton factors could keep an eye on the quality of the crop and decide what to buy and sell. The area had what one historian described as a "marvelous confusion and bustle." Planters came to the city to check on the prices that their crops could bring. Buyers from the enormous English mills set up shop to buy bulk cotton directly.[13] By 1900 the business of cotton was booming; nearly a million bales of cotton moved through Memphis every fall.[14] The 175 men who held seats on the exchange not only became the principal source of money for Delta planters; they also embodied the city's social elite for generations.[15]

The class of white men who controlled the cotton industry were not the only people moving in and out of Memphis. While David Cohn positioned the start of the Delta in the Peabody lobby, the connections between cotton country and cotton city were no less clear five blocks to the south on Beale Street. This avenue through the heart of the black business community was the epicenter of African American life not only in Memphis but the entire Mid-South. The Delta and Memphis needed each other; movement of cotton between the two meant necessary movement of people.

Migration between Memphis and the cotton fields outside the city was constant in the decades around 1900, and it was a movement that both city and farm depended upon. "The Memphis of 1900 was a rural city," historian William D. Miller wrote, "fiercely upholding rural customs."[16] Alongside cotton, Jim Crow rules that governed black life followed African Americans from country to town. By the 1930s many—if not most—black Memphians had come from what had been the surrounding cotton lands, either in their own lifetimes or their parents'. They brought with them a rural sensibility, but also the experience of life under King Cotton's regime. This included both scars and a tradition of resistance. In the Delta, African Americans had long pushed back against white power with whatever tools they had. When the boll weevil arrived in 1908, for instance, black sharecroppers lobbied for greater control over where and how they planted; some even used the threat of infestation to demand better contracts and land. The story of African American migration—field to field, rural South to urban South, South to North—is one of the most enduring expressions of resistance to Jim Crow. And the ways the composition, pace, and determination of that migration changed from 1900 to the 1960s are a revealing source of how much the Delta itself changed over time. Though black Memphians were now miles from the flat, hot cotton fields of Mississippi, Tennessee, and Arkansas, these women and men were still very much in a landscape ordered by King Cotton.

NOTHING CAPTURES HOW cotton organized the Mid-South quite like Cotton Carnival. Begun during the Great Depression as a celebration of the cotton industry, the event grew into the world-famous "party with a purpose" that attracted attention from across the globe. It became *the* stage for the region's political, social, and business elite to show off their wealth, as well as their commitment to the blooming white crop. It was also a stage to show off Jim Crow rules on the streets of the growing metropolis. From its beginning, Cotton Carnival organizers placed public displays of white control over the cotton industry at the heart of the festivities.

While nationally the cause of the Great Depression was a web of economic issues, in Memphis there was basically one: the cotton price. While the value of a pound of ginned cotton reached thirty-five cents during World War I, it fell below six cents in 1931. This cratering hit not only the sharecroppers and hired tenants working in the fields outside the city but also the buyers and sellers on Front Street, the workers in the warehouses, and the women and men across town who worked in the cotton-related businesses. The commodity's impact on the city can almost not be overstated. In addition to the sheer number of people employed directly in cotton shipping, warehousing, grading, buying, and selling, there were dozens of ancillary businesses dependent on housing, feeding, and entertaining employees in the main industries. As these cotton businesses staggered, Memphis's population continued to grow, increasing more than 50 percent from 1920 to 1930, reaching a quarter of a million residents by the 1929 stock market crash.[17] When cotton prices fell and the world economy tanked, Memphians were left wondering what might pull them out of the collapse.

Department store owner Arthur H. Halle thought he had an answer. In 1931 Halle gathered other merchants and the president of the Cotton Exchange and laid the groundwork for an event that they hoped would spur tourism and local spending by celebrating the commodity that sat at the center of their economy. The organizers dreamed up a multiday festival to not only remind locals and outsiders of the importance of the crop to the city's economy and culture but also "promote bigger and better uses of cotton." They imagined turning the city into a cotton wonderland, with parades, the cotton bale arch over Second Street, more cotton sitting on random corners around town, and special store window displays and sales of cotton clothing. With little official backing from the city, but with hundreds of volunteers and thousands of dollars in support from local businesses, the first Cotton Carnival took place in March 1931.[18] That first year set a tone for the event that would last for decades.

In a city in the upheaval of the Depression, with an exploding population of new immigrants from the surrounding farms, Carnival leaders chose an inaugural theme meant to anchor cotton to what they considered its most important moment: the Old South. The events dripped in Lost Cause ideas about the antebellum South, images that certainly had little basis in reality in the newly built Delta to the city's south.

From the arrival of the king and queen on a Mississippi River barge until the closing parade, each element of the three-day festivities reflected this fictionalized interpretation of antebellum plantation life. The boat that delivered the king and queen to the Monroe Avenue dock was literally powered by shirtless African American men who sat at the corners of the floating boat, feet in the water, paddling. After docking on the levee, the king and queen came ashore where they sat atop thrones made of stacked cotton bales. They were then escorted around town in "old-time carriages" driven by black men playing the part of royal servants.[19]

The parade was the cornerstone of Carnival that first year as it drew a crowd of thousands to its downtown route. It was comprised of eighty-six floats decorated in scenes depicting plantation life—including white men and women in blackface—the Civil War, and cotton machinery. Many of the floats were pulled by mules, but some were pulled by African American men.[20] The segregated crowds cheered as floats went past. A number featured black women in mammy dress sitting atop cotton bales. Other African American women were paid to stand on street corners in plantation garb and greet the crowds.[21] As historian Cynthia Jones Sadler has written, Carnival leaders' placements of African Americans in certain roles during the parade was intended to highlight Old South fantasies of black labor, the mythical ideas about how cotton and race divided labor in the antebellum South. Floats depicted scenes of a mammy watching white children, an African American fortune teller reading tea leaves for white women, slave women doing washing and folding laundry. Nearby, African American men wore overalls and played the banjo, sang, and danced on street corners. "Black children sat on street curbs or cotton bales eating cotton candy as white spectators tossed pennies at them," Sadler wrote.[22]

Near the parade route, Carnival organizers staged a fashion show along the levee dock, a site where for decades African American stevedores unloaded cotton bales from paddleboats. The stage for the show was built on top of stacked four-hundred-pound cotton bales, on which young white female models in cotton dresses paraded back and forth for the onlookers. The fashion show, like many of Carnival's disparate events, celebrated cotton by demonstrating white standards of beauty within an imagined Old South context.

FIG. 11. The "royal barge" unloads at the levee. Note the shirtless African American men holding the sides of the gangplank and the cotton bales stacked on the barge. Arthur A. Halle Papers, Memphis Public Library.

The 1935 carnival offered another example of how the entire week was a claim for the importance of contemporary cotton with backward-looking Lost Cause ideology with gender and whiteness at its heart. The year's theme, "A Dream of Fair Women," had several connotations, from "fair" as carnival, to "fair" as white, to perhaps "fair" as legitimate. Sixty of the floats that rolled down Main Street during the Grand Parade featured specific historical women like Queen Victoria, Joan of Arc, and Martha Washington, or representatives, like the float dedicated to the "Belle of the South." As Sadler aptly described it, "the lavish street production blended history and mythology to portray the 'unsurpassed loveliness' of white women."[23] White supremacy was never far from these gender portrayals; in at least one year, small

FIG. 12. African American men pull a float during the Cotton Carnival parade. Photographic Collection, Memphis and Shelby County Room, Memphis Public Library.

black children sat next to carnival princesses on the parade floats. A 1941 photograph in Arthur Halle's papers shows a young African American boy of not more than six years, wearing nothing but a white loin cloth and head wrap. The child stood next to seated white women, waving an ornate peacock-feather fan over them.[24] Another year, white children dressed as "Hawaiian Beauties, Spanish Banderilleros, . . . Indian Chiefs and Red Skins from the Western Plains [and a] Wandering Tribe of Roumanian [*sic*] Gypsies."[25]

Though each year Carnival had a new theme, aspects of this Lost Cause vision of the Old South permeated the event for decades. The festival's public events were paeans to the social order that white Memphians believed cotton dictated. Blackface and plantation scenes were a regular part of the parade well into the 1960s. And while certainly some of this performance of white supremacy was merely a reflection of the roles white and black Memphians played in their contemporary Jim Crow society, much of Cotton Carnival's overall ethos

FIG. 13. A crowd surrounds the Carnival king and queen as they are driven by African American men in a carriage. Photographic Collection, Memphis and Shelby County Room, Memphis Public Library.

remained a performance, or at least a public interpretation, of labor and life in the Old South. From 1931 until the 1960s, many of the annual themes were self-consciously historic, celebrating "George Washington," "King Cotton's Happy Memories," or "King Cotton Reviews American History."[26]

Tellingly, organizers believed that Memphis's Cotton Carnival was not just for white Memphians but for all its citizens. In his history of Cotton Carnival, Halle wrote that the organizers were proud to have created a public spectacle "for ALL the people, for ALL kinds of professions and businesses and for the City as a whole regardless of . . . social standing, wealth, prestige . . ." To his eyes, there was no contradiction between these portrayals of cotton's racial regime and the city coming together "to do something outstanding for Memphis and COTTON."[27]

AS CARNIVAL HIGHLIGHTED Lost Cause history, it did so with a conscious effort to bring Memphis closer to the contemporary agricultural business of its hinterlands. This happened by both transforming the city to look like a plantation and having Carnival activities literally reach out to the country. As early as 1935, Halle and other representatives began a "Good Will Tour" that took them around Mississippi, Tennessee, and Arkansas to promote the Carnival.[28] For the first few years, a series of one-day bus tours carried the president of the Cotton Carnival Association, the cotton king and queen, princesses, and the Maid of Cotton out into the hinterlands. They'd roll into a small farm town, set up a loudspeaker, and drum up attention for the Carnival. Eventually the tour grew in size and range, with airplanes replacing buses.[29]

For example, prior to Elvis's opening concert in 1956, organizers spent time in many states, but they saved the "biggest and final pitch of the year" for Mississippi. Nine days before Carnival began, seventy-five representatives—led by Delta planter and Carnival king Oscar Carr Jr.—boarded Greyhound buses and visited nine Mississippi cities in a single day. After a stop in Oxford to meet with the University of Mississippi chancellor, football coach, and "other university dignitaries," the buses rolled into the Delta with stops in various towns. The day ended in Carr's hometown of Clarksdale where "a huge crowd" met the king and his court.[30]

Touring the cotton fields around Memphis was not reserved only for dignitaries. Carnival visitors could also see a plantation in action. From the 1940s into the 1960s, a signature event during Carnival was a tour of nearby plantations. In 1940 several buses full of white visitors representing twenty-two states loaded up outside the Peabody Hotel and drove out for a tour of Mississippi farms. The tourists hobnobbed with local Memphis celebrities and saw what was billed as a "real" cotton plantation experience. The 1947 tour included the Tennessee governor and the Maid of Cotton.[31] The tourists stopped to spend a few hours at each plantation over the course of the day. Usually this included a ride around the cotton fields (which in May did not look radically different from a Northern corn farm; only small green plants sprouted through the Delta soil), followed by various "plantation" activities. One year, tourists could take a "turn at driving a mule hitched to a plow in the cotton fields."[32]

Cotton labor, cotton culture, and white supremacy were on full display. A 1948 brochure claimed that the tours were particularly popular with "Northern and Eastern visitors" who saw "huge cotton plantations in Arkansas in operation," where they could "judge for themselves how the cotton workers live and play."[33] During the 1952 tour, participants had a lunch of "barbecue with all the trimmings and refreshments," while sitting on the porch listening to three African American musicians playing traditional folk and blues songs. Seated on a bench off the porch, the men played a mandolin, a National

FIG. 14. Visitors toured Mississippi cotton plantations as part of the Cotton Carnival festivities. The events were arranged to give the tourists an imagined view of life on a cotton farm. Tourists could take a turn plowing a field behind a mule, eat barbecue, and listen to African American musicians.
Arthur A. Halle Papers, Memphis Public Library.

resonator guitar, and a fiddle; an African American woman wearing a white dress and headscarf stood nearby, completing the picture for the visitors.[34] (See figure 14.) The *Memphis Press-Scimitar* summed up the 1947 tour by claiming that it gave visitors everything they wanted to see: "stately plantation homes—negro workers singing in the fields—jigging pickaninnies—cotton gins in operation."[35]

Even back on the Memphis streets cotton was everywhere, including adorned to people's clothing. The band director at a Greenville, Mississippi, junior high wrote to Halle in 1960 to ask that her band perform in one of the parades. She promised that the teenagers would look the part in uniforms "resembling a cotton boll . . . and headbands with three artificial cotton bolls." The director told Halle that her band performed "King Cotton March,"

"Dixie," and "Old Man River." It even played the song "Boll Weevil," with marching that "featured the outline of a boll weevil with dance steps showing his legs scratching and nose boring."[36]

In addition to the Grand Parade, which by the 1960s attracted crowds of more than 400,000, there was a children's parade with 35,000 marching kids who got the day off from school to participate. The 1958 children's parade celebrated cotton in ways from the ethereal to the utilitarian. The forty-six floats, each sponsored by a white Memphis public or private school, depicted everything from "Cotton Dreams" and "Cotton Wonderland" to "Cotton Nets" and "Cotton Lamp Wicks." The organizer of the parade wrote at the bottom of his instructions for participants that their move down Main and Front Streets was going to be "THE MOST SPECTACULAR AND DEMOCRATIC EVENT IN THE COTTON CARNIVAL . . . WITNESSED BY HUNDREDS OF THOUSANDS, EFFECTING [*SIC*] THE LIVES OF HALF A MILLION PEOPLE."[37] The all-caps blast certainly captured the grandiose spirit that white organizers had for the parade in the decades after World War II, though its claim of democracy was demonstrably false.

Though books could be written describing the imagery of the parades alone, a quick run over the breadth of Carnival programming demonstrates the ways that the crop was more than an excuse for a festival. From the organization's stationery, which read simply "Always Choose Cotton," to small white children dressed as actual cotton bales walking through the streets, each corner of the Carnival told the plant's story. In the yearly programs, which were sold on the streets and in stores to many thousands of attendees, advertisements from companies like Ford sold pickup trucks only after hailing "His Majesty King Cotton, Long Live the King."[38] The bulk of the promotions were from Arkansas and Mississippi gin companies, rural banks, cotton buyers and sellers, or just planters and their plantations.[39] Famous outfits like the W. O. Shurden Farms in Drew, Mississippi, or Joe Rice Dockery's plantation in Cleveland, Mississippi, bought ads. The Staple Cotton Cooperative Association, "The World's Largest Marketers of Delta Cottons," trumpeted the "rich, alluvial Mississippi Delta soils" with "superior tilth, structure, and fertility." Not to be outdone, the Imperial County Growers' Association from El Centro, California, took a full-page ad sending their "Imperial Greetings" from the West Coast to the "Cotton Empire" of Memphis. Rex Cottonseed's promotion included photos of mechanical cotton pickers rolling through blossoming white plants in a field.[40]

FIG. 15. Jeffrey Wright marched in a Cotton Carnival parade clad in a miniature replica of a cotton bale. *Memphis Commercial Appeal*, May 19, 1956.

It was clear to even a casual observer of the Memphis Cotton Carnival that its organizers, at least for the first thirty years, were trying to exalt cotton in two ways. First, Halle and the rest of the white political and business elite wanted to show off the business connection of the Bluff City to the Mississippi Delta and the other cotton lands that fed its warehouses with ginned fiber every fall. The culture of cotton that flowed from country to city followed the bales themselves and their economic value. Money flowed into Memphis warehouses, department stores, and banks along cotton shipping routes. Making Memphis into an urban plantation vignette was important to accomplishing white organizers' aim of showing off this connection.

Second, organizers needed to couch this crass economic interest in the drama of the Old South narrative. The blackface and demonstrations of white female beauty, the performances of black Memphians acting out roles once played in cotton agriculture—part fantasy, part reality—was also crucial to selling Memphis as cotton's capital. For a week each spring, the regular Jim Crow expectations for African American behavior were ratcheted up, fictionalized, and sensationalized. White Memphians demonstrated cotton's organization of the regional economy and society both on the streets and cloistered away from the public in Peabody Hotel ballrooms. They celebrated cotton landscapes and Jim Crow together. Black Memphians noticed.

CHAPTER SEVEN

A Jubilee for Cotton Labor

FROM THE COTTON CARNIVAL'S inaugural year, critics saw its parades and fashion shows as racist, elitist, and just plain gauche. One of them was Southern Tenant Farmers Union (STFU) member John Handcox. A poet and songwriter who grew up in a large African American family across the Mississippi River in Arkansas, Handcox joined the farm labor group in 1935. By then he had spent his life as a sharecropper fighting against crooked landlords who tried to cut his rightful share of the crop. He considered himself part of only two percent of tenant farmers who kept track of their debts at the landowners' commissary, and he pointed to cotton's grip on the Delta's financial structure as the main culprit. "Lots of places you couldn't have a cow," he remembered, so that every tenant would have to "get butter and milk from the commissary," which would increase your cotton debt. "And they wanted you to put [all debts] in cotton," he wrote, so that workers would have to produce more and more to settle. "King Cotton was the financial part of the farming . . . the only thing sold by the poor people," Handcox asserted.[1]

It is no wonder, then, that images of the 1936 Cotton Carnival, with its white king and queen riding floats pulled by black men, struck a chord with the labor organizer. He must have seen newspaper coverage of the festival, or even visited Memphis during the celebration. It made enough of an impression that he wrote a poem lampooning the event. In "King Cotton," he wrote:

The planters celebrated King Cotton in Memphis, May fifteen
It was the largest gathering you most ever seen
People came from far and near—to celebrate King Cotton
Whom the planters love so dear.
Thousands of flags hung in the street,

But they left thousands of sharecroppers on their Farms
with nothing to eat
Why do they celebrate Cotton? Here, I'll make it clear,
Because they cheat, beat and take it away from
labor every year.
Cotton is King, and will always be,
Until labor in the South is set free.
The money spent for decorations and flags,
Would sure have helped poor sharecroppers who are hungry in rags.
Oh! King Cotton, today you have millions of slaves
And have caused many poor workers to be in lonesome graves.
When Cotton is King of any nation,
It means wealth to the planter—to the laborer Starvation.[2]

Handcox's poignant juxtaposition of wealth and starvation, of plantation violence with the Carnival flags and decorations, was more than a simple critique. It reveals how, for black Southerners as well as white, cotton had become the language in which stories of labor, oppression, and freedom could be told to contest the Lost Cause interpretation. Cotton could carry these ideas because the reality of the rural South was that whites relied on African Americans. As a result, the rural black community had at least a limited say in the crop's world. King Cotton, whom "planters love so dear," was not only a white metaphor but a black one as well.

Handcox was one of many African American observers to bristle at the Carnival narrative of agricultural life in the South, though most would not react to it with poetry and union organizing. In 1935 Ransom and Ethyl Venson took their five-year-old nephew Quincy to see the Cotton Carnival parade. They found a section of the route where African Americans were allowed to gather, most likely near Main Street's intersection with Beale Street. Ransom owned a dental practice on Beale a couple blocks away. Carnival parade grandstands and most other areas to watch the parade around town were whites-only, but there were segregated areas where African Americans could stand.

As the Old South floats moved down the street, showing off African Americans dressed as draft animals and mammies sitting on cotton bales, the older Vensons waved, while their nephew looked on quizzically. Ransom asked Quincy if he liked all the floats and pageantry. "No, I didn't like the parade," he told his uncle. "All the Negroes were horses."[3] His

FIG. 16. Ransom Venson, Ethyl Venson, and Nat D. Williams, the three longtime leaders of the Cotton Makers' Jubilee. Dr. R. Q. and Ethyl H. Venson Cotton Makers' Jubilee Collection, box 1, Memphis Public Library.

comment took the elder Vensons aback. "It horrified me and my husband," Ethyl remembered.[4]

Quincy's comment seems to have shaken the Vensons into recognizing what they were witnessing: a version of the cotton industry that diminished or just plain ignored the black labor that sustained it. Ransom later recalled that the parade's cotton scenes reflected a romanticized image of the plantation South—one he knew was a lie. Standing there in 1935, he "pledged . . . to make an effort to have the Negro citizens of Memphis identified" in the "great enterprise" of cotton farming and production. "It is impossible to exclude the Negro from cotton."[5]

Ransom went straight to Cotton Carnival founder Arthur Halle and the other organizers. He asked how the black business community could participate in a positive way, as more than horses and props. "They told him, in no uncertain terms," recalled Ethyl, "that they used the best liquor, the best stationery, and they weren't fixin' to have any niggers come in there." Privately, Halle apologized and told Ransom that while black Memphians could not have a respectable part in the white event, the Vensons were free to start a black version of Carnival.[6] With remarkable speed and detail, they did. The Vensons put to work their contacts across Memphis and later that same year, 1935, put together the Beale Street Cotton Makers' Fiesta. After two years the event changed its name to the Cotton Makers' Jubilee, which became a staple in the Memphis civic calendar for nearly five decades.

From 1935 until the 1980s, thousands of African Americans from across Mississippi, Arkansas, and Tennessee flocked to the city each summer to parade, hear music, listen to speeches, see fashion shows, and just have fun together, all under the banner of cotton. The middle fifty years of the twentieth century were a time of remarkable change in the South, but perhaps no city was more emblematic of that transformation than Memphis. One of the striking aspects of the Cotton Makers' Jubilee is that, amid economic turmoil, political upheaval, and unrelenting violence, African Americans continued to organize a celebration of cotton every summer. Black Memphis's embrace of the crop through Jubilee is a revealing window into the fiber's power as a lever for inclusion *and* resistance, though its exact use changed radically over the twentieth century.

As this chapter will demonstrate, rather than running from the crop because of its tangible historic and contemporary connections to slavery, economic oppression, and violence, thousands of black Memphians seized it as their own. They sidled up to cotton's power, and in everything from essays and speeches to floats and dances, made the Jubilee an annual, weeklong, public argument about how cotton could not be king without African American contributions.

These arguments, however, were never static. During its fifty-year run, Jubilee planners and participants reoriented the event's relationship to cotton as both farming practices and social structures evolved. Black Memphians contested and reshaped the crop's symbolism in telling ways, responding to shifting agricultural realities in the surrounding countryside and the advance of civil rights within the city. Yet even as Jubilee expanded in size and influence, it remained anchored to cotton, holding fast to the crop's centrality even as the world around it—and the struggle for justice in the Bluff City—changed dramatically.

In the 1930s and early 1940s, the white Carnival offered African American organizers a foothold from which to claim greater cultural, economic, and political power. After all, since white Southerners were spending so much time, money, and effort exalting cotton, black Southerners could write themselves into that importance through direct claims to historic and contemporary African American labor in cotton fields, gins, mills, wharves, and warehouses. Jubilee celebrated that work. In most ways, the early Jubilee events mirrored those of Carnival, though they occurred in smaller numbers and in segregated spaces. There was a children's parade, a "coronation parade" that ended in W. C. Handy Park with the crowning of the Jubilee king and queen. Over the years the events expanded to include balls, a publicity tour, history essay contests, concerts, fashion shows, and dances.

After World War II, however, organizers reacted to changes in both the cotton industry and the structure of Memphis itself by massaging their connection to the plant. Generational fissures emerged. The Vensons gave way to younger Jubilee leaders who found themselves performing greater and greater feats of rhetorical gymnastics to make the cotton celebration a statement about equal rights. The dueling celebrations of Carnival and Jubilee in the 1950s and 1960s reflected new tensions, as both festivals grappled with what it meant to celebrate a crop that was no longer central to the lives of the attendees. Even before the 1968 assassination of Martin Luther King Jr., only seven blocks from Beale Street, Jubilee participants no longer used cotton as a call for inclusion, but as a weapon against segregation and white supremacy. Young members of the movement called for boycotts of all things cotton.

As this chapter demonstrates, the two forces, agricultural changes in the fields outside the city and the civil rights reckoning inside Memphis, were constantly pushing and pulling at both Jubilee and Carnival. Technological change and the corporatization of plantations outside the city meant fewer workers in the cotton fields. This changed Memphians' connections to the fiber. By the 1970s cotton was no longer important in the lives of the people of the city, and the crop no longer worked as a reason to meet on the streets every summer to celebrate together.

From the beginning, however, Jubilee was no simple "black version" of Cotton Carnival. As historian Charles L. Hughes points out, "the Cotton Makers' Jubilee defied the physical *and* ideological restrictions of the whites-only celebration."[7] It's an important point. Physically, Carnival remade the city into a cotton metropolis with reminders everywhere of the plant and its fiber. Jubilee also remade the segregated African American part of town into a cotton wonderland, which erased what could have been yet another Jim Crow boundary.

Ideologically, Carnival's attempts to make cotton a whites-only embodiment of the Old South could not work nearly as well alongside black celebrations of their contributions to the cotton industry. While the social spaces of the city were defined by Jim Crow, the "ideological restrictions" of King Cotton were up for contestation.

One place African Americans contested white versions of cotton's culture was right there in the name. The possessive "Cotton *Makers'* Jubilee" claimed ownership of not just the parades and parties but the crop itself. African American organizers asserted their labor, the *making* of cotton. It highlighted the work that African Americans did at every stage of the plant's movement from field to fiber. And though it was a seemingly small thing, the apostrophe in the name became an important marker of this ownership. Over the decades that followed the first Jubilee, white newspaper descriptions often dropped the punctuation mark, implying that "Cotton Makers" was merely an adjective description for the Jubilee. In official documents and in the black press, however, the apostrophe remained.

"Jubilee," too, had a specific meaning. In the Bible the term refers to a time of emancipation when workers left farm fields uncultivated for a year and returned home to live on ancestral lands.[8] The Bible promises that in the Jubilee year, the poor will be taken care of and anyone who sells their property because of poverty can redeem that sale later. In the early twentieth century the word meant a time of restitution, release, and public celebration. In the African American lexicon it was associated with singing and more generally "sounds of jubilation."[9] The name conveyed a celebration of African Americans' pride in the ownership of the crop. Contrasted with the white event, Jubilee was more than a mere carnival.

FROM THE BEGINNING, Jubilee organizers walked the delicate political line between asserting their place in the history and contemporary culture of cotton and recognizing the power of the white cotton establishment. In the pages of the program, Ransom Venson endorsed the white Cotton Carnival's recognition of the crop as the "life sustenance" of Memphis, "the Capital of the Cotton Kingdom." "Cotton is the basis of all progress made in the Mid-South," Venson stated plainly in 1938. "It is imperative that some united effort be made to keep cotton king."[10]

Jim Crow demanded a careful balancing act between asserting cotton's significance and offering tributes to segregation. The early Jubilee programs not only honored Carnival's efforts to save the cotton business but also paid specific attention to white political and economic powerbrokers. There was a regular page devoted to white Memphians like Mayor Watkins Overton ("a friend of progress and development for all Memphians, regardless of class or color"), Cotton Carnival president Vance Norfleet ("sympathetic . . . and patient"), and Bailey Walsh, assistant publicity director of Carnival ("a well-known friend to all classes of citizens").[11]

Yet, at the same time, Jubilee organizers did not leave Carnival's presentation of African Americans in the cotton industry unchecked. Ransom wrote in 1937 that "no celebration [of the crop] is complete without his participation."[12] The 1940 program pointedly criticized how during the Carnival "Colored women used to perch atop cotton bales on Main Street" and argued that "the Negro played a much more significant and conspicuous part in the production of the South's greatest staple." African Americans were "more important personage[s] in the Memphis scene than a mere menial to be presented as a clown and mountebank."[13]

Ransom Venson had a keen understanding of cotton's power in Memphis and throughout the South, and rather than run from it—to claim that African Americans could or should gain economic, political, and cultural strength outside of the commodity's grasp—he embraced it. If the white Southerners liked cotton so much, Venson seemed to argue, the Jubilee would remind them that without African American labor there would be no King Cotton. His writings made it clear year after year, in the 1930s and into the 1940s, that if white Memphis was going to celebrate this monarch, African Americans would take seriously their role in the kingdom. In 1939 he positioned Jubilee as creating favorable publicity for "colored residents of . . . the cotton country" and for cotton itself. The three-day event would "publicize the varied and possible uses of the South's greatest staple, the 'money-crop,' the key to Front Street's prosperity and Beale Street's gaiety, Cotton." As the Southern crop succeeded, so too would African Americans. "As workers toiling in the fields, making cotton, we realize what the 'silver fleece' means in the economy of our section. For this reason, we . . . 'help sell cotton' to the world at large and at home. We seize it because, as part of the scene and as active workers in the 'Cotton hegemony,' we know it is our duty to 'help ourselves.'"[14] The message was clear: Cotton ruled the South, and it was in African Americans' self-interest to work to keep the crop in power.

Venson's argument was not simply economic, however. He put cotton's history at the center of Jubilee and took direct aim at the Lost Cause story offered by Carnival, which portrayed a white planter's vision of cotton agriculture, and he did so at events that were whites-only. The Vensons objected to Carnival's diminishing, or worse, ignoring, the black role in cotton's past and present. In contrast, "the principal objective of the Jubilee" was "to symbolize the great and important part which the colored people of this area have played in the history of cotton." This intellectual element—the arguments about cotton that Jubilee offered to counter Carnival's versions—were baked into the festivities. The 1937 Jubilee included parades and concerts dedicated to cotton, for instance, but also a speech contest between "local Colored grammar schools" on the subject "How Cotton Affects Life in [the] South."[15]

Venson's essay in the 1941 program deserves a close read because it lays bare the logical gymnastics required to square a celebration of cotton with a celebration of African American life, but it also details how he saw African Americans as agents in their own discrimination. Venson begins with an admission that he faced criticism for celebrating cotton. Some claimed the crop "has been the excuse for the economic slavery of the Negro, and a medium for his exploitation and robbery by those whom his economic station has forced him to serve." But life outside of cotton for African Americans, Venson argues, was limited. He attacks the black education system, which he claims turned out "proper-phrasing, smart talking, over-stuffed jelly-fish." African American schools patterned after Harvard and Yale teach "the Negro . . . to be a White man while he is in school . . . then speedily [place] a mop and bucket in his hand." It was a continuation of a dynamic formed during slavery, when "Big House" slaves "gazed in admiring awe upon the ways of their White aristocratic masters." This "play acting" group of "ten-cent millionaires" look down, Venson writes, on the "'Po White Trash,' and 'Field Nigger' . . . who . . . they deem their inferiors." This "pseudo Negro elite" painted work in the cotton fields as dishonorable.[16]

Cotton work was not menial or degrading, Venson counters; it had brought a generation of black Southerners out of slavery into freedom. Many, he claims, owned land and farms "built out of the toil and sweat of their bodies and the tenacity of a desperate determination to 'amount to something.'" Yet this toehold was "being lost by the present generation, who regard it beneath their dignity to cling to the earth from which all our real blessings flow." Farming was "honest and productive" work. It was not black farmers who were facing hardship, Venson argues, but the "vast hordes" that had left rural areas to "crowd into the already over-crowded cities."

Venson's rebuff of elite black education *and* his criticism of migrants who left cotton country present a surprising point of view, considering he was a trained dentist who had settled in Memphis after growing up in rural Louisiana. His defense of cotton seems genuine, if devoid of all discussion of the ways that white supremacy, tenant farming, and farm credit limited black opportunity in the rural South. The Jubilee, he writes, was designed to dramatize "the Negro's contribution to the agricultural South." It was not an attempt to offer a makeshift, secondary, or "'sun-down' interpretation to the serious purposes of the great Memphis Cotton Carnival." The festival was an earnest attempt to "focus attention on the part the Negro has played in the cultivation and processing of the great staple . . . cotton . . . which has played and still plays, so great a part in the life and economy of the Old and the New South."

This was not an accommodationist stance, in his view, but a "progressive" one. Jubilee could "create good-will between the races." It was an antidote, he believed, to popular portrayals of black life in cotton country as debased and wretched. There was "much lamenting comment and many literary tears" about rural life, Venson complains. In a direct reference to novelist Richard Wright, Venson calls out "top flight writers [who] give the country the impression that many of us are 'Bigger Thomases of Native Son' extraction, choking and dying in frustration like cornered rats." Jubilee would endeavor instead to "avoid the description of 'clowning.'"

Venson's defense of cotton as expressed in the 1940s Jubilee programs laid important groundwork for those who stepped in to replace him in the decades to follow. Future organizers frequently referred to his stories and quoted his essays. But there was always a disconnect between the stated philosophies of the programs and the reality of Jubilee out on the streets of Memphis. For all of Venson's talk defending cotton, in fact, there was little evidence of the crop in the rest of the printed guide. While the white Cotton Carnival's program was full of advertisements for cotton gins, warehouses, and plantations, Jubilee's had no advertisements related to the crop. And while Venson's team of volunteers marketed the event in Arkansas, Tennessee, and throughout the Delta, they sold it as a break from rural life. Even by 1939, "practically all the towns" of the north Delta sent "representative colored citizens" to build and ride in floats or take part as princesses and maids of honor in the parades. Those Jubilee marketing materials depicted it not as a celebration of cotton but rather as "the nation's greatest 'Negro Party.'"[17]

LIFE IN THE COTTON fields outside of Memphis, however, was no party. The political, economic, and social oppression—not to mention the personal violence—that characterized rural Southern life for African Americans meant that Memphis and places north were attractive destinations. Mississippi Delta bluesman Charley Patton was right to sing "Every day seems like murder here." His solution, as for so many of his fellow rural dwellers, was to move. "I'm gonna leave tomorrow," he promised in "Down the Dirt Road Blues."[18] But the material conditions—the changing agricultural and environmental realities for farmers in the cotton South—were important factors in this movement.

Two developments in the Delta had significant impact on African American life in its metropolis. First, the invention of the mechanical cotton picker just seventy-five miles south of Beale Street forced thousands of farmworkers out of sharecropping work. Second, the New Deal and World War II opened up some industrial, nonagricultural jobs to African Americans. Those two factors pushed black workers toward Memphis. The city's population grew from 162,351 in 1920 to almost 400,000 in 1950, with a larger percentage of African Americans making up the urban population than ever.

For these new Bluff City residents, many of whom had self-consciously decided to leave farming and rural life behind them, cotton remained a tangible, connected part of their lives. Even after World War II, farm owners in the Mid-South relied on seasonal workers to pick the cotton in the fall. The *Memphis World* reported that thirty thousand laborers who lived in the city traveled out in buses or the backs of trucks to cotton fields at harvest time. No longer working for a share of the crop on a patch of land on which they lived, these urban-based pickers earned between two and three dollars for each hundred-pound sack of cotton they filled.[19] Even for those not returning to the fields to pick, cotton was no distant memory but a visible feature of urban life.

The Cotton Makers' Jubilee reflected that connection into the 1950s and 1960s. In the postwar period, new leaders emerged who, subtly at first, changed the focus of Jubilee politics. As the Vensons began to do less in the day-to-day planning of the festival, Nat D. Williams stepped in to take on greater responsibilities both behind the scenes and, more importantly, as the public voice of Jubilee. Williams was only twelve years younger than Ransom Venson, but in their personas the difference seemed much greater. Venson was from rural Arkansas and had moved to Memphis, where he had established his dental office on Beale Street. He was a Mason, a member of the Elks Club, and a Sunday school teacher at St. John's Baptist Church.[20]

Williams, by contrast, was literally born on Beale and seemed to many to embody the spirit of the street, which he called "Chocolate Avenue."[21] After earning degrees at Columbia University and Northwestern University, Williams taught history at Booker T. Washington High School. One student, Rufus Thomas, who would gain fame as a singer and comedian, remembered

FIG. 17. Dorothea Lange photograph for the Farm Security Administration of "Cotton hoers loading at Memphis for the day's work in Arkansas; June 1937." Schomburg Center for Research in Black Culture, Photographs and Prints Division, New York Public Library.

him as more than a stodgy academic.[22] Williams developed an annual dance for the festival—the Jubilee Jerk one year and the "'sensational' Jubilee Dip" the next—and taught it to his students.[23] The teacher also worked for the *Memphis World* and *Tri-State Defender* writing a column and reporting and editing stories, and he hosted a weekly amateur night revue at the Old Palace Theater. He was already a public figure among black Memphians in 1948 when he sat down in front of a microphone at WDIA radio and became the first African American disc jockey in the United States.[24] As his fame grew—at one point his voice could be heard on the radio by 10 percent of African Americans in the entire country—he remained committed to the Cotton Makers' Jubilee.

At the end of the 1940s, Williams wrote an article in the Jubilee program trumpeting the event's seven greatest accomplishments since 1934. He began big. Jubilee was "one of the most significant developments on the inter-racial 'front' in America," because it was a display of black patriotism. The event offered the "truest expression of the basic 'abandon' of the American Negro in his enjoyment of the 'great United States of America.'" Yet, alongside improved "social and inter-racial relations" and promotion of civic and political groups, Williams only made one mention of the crop itself, an unenthusiastic line about an annual essay contest in which elementary students "write essays on cotton."[25] The community leader's ambivalence toward the staple foreshadowed a winnowing of cotton's importance to the Jubilee, and Memphis itself, over the 1950s and 1960s.

Despite Williams's claims about improved race relations, several changes in the economy and demographics of Memphis worried the white elite. First, the decreasing importance of cotton *work* to black Memphians—and the increasing stretch of time since immigrants to the city had actually lived in cotton country—meant that the crop was a less tangible reality in the city. It also meant that, as a cultural icon, cotton no longer carried the weight that it had years earlier. The "plantation mentality" that characterized race relations in the city since the end of the Civil War began to fade as the plantation itself became less central to black life. African Americans resisted public and private rules seen as "country," even as the Negro Chamber of Commerce encouraged black Memphians not to give up seasonal work on cotton farms.[26] Middle-class whites, as Michael K. Honey argues, "feared 'uprisings' of the 'coloreds'" and "complained to the mayor that blacks 'shopped around' for the highest-paying jobs." White Memphians were upset that African Americans no longer left the city each summer to work in cotton fields. As Honey writes, "The problem was not black laziness, for no one worked harder than blacks in low-wage occupations; the 'problem' was that blacks finally perceived the possibility of doing better."[27] "Doing better" meant literal and, as the changes in Jubilee and Cotton Carnival would make clear, figurative distancing from cotton and all its encumbrances. Changes in the agricultural and environmental scene outside the Bluff City were changing race relations and the reality of its grandest public performances.

One of the clearest examples of this is in the vignette that opens chapter 6. By 1956, when Elvis Presley rocked the Cotton Pickin' Jamboree at Ellis Auditorium, the historical forces of postwar America were in full effect in Memphis. The structures holding up racial division were being supported just as energetically as were the forces testing them. Elvis was mixing up traditional black and white music for a segregated crowd. Oscar Carr Jr. and

Clare Mallory, the Carnival king and queen, were ferried on a barge adorned with black bodies and cotton bales. Meanwhile, black workers across the city were organizing, membership in the NAACP and local civil rights organizations blossomed, and African American culture was pushing its way into formerly all-white radio stations, magazines, and music charts.

From the Civil War through World War II, cotton had ordered Memphis society because of the commodity's importance to both the city economy and the life experiences of so many Memphis workers. The fiber was connected to the day-to-day life of the entire metropolis. World War II and its aftermath shook the very foundation of the city, however. In the 1950s and 1960s the South produced less and less cotton, and farms employed fewer and fewer people. At the same time, African Americans increasingly saw their futures in urban areas with access to integrated spaces; they emerged from wartime ready to fight for that access. Therefore, white and black Memphians saw cotton two contrasting ways. The planters, merchants, and shippers who had sat atop the city's economy perceived threats to cotton in the market and sought marketplace solutions. Most African Americans, however, no longer saw cotton lining up with their political, economic, or social priorities. Cotton Carnival and Cotton Makers' Jubilee both pivoted as a result.

At Cotton Carnival crowds continued to grow over the decades, but the emphasis on the crop's agricultural roots—and the reliance on public performances steeped in black stereotypes—began to fade. At first the shift was almost imperceptible, but it became more apparent with each passing year. Historian Robert Emmett McLean argued that "by the end of [the] 1960s," parade goers and concert attendees sensed that the event's "priorities, attitudes, and histories" no longer aligned with their own. Yet the evidence suggests that this disconnect had begun well before the decade's end.[28]

The theme of the 1964 Carnival, for instance, was retrospective: "King Cotton's Happy Memories." The program that year was filled with advertisements from Mississippi, Arkansas, and Tennessee plantations, gins, and chemical companies. But the images were starkly different in that they went out of their way to avoid showing farmworkers. Whereas the prewar programs and events were structured to highlight black labor, these mid-1960s ads showed cotton in an entirely new light. Rex Seed Company of Parkin, Arkansas, for instance, sold its Crown Brand cottonseed with not photos of black laborers in a field but a chart and a case for the modern science behind the product. The photo atop the full-page ad showed a blooming field ripe with white bolls with four mechanical pickers—not people—rolling through. The ad for Greenwood, Mississippi's Staple Cotton Cooperative Association featured two mechanical pickers, though its multipage spread did not stop there. Two large photographs told a modern, nearly laborless story of commodity production. The first shows the floor of its gin building, with six state-of-the-art Chief Supreme gins whirring away, and two motionless African American men just standing, posed, staring at the machines. The second image depicts a white woman in a shirt embroidered with the company name seated at a table, with her hands on a fiber-testing machine. The caption echoes the modern message, trumpeting "new service to buyers," "accurate classing," and "dependable fiber lab measurements."[29]

While the Cotton Carnival tried to pivot to keep the crop relevant, the Cotton Makers' Jubilee seemed to be at even greater odds with the zeitgeist of postwar Memphis. For instance, while organizers renamed the "Spirit of Cotton" talent show for African American high schoolers to the "Ms. Jubilect" competition, the prize remained an all-cotton wardrobe—to be worn while the winner marched in the Jubilee processions. It was an updated name, but the loyalty to cotton remained.[30]

DESPITE THE ORGANIZERS' efforts to keep cotton central to the festivities, by 1960 that connection labored under the weight of the plant's history. Across the South, African American college students began putting pressure on segregated facilities with direct action. The sit-in movement had begun in February 1960 in Greensboro, North Carolina, but was enlivened by the leadership of black activists in Nashville. In Memphis students at the historically African American LeMoyne College quickly followed the lead of these other young activists. Marion Berry, a LeMoyne graduate who had been a vocal civil rights advocate as a student, returned to campus in the wake of the 1960 sit-ins and encouraged more student protests.[31] The burgeoning activism of these students put pressure on the older generation of African American leaders in Memphis, especially those like Nat D. Williams and the Vensons who had built Jubilee as a segregated institution celebrating cotton.

As Shirletta Jeannette Kinchen describes in her history of student activism in the city, college-aged African Americans no longer waited for their elders and their traditional organizations to lead on civil rights issues in the city. Protests targeted segregated public facilities at the library, zoo, and train station, as well as private businesses. White city leaders mostly rebuffed the protests and dug in their heels to protect segregation.[32]

Not surprisingly, given both the agricultural and political changes, in summer 1960 activists turned their attention to both cotton festivals. "Memphis Negro college students," reported the *Tri-State Defender*, "temporarily shifted their fight for integration from public facilities to a battle against a 24-year-old segregated negro celebration—The Cotton Makers Jubilee."[33] The crux of the demonstrators' complaint was not the segregation of Jubilee but its allegiance to cotton. Students surrounded Jubilee headquarters, marching with signs that asked, "What has King Cotton done for the Negro?" Another sign answered: "All Negroes have got from King Cotton is a stiff back and blistered hands."[34] The activists called for an all-out boycott of both Carnival and Jubilee. One student, who asked the *Defender* not to publish his name, explained why the African American event in particular should stop: "Cotton does nothing for Negroes to cause them to celebrate. . . . By condoning a cotton celebration," the young man argued, "Negroes are paying tribute to the system that undergirded the entire slavery period." His critique was not limited to the past. "If Negroes were integrated into all phases of the cotton industry, then we'd have something to celebrate. But because they have been restricted to the lowly chore of picking cotton, all Negroes have done is make the white man rich." The protester then turned his attention to Venson, Williams, and the other Jubilee organizers. "The persons who are sponsoring the Jubilee have brainwashed the Negroes who participate into believing that a segregated celebration is better than none at all," the young student told the *Defender*. The paper's bold headline blared "Why Students Picket Cotton Jubilee," which was the weekly's top story during Jubilee in 1960, indicating that the protest had captured the attention of black readers. Venson, perhaps missing how quickly the burgeoning civil rights issues were moving against Jubilee, told the newspaper he thought the protests were "foolish."[35]

By 1961 civil rights activities across the South picked up steam, and the focus on the Jubilee did not abate. The Memphis chapter of the NAACP issued a statement narrowing in on the role of Venson, Williams, and other African American festival organizers. "The fact that this affair is sponsored by negroes does not alter its evil effects," the group argued; "this only serves to make it more odious."[36] Perhaps revealing the generational differences in approach to the boycott, the NAACP executive secretary noted that Jubilee protests had been handed over to its own "College Chapter." The growing divide—a tension that was present across NAACP chapters as well as in other civil rights organizations—was clear in Venson's immediate response to the local chapter's anti-Jubilee statement. He implied that protesters were merely "using the name of the NAACP." After all, he said, "I'm a life member of the NAACP myself. It is not the NAACP that is against the Jubilee."[37]

Rather than running from cotton to defend Jubilee, over the next few years the Vensons and other organizers pushed back against protests by employing the argument that had served them for more than two decades: African Americans' history with cotton gave the community social, cultural, and economic power. Venson fired back at what he saw as protesters' ignorance of the past. "They say cotton kept negroes in slavery. That's nonsense."[38]

In the 1961 program Nat D. Williams argued that rather than holding African Americans back, Jubilee had created a tradition of black empowerment across the South. He argued that the event itself had flipped the narrative of African Americans having demeaning positions in the cotton industry: "Long aligned with the mule in the cotton fields of the Deep South, the Negro felt hurt and insulted to be relegated to pulling floats in the main Cotton Carnival parades, serving as plantation singers on the banks of the Mississippi River when the Royal Carnival barge landed . . . seeing his children perched on cotton bales serving as pickaninnies on Main Street, to lend atmosphere to Carnival Week."[39]

When it started, the white Cotton Carnival had been, in Williams's words, "an annoying situation" that Jubilee sought to fix. And he believed it had. Williams claimed that "a new 'image' of the Negro was being created in the minds of the world." Integration supporters who criticized Jubilee were in danger of "destroying or casting aside all things suggestive of the Negro," in the name of equality.

Jubilee president Frank Scott echoed Williams's words in his own program editorial. "There is a marked difference between 'All-Negro,'" he wrote, "and 'Segregated.'" Jubilee was the former, Carnival the latter. Yet Scott's language suggests that internally he was struggling to find the place of the white fiber within the Jubilee tradition. The event was "a salute to men and women . . . in this our beloved Southland who are a part of the struggle for dignity of all mankind *with* King Cotton in a changing world." It may have been unclear to readers if this fight was "with" in the sense of "alongside" the regal crop, or if "with" meant against it.

Despite these defenses of Jubilee tradition, resistance increased. Local news coverage in 1961 made special note of "opposition" and "some negro protest." The presence of protesters was enough that Williams, while emceeing from a stage off Beale Street, felt the need to explain why Jubilee was good for the African American community. The event "helped sell cotton," which was vital to the economy. "We use cotton from the time we are born, when we are wrapped in it, until we shuffle off this mortal coil, when our coffins are lined with it.... We even eat cotton, and when we graduate from high school we wear a cotton gown," Williams told the crowd, attempting to tie the celebration of the fiber with every milestone of black life.[40]

Newspapers made it clear that something else was noteworthy in 1961: a modicum of integration. One report noted the presence of "a score or more of white persons in the stands with negroes."[41] More dramatically, white Carnival king Joe Rice Dockery, a Mississippi planter, and queen Lida Willey Black visited the Jubilee viewing stand at the end of the parade. The *Commercial Appeal* ran a photograph of Rice and Black meeting the Jubilee king and queen, John Kohleim and Joyce Ford. The paper also reported that protesters in the audience booed and held signs saying "Go home, King Kohleim! You are a disgrace." NAACP activists had homed in on Kohleim, despite being an African American principal of a segregated high school, because he was from Fayette County, Tennessee, where landlords had evicted more than two hundred black sharecroppers for trying to register to vote. The families were still living in a tent city when Kohleim donned his crown and robe. Protestors pointed out that "so many hundreds of our people have suffered unknown hardships and indignities in their struggle to raise the yokes of segregation and discrimination," and yet Kohleim was celebrating cotton. Other placards struck at both cotton's history and the perceived conservatism of some leaders. "Local Uncle Toms have brought Mississippi whites to rob you of your money," one said. "Cotton was the cause of slavery, why celebrate it?" When Halle, the white founder of Carnival, was asked to speak to the Jubilee crowd, he directly referenced the protests, telling the African American audience, "This is the most respected Negro festival in the country. Don't let anybody take it away from you. I hope you guard it jealously."[42]

Jubilee organizers took Halle's charge to heart. Throughout the 1960s they doubled down on cotton as the central metaphor through which to explain both the event's importance to Memphis and its possibility of influencing the freedom of African Americans. While cotton remained central to the pageantry of Jubilee—even in 1963 African American children competed to be crowned Master White Gold and Little Miss White Gold—Williams and Venson wrote about the importance of cotton's history, and they argued that remembering the relationships between white and black in cotton's past was an important piece of modern calls for civil rights. Venson wrote, "If Cotton is to remain King, he must not only realize the fact that there are economic, political, and educational and social inequalities, and injustices existing in his domain. He must have the courage and the will to overcome the complications." It was a kind of dance with the importance of the crop's history. "King cotton"—clearly a stand-in for the white leaders of the cotton industry rather than the crop itself—"must forget about the glory and splendor of yesterday" and "rid his kingdom of these inequalities toward Negroes, giving them an opportunity to qualify for technical and white-collar jobs in the cotton industries." "It is much cheaper to accede than it is to secede," Venson wrote. Williams argued that the Jubilee continued on, not "to distract nor to ignore, nor to question the justice of the Negro's cause," but rather to work as "oil in the midst of friction."[43]

Even in the shifting climate of the mid-1960s, Jubilee organizers stuck to their script, finding new ways to defend the old focus on cotton. "Keeping Stop with Progress in This Changing World," read one program headline; "Battle for an Image" ran another.[44] In one editorial Nat D. Williams forced a connection between the civil rights marches and the Jubilee's parade, claiming that both "show that the Negro is 'for' the growth, progress, and glory of America." "The Jubilee has no fuss with 1960's Marches on Washington," he continued. "There is no denying that [they] have just about shaken America awake to what the Negro wants and means. But it is still felt that the Jubilee was something of a pioneer in the Negro Revolution." He concluded, "There is still a place for the Jubilee in the Negro protest."[45]

It remained to be seen, however, if cotton itself had a place in the Jubilee. When Carnival pioneer Arthur Halle died in 1963, his obituary made the front page of the Memphis papers, running next to articles about the Kennedy administration's struggle to pass a civil rights bill. Five weeks later, after the assassination of the president in Dallas, the bill received new support.[46] The juxtaposition of the news coverage on Halle's death and the national debate on civil rights legislation was more than serendipity. It revealed the dueling historical moments in Memphis, as many white and black residents clung to their cotton celebrations while the social fabric of the South was being tested more acutely than ever.

As historians have long argued, the impetus for national rights legislation was the activism of the local people of the South. Memphis had been an important epicenter of civil rights activity, for many of the same reasons that it had become cotton's metropolis. The city's relationship with the Delta and the farm hinterlands, as well as the back-and-forth of cotton workers to and from the fields and city streets, had played a part in African Americans' postwar organizing and their intensifying tests of Jim Crow.[47] But the streets of Memphis soon became more than a site of civil rights organization and protest. Visiting the city to march in support of striking city sanitation workers, Martin Luther King Jr. was assassinated on the balcony of the city's Lorraine Motel on April 4, 1968.

It is of course impossible to know what direction the Carnival and Jubilee would have followed if not for the enormous tragedy and subsequent social, cultural, and political disruption in the aftermath of King's death. Even in the first weeks after the murder, it was clear that whatever social and political norms had existed before the assassination were now up for grabs. The day following the leader's murder, Cotton Carnival organizers canceled the parties planned for the weeks leading up to the May event, but they issued a statement that said they hoped to be able to continue with the main festival.[48] Less than a week later, however, Carnival president S. Toof Brown announced that "a week of gaiety would not be appropriate at this time" and Carnival would be postponed to "a date which would be right."[49] A few months later he announced the total cancelation of the event, whose theme was to be "A Cotton Pickin' Bale of Fun."[50]

Despite Brown's public statement, in September, behind the closed doors of the Memphis Country Club, organizers threw a lavish private coronation of the year's king and queen. While the crowning occurred in a private space, it still made the papers. The *Commercial Appeal* reported on Queen Gaye Giles's white dress with "short sleeves resembling cotton bolls about to burst into bloom" and "raised cotton boll designs [that] outlined the bottom of the skirt and the trail." Imitation cotton stalks seemingly grew from the dress's neck; bobbing atop the shoots were "full-blown cotton bolls touched with silver."[51] If there was any sign of restraint or of questioning the cotton imagery in the aftermath of the King assassination, it was not on display that night.

Venson, Williams, and the leaders at the Cotton Makers' Jubilee canceled their 1968 event as well, and like Carnival, they pressed on with the public celebration in the summer of 1969. The Jubilee's tone was strikingly different, however. Under the theme "Black America Moving Forward," Jubilee organizers sought to publicly honor King and his movement. How they did so, however, is revealing of the moderate politics of the leadership. Clyde Satterfield, a longtime Jubilee board member, encouraged attendees to "uphold and defend law and order" and oppose "illegal looting and property damages in opposition to non-violence." Nat D. Williams, as he had for several years, encouraged black Memphians to think about the Jubilee in light of African American history. Citing black protest movements in America as early as the seventeenth century, Williams argued that Jubilee's origins too were in a protest of the African American "stereotypes of the past . . . as slaves, lackeys, and clowns." Williams even directly compared King to Venson, writing that the latter "also 'had a dream' . . . of seeing black kings and queens riding through the main section of Memphis. . . . He dreamed of black children being inspired . . . by seeing the history of their people portrayed in the pageantry of the Jubilee floats and the themes of Negro history symbolized."[52]

For his part, Venson's 1969 essay reads as jarringly out of step with the frustrations of so many African Americans in the city. He called for "Moving Forward" not with activism but with work. "Only the forces that are within man can control his behavior," he wrote; labor itself is "the key to living, a punishment for transgressions, and the main source for rewards." A year later, Venson wrote his final program editorial in which he lambasted critics of the American system and called slavery "a blessing in disguise." He died in 1970 at the age of seventy-six.[53]

DESPITE EFFORTS by Jubilee and Carnival organizers to center cotton and maintain cultural relevance in a rapidly changing nation, it was a losing battle. As historian Robert Emmett McLean has written, the single most important moment in this decline was King's assassination. "Cotton Carnival and Cotton Makers Jubilee were never the same after April 4, 1968," he wrote, and "neither was Memphis."[54]

The litany of changes to both events portray a city benefiting from the successes of the civil rights movement and reeling from white backlash to it. In the 1970s, as Jubilee and Carnival declined in importance separately, two new trends emerged. First, the two celebrations started to combine some events, and second, they made cotton even less central to their pageantry. In 1971 the Memphis Chamber of Commerce created the Memphis in May International Festival organization, which laid the groundwork for combining the organizational work of the two events under one umbrella and offered a new name, one absent of any cotton connotation. A year later, the Jubilee and Carnival king and queens, still separate royal courts, were presented in public at the same time. The Carnival children's parade went away in 1973, and the Carnival events and main parade moved from downtown Memphis to the fairgrounds. This move reflected the demographic shift of the city—as whites had increasingly fled integrated schools for suburbs and private suburban academies—but it also attested to the end of cotton's geographic importance to the city. The Mid-South Fairgrounds were more than five miles from the (now mostly vacant) Front Street cotton-trading buildings, warehouses, and docks. The entire cotton industry had changed; men no longer sat in dusty offices grading the fibers as they arrived from Delta plantations. While the Carnival had fled from the city center, Jubilee events remained centered around Beale Street and downtown through most of the 1970s.[55]

More changes happened, albeit haltingly and incompletely. In 1975 Debra Trammell, an African American woman, was selected as the queen of the Carnival's Crown and Sceptre Society, which had its own party during Carnival. She was the first African American to play a royal part in the event, though she admitted to the newspaper that she was not invited to "some social events" that the queen usually attended. In 1977 Jubilee and Carnival integrated several public functions. The royal courts were presented together at an event at the Memphis Naval Air Station and rode together in the Carnival parade. The Carnival king and queen also attended a Jubilee party.[56] In 1981 Jubilee planners agreed to participate formally in Carnival as a "grand krewe," which meant full participation with control over their floats and events. Four years later Carnival changed its name to the Great River Carnival, and the Maid of Cotton pageant broke free from Carnival and moved to Dallas.[57]

Ethyl Venson lived to witness all these changes. "It has been worth hanging on," she told the *Commercial Appeal* in 1977. She recalled the years of criticism that Jubilee had faced, from white Memphians as well as "some blacks who resent celebrating the fiber which helped enslave them." Cotton, however, had been an important part of black life in Memphis, Venson argued, and African American participation in the industry deserved celebrating. "I can understand why the affluent black community does not come in with us," she explained, but "the early support for Jubilee came from the blue collar workers who actually worked with cotton."[58] While many critics said that "cotton had produced only slavery for Negroes," Venson understood Jubilee as "a different kind of protest" of white supremacy. Even in her late eighties she stood by the event's organization around the central theme and language of the cotton plant.

FROM THE GREAT DEPRESSION to the end of the twentieth century, as the fiber's place within the Mid-South agricultural economy changed—from the fields outside of town, along the shipping routes, to Bluff City warehouses—white and black Memphians manipulated the culture of the crop to fit their own interests. Its central place in the city's economy spawned its initial celebrations. White Southerners trumpeted their role in producing, shipping, marketing, and processing the plant, and they developed a backward-looking history of the crop to remind everyone of the role of white supremacy in its past and future. African Americans responded not by dismissing cotton but by embracing it. For decades, their story was one of the central importance of black labor to the agricultural and industrial worlds of the plant.

Throughout this time, cotton was never simply a replacement for white supremacy. It was a metaphor contingent on the realities of its production. As the next chapters show, black labor in the Delta and in the city dictated how the crop could be celebrated. As technological advances reshaped cotton farming and pushed African American laborers off the land, many moved to cities like Memphis. At the same time, the industry no longer depended on the city's white-owned businesses, and black Memphians were pressing more effectively for full inclusion in Southern democracy. In this changing landscape, cotton could no longer anchor the culture of the Mid-South.

The story of the plant's public fate in Memphis was tightly linked to the human and environmental changes of twentieth-century rural Mississippi. In the muddy fields south of the city, changes in the agricultural and demographic picture of the world's richest cotton lands were, at the same time of Carnival and Jubilee's rise and fall, altering how the people of Memphis and of the world would come to understand the meaning of cotton.

CHAPTER EIGHT

Pickers and Polyester on a New Delta Landscape

ON THE FINAL NIGHT of the 1956 Cotton Carnival, King Oscar Carr Jr. and Queen Clare Mallory boarded the royal barge that a week earlier had carried them up the Mississippi River into Memphis. The Elvis Presley concert was over; the days of parades, parties, and pageants had come and gone. The secret societies' masquerade balls concluded the previous night, with "Mrs. Jack Ross" winning first place for a dress shaped like a cotton boll; her torso emerged from the waist like an extended white fiber.[1] After closing ceremonies along the Front Street landing—with still more music, pageantry, and speeches about cotton's importance to Memphis—Carr and Mallory boarded the royal barge and, as the *Commercial Appeal* put it, "slid away . . . in solemn grandeur."[2] In reality the barge only carried the cotton king and queen across the Mississippi River to a dock on the Arkansas side, but the journey symbolized the royal couple's return to the hinterlands, to the cotton fields themselves.

After he stepped off the ceremonial barge and said goodbye to his queen and court, Oscar Carr pointed his automobile south, away from West Memphis, down Highway 61. The storied road was already the subject of a number of blues songs composed by African American migrants, thousands of whom had recently moved up Highway 61, the opposite direction that Carr traveled that 1956 day. The road loosely traced the Mississippi River and the Illinois Central rail line, the two important conduits that had themselves decided so much of the histories of Memphis and the Delta. Carr traveled through the towns of Tunica and Lula until he drove into Clarksdale, one of the largest cities in all of the Delta with a population near twenty thousand. He drove toward downtown, straight through the crossroads with Highway

49, where bluesman Robert Johnson supposedly sold his soul to the devil, and then turned south onto New Africa Road. Eight miles later he pulled into the dirt driveway of his 3,500-acre Mascot Plantation, nestled against the Sunflower River.

Mascot Plantation had been in the Carr family for generations, and Carr's Delta credentials were as good as any planter's. His family had been among the first generation of white "settlers" to buy up land after Native American removal and to bring slaves and later free laborers into the swampy region to clear and drain the soil. Clarksdale itself was the namesake of his great-uncle, John Clark.[3] His family connections did not end there. Carr's maternal grandfather, James Alcorn, was one of the state's leading lawyers and planters who became Mississippi governor and later U.S. senator during Reconstruction. Carr's parents, born in the 1860s, had lived in a Delta that was still very much a frontier.

In many material ways, Oscar Carr Jr.'s mid-twentieth-century cotton operation had the trappings of a remote nineteenth-century plantation, but if one looked closely, they would find antebellum fantasy mixed with industrial, mechanized, and cosmopolitan reality. In fact, Carr's enormous, flat, well-drained, organized plantation would have been William Henry Gist's greatest dream. As historian James C. Cobb has described, planters like Carr (and his father before him) wrapped a fictional antebellum culture around their modern enterprises. "Fancying themselves heirs to an aristocratic antebellum tradition," he wrote, "this cadre of white leaders sought to create through an ironic combination of economic modernization and racial subjugation a prosperous and politically insulated cotton kingdom where the Delta planter's longstanding obsession with unfettered wealth and power could be transformed from Old South fantasy to New South reality."[4]

As much as white Delta planters may have thought of themselves heirs to antebellum slaveholders like Gist, the twentieth-century Delta was nothing like the Piedmont, or even the famed Natchez district, where before the war, as the common saying goes, there were more millionaires than any other place in America. In fact, the key to Carr's and his colleagues' success in growing cotton was that the Delta was *so little* like these other places. The reasons for that were simple: Two generations of African American laborers had felled gums and cypress, hand-dug drainage ditches, built levees, and cleared stumps. They had remade the landscape to give access to that rich soil. The result, from Carr's perspective, was a cotton paradise. It is no wonder, then, that by the early twentieth century, white Deltans looked out on the land they owned and the flowering white cotton plants and fancied themselves the new kings of Southern agriculture and society. They self-consciously embraced the antebellum metaphor because it was a world their white predecessors dreamed about. They oversaw not only a massive, connected cotton empire but also a large, mostly black labor force that they tried to control in a number of legal and extralegal ways.

At the heart of this white elite oversight of land and labor was cotton itself. From the beginning of white settlement in the region, the ruling Delta landholders celebrated their management of the environment and people by making the cotton plant the heart of their society. As the story of Cotton Carnival reveals, there was no separating the celebration of the crop from the glorification of planters who thought they ruled this world.

In reality, African American men, women, and children carved out existences in cotton's bleak circumstances. They used every tool at their disposal to resist Jim Crow when possible, and in many cases they invented new tools of resistance. Though too much can be made of the power of blues music, foodways, and similar forms of cultural resistance, it is not a coincidence that some of the sharpest critiques of tenancy, violence, and cotton culture itself come from African Americans living in the Delta during this period. For instance, when the boll weevil arrived to threaten the crop, many black tenants used its disruption to access more and better land, to bargain with landowners for better conditions, or simply to leave the area altogether. Black Mississippians seized and maintained real power despite cotton's grip, but it remained the exception over most of the Delta's history.[5]

One reason for white supremacy's long and unique presence in the region was how integrally white planters had woven it with the thread of cotton. The very language white Mississippians used to describe black laborers evinces this relationship. As geographer Brian S. Williams has pointed out, Delta whites flattened African American lives, calling them "hands," "hoes," and "pickers." The labels defined these men and women only in terms of their "capacity to work and produce cotton."[6] That white Deltans used racist language to describe black members of their community will surprise no one, but it is the very frequent pairings with cotton and farming metaphors that make it so revealing.

The two ideas—white supremacy and cotton growing—were fused in their minds and reflected in their racist language. Walter Sillers Sr., a politically powerful Rosedale, Mississippi, lawyer and planter, wrote a friend in 1907 that his time was occupied by "niggers and cotton, and 'future cotton,' and law and niggers and mules."[7] A superintendent at what was at the time the world's largest cotton farm, Delta and Pine Land Company, eschewed the idea of mechanization or global markets when he explained the essence of the mega-plantation's operation: "It takes niggers and mules to make cotton." Another Delta and Pine manager admitted that the farm's future relied on only two things, "a good many mules" and "worlds of niggers."[8]

African American labor and cotton production were so connected that the work became naturalized. Across the South, tenant farming was the occupation of white, black, Chinese, Native American, and Mexican women and men, but in the Yazoo-Mississippi Delta it was almost entirely African American work. As one planter recalled, laborers were "secured wherever, whenever, and however they could be had."[9] At the turn of the twentieth century the region had the highest concentration of black labor in the whole country. A decade later, the USDA found that 95 percent of black farmers in the Delta were tenants and 88 percent of people living in the rural areas were African American. This was not by accident. Historians have described in detail how these conditions arose out of a Reconstruction-era need for labor, a scarcity of credit, and the social, economic, and political weapons of white supremacy.[10] The first Great Migration had changed the demographics somewhat, but even in Carr's time, cotton work depended on black labor.

That dependence, though baked in to the plantation system, was not something that all white Mississippians recognized. Carr's own transformation underscores this point. The day he drove south from Memphis in 1956, he was a man beginning to see differently the world that cotton had made. His friend Betty Bobo Pearson, herself a member of an established white planter family, recalled that during the early 1950s, Carr was quite conservative. When Pearson talked to Carr about the 1955 murder of Emmett Till or the burgeoning civil rights activism of African Americans across the South, "Oscar listened, but did not say much." She chalked it up to his work as a planter. "He was busy establishing himself at Mascot [Plantation] . . . [and] in the establishment of the First National Bank of Clarksdale." Then, out of the blue, "about five years after the Till trial," Oscar told her "the most 'amazing' story." Carr told Pearson: "I was driving home from Memphis, and when I came down that last hill into the Delta, all of a sudden I saw one of those tenant houses for the first time. Although I had seen such houses all of my life on Mascot and other plantations, I never before thought about people living in that shack with no electricity, no plumbing . . ." Pearson described Carr's awakening as "a thunderbolt out of the blue . . . one of those 'road to Damascus' things where you have a sudden conversion."[11]

Carr's Clarksdale-via-Damascus epiphany is more than symbolic; it is profoundly revealing. His unexpected realization, at the age of thirty-seven, of the human value—of the humanity itself—of the African Americans living around him is a shocking window into just how Jim Crow closed off not only black lives from white but also the minds of white Deltans. Of course, a sudden awareness of black lives did little to help Carr untangle the connections of African American tenants and the cotton industry on which so much in the region depended. Sure, he might now recognize the humanity of the African Americans around him, but could he imagine a better life for the women, men, and children in those "shacks"? If he could, did that vision see African Americans still working in cotton? Were they still in rural Mississippi at all?

It would be enticing to argue that Carr's opinion on how to improve black life just did not matter, that African Americans had the agency to improve their lots on their own. And while the story of outmigration is some limited evidence that this was the case for thousands of black Mississippians, the stark reality is that Carr and the rest of the white elite had engineered an economy and society to conscribe black freedom. Carr's ignorance of black life mattered in very concrete ways and, surprisingly and at long last, the planter had recognized it. After his epiphany in the late 1950s, Carr spent much of his life trying to right the wrongs of his ignorance, racism, and complicity in white supremacy. Throughout the 1960s the former king of Cotton Carnival worked closely with civil rights leader Aaron Henry, helped court War on Poverty funding and programs to Coahoma County, founded the first bank in the area that offered loans to African Americans, and was part of the group that gave Robert Kennedy his famous tour of Delta poverty in 1968.[12]

Carr had a front-row seat to the fundamental disruptions going on in Delta life in the post–World War II era: black soldiers returning from war with a newly found insistence for civil rights activism, rural outmigration of white and black farmers pulled to cities by the promise of better industrial jobs, the invention and application of new farming methods like the mechanical cotton harvester, new federal intervention in the cotton economy and Southern politics writ large, and new competition for the crop that was the Delta's raison d'être. Each of these forces was powerful on its own, and it is hard to pull one from the others, even with the hindsight of history. But for a society created out of a swamp by black hands and white capital and engineered for one productive end, cotton growing, it is perhaps most revealing to understand this moment in Delta history as a crisis of the staple crop itself.

THE TRANSFORMATION OF the Yazoo-Mississippi Delta landscape in the postwar period is in large part a history of mechanization. Work to build a machine that could pick ripe cotton bolls from plant stalks began as early as 1850. The patent office recorded more than 250 ideas for various machines that promised to move through a field and use spindles, blasts of air, electricity, or a thresher to harvest cotton. Large-implement companies like John Deere and International Harvester (IH) experimented across the South hoping to perfect an apparatus that could work faster and for less cost than human hands.

In the 1930s national newspapers took interest in Texans John and Mack Rust, whose mechanical cotton picker prototype looked like it might industrialize farming, but local reactions in Mississippi were far from optimistic.[13] The prospect of mechanization tested white Southerners' thinking about not just farming but also race. The promise of a machine that could replace all the people planting, chopping, and picking cotton was exciting for many white state leaders and landowners. But others saw it as a nightmare. Many white Mississippians wondered aloud, What would all of these black people do? As Gerard Helferich has written, "The idea of millions of unemployed, homeless African Americans was more than southern whites cared to contemplate." The *Jackson Daily News* suggested the machine "be driven right out of the cotton fields and sunk into the Mississippi River."[14]

Though the Rust brothers' experiments bore little fruit, experimentation picked up pace during World War II. IH sent convoys of experimental pickers through the South, trying them out in Texas, Arkansas, and Mississippi. In 1940 and 1941 the company brought their latest models to the Mississippi State Extension Service's Delta Experiment Station in the town of Stoneville, as well as to the Hopson Planting Company, which was only about eight miles up the Sunflower River from Carr's plantation.[15]

The Hopson plantation had relied on enslaved people handpicking cotton when the family bought the farm in 1852, and on sharecroppers after the Civil War.[16] In the 1920s the Hopson brothers, Howell Jr. and Richard, embraced mechanization. They adopted tractors to replace mules, experimented with all kinds of crops and planting techniques, and eventually eschewed tenant arrangements all together. By the end of World War II, the Hopsons had replaced sharecroppers with wage workers on 80 percent of the plantation.[17] Between the brothers' willingness to experiment and the wartime need, Hopson was an obvious place for IH to try out their new pickers. By mid-war, the company was running several mechanical harvesters on the Delta land, and when its engineers finally believed that it had a prototype worth making public, they returned to Coahoma County to show it off.[18]

Howell Hopson Jr. explained that his plantation's experiments with mechanization came from their inability to pay laborers a high-enough wage. Despite wartime government subsidies, he wrote in 1944, in order for the farm to "survive," he and his brother could only "pay wages to the employed labor that were not commensurate with a desirable scale of living." Workers were leaving, "drained off by industry." It was an odd argument that boiled down to the notion that in order to "more successfully bid against industry for . . . labor," the farm managers had to find ways to replace them. Making farming more efficient, Hopson argued, would save African American workers from the drudgery and low wages of work in the Delta cotton fields. Indeed, he happily reported that his farm's mechanization efforts had kept in place the racial caste system. "All salaried employees are white," he wrote in 1944, "while the wage labor and share-croppers are colored. Both negro and Mexican labor is imported for cotton chopping and picking."[19]

Mechanical harvesters spread across the Delta, taking advantage of the miles of broad, flat, treeless fields, but not all cotton laborers left. Hopson pointed out the seeming contradiction of human laborers working with centuries-old tools laboring alongside the latest technical machinery. "It would seem the incongruous sight of a laborer with a hoe laboriously weeding . . . working in the same crop with the operator of a four-row cultivator . . . while in adjacent fields an airplane is busy dusting several hundred acres."[20] He made the point clear in the images he used in his self-published, self-aggrandizing color magazine. (See figure 18.)

While economic historians have debated the chicken-and-egg effects of mechanization and migration, it was not an either-or proposition. Movement of farmworkers in and out of the Delta had been constant since emancipation. White landowners sought to control, or at least harness, some of that movement, particularly when there were disruptions in cotton production like

FIG. 18. Howell Hopson Jr. publicized his farm's mechanization in a self-published magazine that trumpeted his forward-thinking approach to cotton farming. He was clear about the improvement that machines made over human labor. The two images in the figure were juxtaposed on the same page. The original captions make his point clear: "Laborious process of hand picking cotton" and "A mechanical cotton picker at work." H. H. Hopson Jr., "Mechanization of a Delta Cotton Plantation as applied to Hopson Planting Company, Clarksdale, Mississippi, by the management" (October 1944), 5, in Special Collections, Mississippi State University.

those caused by the boll weevil. And it is impossible to sort the pull effect of industrial jobs in Southern and eventually Northern cities from the push effects of the drudgery of farm life or the violence and political oppression of Jim Crow. What we can say for sure is that millions of Southern African Americans moved off farms over several decades. Many white landowners like the Hopsons took the checks they received from New Deal programs—money that was intended to be passed along to their tenants—and bought tractors and later harvesters. As Greta de Jong argues, when civil rights activities came to plantations in the 1960s, "economic and political considerations drove plantation owners to get rid of their remaining laborers as quickly as possible, leading to mass evictions."[21]

When historian Donald Holley crunched the numbers, the dual effects of mechanization and outmigration appeared stark. In Mississippi the number of tenants fell from nearly a quarter million in 1930 to less than four thousand by 1974. As a percentage of all farm operators, tenants fell from 66 percent before World War II to less than a quarter by 1964.[22] The Census Bureau estimated

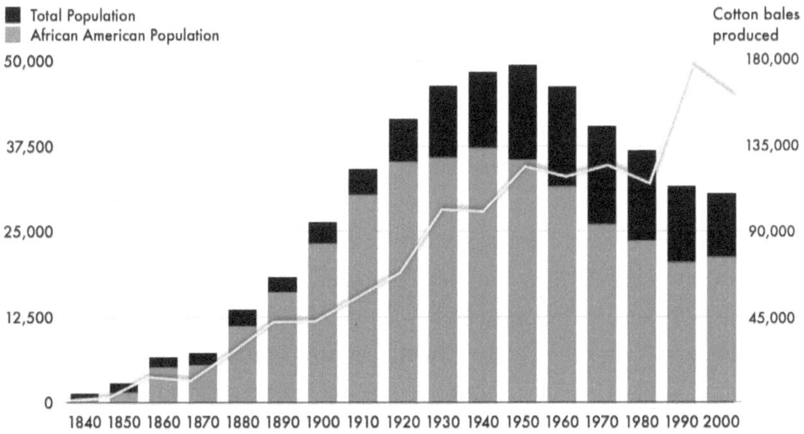

FIG. 19. African American population, total population, and cotton bale production, Coahoma County, Mississippi, 1840–2000. From Population and Agricultural Censuses, 1840–2000. Note the contrast with the Union County chart (figure 2).

that overall outmigration of Mississippians to other states was equally dramatic. While 240,000 white residents left the state between 1930 and 1970, four times as many—nearly one million—black Mississippians moved out.[23] Across the Cotton Belt, the appearance of cotton-picking machines was just as dramatic. At the end of World War II, 98 percent of the crop was picked by hand; only ten years later the amount had fallen to 68 percent. In 1962 it was only 30 percent, and by 1970 only 2 percent of U.S. cotton was handpicked.[24]

In places like Coahoma County, these stark demographic and mechanization changes reveal a great deal about the day-to-day life for Mississippians over these decades. Figure 19 juxtaposes some of the forces of these demographic changes at the local level. The African American population in the county peaked in 1940 and fell relatively consistently after that point, though the black share of its total population had been declining since the remarkable 89 percent tally in 1910. Cotton acreage fell too, though at the same time productivity rose. The result demonstrated the odd mix of agricultural and demographic changes: By 1980 there were fewer Coahoma farmers, but those left were growing more cotton on less land. As figure 19 illustrates, as the African American population dropped, cotton production increased.

This relationship between the black population and cotton production was important for everyone in the Delta. The decline of the African American presence in places like Coahoma County was not the lever for cotton production increases, of course, but many white landowners and white Southerners in general tied these two phenomena together. They explained many of these social and agricultural changes in terms of the declining black population. In actuality, machinery, along with fertilizers, pesticides, and other agro-technical innovations, are the reason cotton production increased, not somehow the new relative absence of black laborers.

The decreasing African American population was not just from the ranks of tenant farmers. In the decades after World War II, economic pressure, government policy, and the racism of white landowners pushed African Americans off of Delta farms with devastating effects, especially for the hundreds of black landowners. African Americans in Mississippi owned more than two million acres in 1910, which comprised nearly 15 percent of all the black-owned land in the United States. As a percentage, more black Mississippians owned land than African Americans in any other state. But in the 1940s a combination of factors pushed most of them out of farming. It was "a war," Vann Newkirk wrote in *The Atlantic*, "waged by deed of title." A concert of factors, from banks refusing to loan money to African Americans involved in civil rights activities, to the simple economics caused by the consolidation of farming generally, specifically hurt black farmers. But for all small cotton farmers in the South, the economy of scale worked against them; many banks and government programs simply wouldn't extend credit to the smaller operations. This disproportionately hurt black landowners. There was also well-documented discrimination in the USDA and the state's extension service. The results were massive loss of black-owned land: nearly 800,000 acres between 1950 and 1964, an amount conservatively valued at $5 billion in twenty-first-century dollars.[25]

Wage hands and day laborers too felt the squeeze of agribusiness on the African American presence in the Delta as human labor as a whole became less integral to the daily life of a cotton plantation. These changes did not put a stop to the cotton growing for planters like the Hopsons and Carr. But their impression of what farming meant, and specifically what being a cotton planter meant, did begin to change in revealing ways.

THE MECHANICAL HARVESTER wasn't the only force reshaping the cotton world in the mid-twentieth century. Even as machines displaced thousands of black laborers in the Delta, a quieter but equally significant threat was emerging far from the fields. Advances in textile manufacturing and the rise of synthetic fibers like polyester were beginning to undermine cotton's dominance in the marketplace. By the mid-1950s consumer tastes were shifting, and the consequences rippled all the way back to the Delta—changing not just the economics of farming but the cultural meaning of the crop itself.

Again, Oscar Carr Jr.'s reign as Cotton Carnival king in 1956 helps tell that story. Carr had spent Carnival week not only presiding over balls and meeting Elvis but also putting in what one newspaper called a "serious performance" in a speech to Memphis business leaders. In the ballroom of the Peabody Hotel—the symbolic northern terminus of the Mississippi Delta—he assured industry powerbrokers that not only was cotton farming changing but the whole fiber industry was in peril.

After reminding his audience that cotton was a $900 million industry in the Mississippi Valley, and that it was "the most important single factor in the economy of the Memphis trade area," he warned that King Cotton was sick.[26] "Synthetics have captured markets from cotton." Not only were some consumers choosing polyester, rayon, and nylon fabrics over the natural fiber, mills had begun blending the synthetics with cotton, depleting the plant's use even further. Carr warned his audience that customers were demanding these new blended fibers.[27] "Cotton has slipped from a total of over 90 per cent" of clothing "to less than 70 per cent." The reason, the Mississippi planter argued, was not that these fabrics were better. "Although synthetics can be outstanding in one or two traits," he admitted, "cotton is the only 'all-around' fiber on the market today. It is cool, comfortable and good looking."[28]

One only needed to look at the advertisements that ran alongside news coverage of the 1956 Carnival to illustrate Carr's point. On the very newspaper page with an article describing his talk at the Peabody, there was an ad that touted a "100% Nylon Jersey Dress" for $12.98. "Washes . . . drips dry ready to wear without ironing," the copy claimed, implying that it was superior to its common cotton counterpart.[29] There were plenty of other examples of synthetics' inroads. On the back page of the paper, Memphis's leading department store noted its plan to close early because of the Cotton Carnival parade, but it also advertised a "Bolero Sundress" that was "slim and slimming" because of its "Rayon Linnenette" blended fabric—the very cotton-synthetic hybrid Carr warned about. There were still cotton goods on sale across town, but Dacron slipcovers, rayon underwear, and nylon socks filled both newspaper ads and the shopping lists of Memphis consumers. Writing in

1956, Deltan David Cohn was enthralled with the "spectacularly successful synthetic fiber called rayon staple." He listed more than a dozen uses, everything from "sport shirts, summer suits" to "diapers" and "casket linings." "Cheaper than wool, more luxurious and durable than cotton," rayon was "the most gregarious of all textile fibers."[30]

Carr and Cohn were right to raise the alarm about declining consumption figures. In 1955 the USDA reported that cotton purchasing was down to its 1930s levels, while synthetic consumption had risen from 10 percent of the overall textile market in 1939 to 25 percent by 1955.[31] The effect of synthetics was not just seen in the clothing market. At mid-century, 37 percent of U.S. cotton ended up in apparel, but only 8 percent went into women's clothing. Household uses like sheets, towels, and furniture made up 31 percent of the overall market, but nonnatural fabrics were making inroads in these home goods as well.[32] The chemical companies that made these new fibers had not only invented new products; they had won the marketing war. By contrast, the cotton industry seemed archaic and unprepared. As one book claimed, never had "any segment of American agriculture ever presented a fatter, more tempting, more unprepared target" for competition.[33]

Despite these falling numbers and industrial disorganization, Carr's speech was not all doom and gloom. He had a solution to the fabric's falling competitiveness, one targeted neither at labor, nor farm technology, nor tariffs. "The synthetic industry is expending 60 million dollars a year on research," he told the crowd, and "spending 20 million dollars for advertisement and promotion." Together, the U.S. Department of Agriculture, cotton-growing states, land grant colleges, extension services, and the planters' own industry group spent only $14 million on research and $1.5 million on marketing. Without new textile research and a wholesale rebranding of cotton's image, Carr predicted cotton's swift collapse. "Each person in this room has a stake in cotton's future," he told the businessmen. A new research and marketing program, supported not just by planters but also by ginners, wholesalers, shippers, spinners, and retailers, would "go a long way toward staving off ruin," Carr argued. Despite Carnival's gaiety and pomp, it was a grim message about a dire moment. "In short gentlemen," Carr concluded, "the King is ailing; let us help him as he has helped us."[34]

The group in the best position to take up Carr's call for better marketing was the National Cotton Council of America (NCC). Founded in 1938 in the same place Carr gave his speech, the Peabody Hotel in Memphis, NCC was comprised of cotton planters, ginners, warehousers, and merchants from across the country, any place from the Atlantic to the Pacific where the crop was grown. The organization's mission was to lobby the federal and state governments on behalf of cotton, find new uses for the crop through laboratory research, and market the fiber around the world. Together, these goals pointed in one direction: sell more cotton. The council was headquartered in Memphis, but it had tight connections to the Delta. Its first president, Oscar Johnston, ran Delta and Pine Land Company, at the time the largest farm (of any kind) in the world.[35]

Before World War II, NCC's marketing and research efforts were relatively narrow. In a laboratory in New Orleans, the organization tested fiber strength and dyeability, then marketed the results to mills and manufacturers. It was the clothing makers, or the industrial buyers of cotton, who then had to find ways to advertise cotton's superiority to their consumers. NCC did not have national campaigns targeted at the consumers walking the aisles of a department store.[36] The closest it came was with events like the Maid of Cotton, a pageant for young white women with the winner crowned by the NCC president each year during the Cotton Carnival. It was hardly a national ad campaign. The organization had done very little to either effectively organize farmers or expand the fiber's reach in world markets.

In the wake of the war and the rise in synthetic competitors, however, NCC slowly woke to these new threats and the changing economic conditions and began some limited marketing in national media. The council aimed these efforts at housewives, whom it had identified as the decision-makers on household clothing and textile purchases. As one expert put it, "the American housewife" is the best "index to the esteem in which cotton is held."[37] Despite a single audience demographic, NCC marketing efforts ran in two often opposing directions. On the one hand, the council began trumpeting cotton's frugality and utility. One campaign encouraged women to deconstruct and reuse cotton feed sacks to make clothing and other items. A grandmother from Shreveport, Louisiana, won her state's NCC-sponsored competition by repurposing the rough sackcloth into "a blouse, curtains, a stuffed doll, pair of pajamas, and mother-and-daughter dresses." The goal of the contest was to show women how the cotton could be used again and again, even while the winner admitted she never actually wore her creations herself. "I never have known what to do with them," she admitted to the local newspaper.[38]

While that campaign focused on durability and economy, at the same the Cotton Council launched promotions trying to make the fiber appear upscale. Advertisements in fashion magazines like *Vogue* and *Mademoiselle* featured the wives of governors (from around the country) wearing cotton fashions.[39] The campaigns fought the general public's perception of cotton clothing as work clothes, not haute couture. While not completely working at cross-purposes, these two types of campaigns were pushing cotton as two different things, a contrast that consumers could plainly see not just in these ad campaigns but in a larger American debate over clothing.

Since the nineteenth century, cotton had been the fabric of work wear: farmers' overalls, factory workers' one-piece coveralls, even the sturdy dresses of mill women and girls. Blue jeans were cowboy wear, though as early as the 1930s, middle-class Americans seeking to appear as "everyman" workers put on denim as a political symbol. In films like *The Grapes of Wrath* (1940) and *Rebel Without a Cause* (1955), jeans were symbols of labor politics and rebelliousness.[40] In the 1960s hippies and activists donned certain cotton outfits to self-consciously appropriate working culture. Volunteers with the Student Nonviolent Coordinating Committee (SNCC), for instance, put on cotton overalls before they walked Mississippi country roads to persuade African American tenant farmers to register to vote. They wanted to fit in among sharecroppers, to be sure, but they also wore the clothes in solidarity. Along with tie-dye, jeans became the uniform of hippies marching against the Vietnam War, dancing in the mud at Woodstock, or gathering to levitate the Pentagon.[41] So while NCC was attempting to broaden its appeal to consumers, its efforts to shape cotton's image were minuscule compared with the larger cultural forces at work in the 1950s and 1960s.

Still, as the Cotton Council worked to sell the fiber as *both* industrial and elegant, researchers were finding that the industrial side was winning, at least in terms of consumer taste. The USDA studied the market in 1950 and found that while women buyers preferred cotton to synthetics for things like housedresses, socks, dish towels, and pajamas, they liked synthetics for products more inclined to be seen in public. They preferred "winter street dresses" and "short-sleeved blouses," along with hosiery and slips, to be made from noncotton fibers.[42] As chemical companies like DuPont were spinning out all kinds of new "miracle fibers"—and marketing them as such—they took cotton's place in an increasing range of products. Timothy Jacobson and George Smith, authors of a book chronicling the history of NCC, point out that even the product names "had become part of the language." Consumers knew Dacron and Lycra from Orlon and nylon. And that language changed buying decisions. Phrases like "permanent-press," "wash-and-wear," and "drip-dry" not only distinguished synthetics from cotton; they also made their way into consumers' expectations for clothes. Between these legitimate advantages of synthetics and the cultural baggage of cotton, producers and marketers of the natural fiber faced a growing crisis. As Jacobson and Smith put it, "cotton was outgunned by synthetics in quality, in costs, and potentially in price."[43]

The efforts made little impact. Unfortunately for the cotton farmers and ginners who comprised the Cotton Council's board of directors, the more money farmers raised, and the more they spent to advertise the fiber, the less cotton consumers bought.

The result was a confluence of events that made the cotton industry seem, to those inside and outside of it, like it was careening toward collapse. Mechanization had pushed thousands of black Southerners from the cotton fields. The biggest planters were able to make more cotton than ever on rich Delta land, thanks to tractors, mechanical harvesters, new seeds, and chemicals. The very essence of cotton in the Delta, which is to say the very essence of the Delta, had changed in stunning ways in only a couple decades. The problem, as Oscar Carr Jr. had said in 1956, was that, despite all these new efficiencies in Delta cotton operations, fewer and fewer consumers wanted to wear cotton clothes.

CHAPTER NINE

The Fabric of Our Lives

BY THE LATE 1960S, the cotton industry was in full-blown crisis. But the problem wasn't rooted in Southern soil. In the Yazoo-Mississippi Delta, mechanical cotton pickers had replaced African American labor, while new seed varieties and fertilizers had improved farmers' cotton yields dramatically. Large and highly capitalized landowners were buying up smaller farms, making the bigger operations even more productive and efficient. These newly efficient planters, however, could not sell all the cotton they produced, or at least not at the price they were looking for. The cotton crisis was happening not on farms but in stores. American consumers increasingly looked for synthetic fabrics in their clothes, and the cotton growers' organization seemed rudderless to turn buyers back to their product.

The pages that follow trace the story of a disparate group of people who fought to revive the industry. Farmers, industry executives, and advertising creatives—a weird alliance of those with Mississippi mud on their boots and others wearing Armani suits—came together to reposition cotton in both international markets and the American mind. They did so first by rewriting the plant's history, imagining a new cotton brand that obviated the historical and contemporary problems of its production. The result was perhaps the greatest rebranding success in the history of U.S. commerce. The makeover came from boardrooms far from the Delta, but the new image relied heavily on the changes on the land—the agricultural, environmental, commercial, and demographic realities of the Yazoo-Mississippi Delta—to make cotton's rebirth possible.

Two events at the end of the 1960s changed the National Cotton Council's strategy and fortune, events that would make a lasting impression on how Southerners understood and celebrated King Cotton. The first was legislative. In 1960 NCC created an offshoot, the Cotton Producers Institute (CPI), which was to be funded by voluntary donations from cotton growers. CPI was to handle research into new kinds of cotton textiles, on-farm improvements, and advertising. In order to boost farmer donations to CPI, the council sent a group of well-connected Mississippi planters on the road to visit growers across the country, selling the idea of donating "a dollar a bale" to the marketing and research cause. By the end of the first year, despite not gaining the support of all producers, CPI had raised $1 million.[1]

Much of that money went to a new ad blitz. In the early 1960s CPI placed print ads within popular catalogs and on store displays at the biggest department chains including Sears, JCPenney, and Montgomery Ward, and bought television advertising space for national audiences.[2] Despite the new marketing push, however, the institute's promotional campaigns highlighted cotton's traditional roles and uses. "The Fiber You Can Trust" was its tagline, an attempt to contrast buyers' long-standing relationship with cotton and the perhaps unreliable synthetics.[3]

Despite the new effort, the campaign did not translate to dramatically better sales. The problem, NCC's leaders thought, was simply that they weren't raising enough money with the one-dollar-per-bale funding system. Holes in the formula's rules allowed underpayment of dues, and to close the gaps the organization turned to an unlikely ally: the federal government. Cotton boosters launched a nationwide campaign to convince farmers that their only hope of competing with powerful synthetic producers like Dow and DuPont—companies with deep pockets and sophisticated marketing operations—was collective action. They argued that all growers should be required by law to contribute funds to promote cotton, creating a unified front for the industry. After much internal debate among farmers hesitant to ask the state to further regulate their business, CPI turned to Congress, which agreed that the USDA could facilitate direct collection of money from all cotton farmers for marketing and research expenses. In December 1966 a referendum of growers passed the new rule with 68 percent of the vote.[4] Almost overnight, CPI's budget jumped to more than $10 million, two-thirds of which was targeted at advertising.

The second change that remade cotton's image involved the question of who would oversee this new advertising budget. Many younger, advertising-minded cotton leaders thought that the Cotton Producers Institute—an old-fashioned name for what was becoming an independent, well-funded research and marketing arm for the entire industry—needed new leadership.

It was an arm of the Cotton Council, organized and founded in Memphis and heavily influenced by Delta planters, and although it was comprised of people across the industry, it gave the impression that it was concerned mostly with improving farm production. CPI's strategy had always reflected production-side thinking. It promoted the idea that cotton would win the fight against polyester and rayon because it was just a better fiber. CPI insisted that mills never blend cotton with synthetics but instead keep things "100% cotton." Following the 1966 referendum, the new funding model, and the growing separation between NCC and CPI, the time appeared right for new thinking on the marketing of the crop.

As CPI's board worked to distance itself from the farmer-dominated National Cotton Council, it searched for a new director, someone free of the grudges and regional loyalties that had long shaped the industry. They succeeded. The man they hired knew none of cotton's power players and felt no pressure to walk, talk, or act like a farmer. At fifty-two, he had never spent meaningful time in the rural South and had no idea how cotton was even grown. On May 12, 1970, CPI president Howard Alford, a cotton planter from Lubbock, Texas, announced that the board had chosen J. Dukes Wooters to run the organization. Wooters was a bold choice, as much of an outsider to the world of cotton as anyone could have imagined.

Wooters, who described himself as a proud member of "the Eastern Establishment," was at home watching polo matches and riding at hunt clubs around his elite New York City suburb of New Canaan, Connecticut.[5] Dukes and his wife filled the society pages, which recorded their hosting a "Gala Champagne Dinner-Dance" one month and a cocktail party at the Waverley Mansion the next.[6] He had gone to Lehigh University and Harvard Business School. His only experience with cotton was, in his words, buying shirts "twice a year (on sale) at that bastion of male traditionalism," Brooks Brothers.[7] Before joining CPI, his previous jobs had been selling ads for Hearst Publications and, most recently, as the executive assistant to the CEO of *Reader's Digest*.[8] News of the hire broke in an "exclusive story" in *Women's Wear Daily*, the leading fashion industry magazine. Papers across cotton country picked up the news and spared no details of Wooters's Yankee heritage.[9] In order to get the deal signed, Alford traveled from his Southern farm all the way to the Greenwich Country Club, a fact that foretold a move of the seat of power from Memphis and the cotton fields of the South to the high-rises and boardrooms of the urban East.[10]

Wooters's hire was unexpected and certainly uncharacteristic of how the Southern-centric cotton industry had always conducted its business. For his part, the new CPI director did nothing to assuage the concerns of cotton growers about his unfamiliarity with the business. In fact, Wooters quickly went out into the Cotton Belt to meet farmers, ginners, spinners, and buyers. In these meetings he sold his unfamiliarity with the region and the crop as a strength. His outsider perspective, he claimed, gave him a unique view on the industry, one that was concerned not at all with cotton itself but almost exclusively on how to sell it. Wooters "knows nothing about producing cotton," reported the biggest newspaper in Mississippi. "But he is a salesman and he aims to promote the sale of cotton as it has never been done before." For his part, Wooters told a group of Mississippi farmers, "Don't break faith with the product you produce, and don't break faith with the people who are going to take it to the market place." But in his first months on the job the new director gave only vague promises to "achieve maximum cotton consumption" and "maintain a healthy cotton economy."[11] These hazy promises soon turned to bold action.

Wooters recognized a single problem facing the cotton industry, one that was even more important than the direct competition from polyester: history. Every move he made in his first few years as director of CPI, in fact, was targeted at erasing the crop's links with the past. As Jacobson and Smith point out, after his first trip to the National Cotton Council offices in midtown Memphis, Wooters came away thinking that the whole location and situation sent the wrong message. The money that cotton had brought to the Bluff City, the mansions lining the streets around NCC's headquarters, connected the industrial group—and the plant itself—to plantations, farms, warehouses, and old-fashioned trading floors.[12] For the person now charged with selling the crop to consumers across the world, this sent the wrong message.

Wooters's employment set into motion a series of changes that made Memphis and the rural South less central to the cotton industry than they had ever been. With the hiring of this single person to an influential post within the business, all of the cultural work that people like the Vensons and Arthur Halle had done to fuse the crop to Memphis, not to mention the actual work done by thousands of Memphians to unload, ship, gin, pick, grade, load again, pack, and trade the fiber, was suddenly not a strength for the community but a liability. Wooters sought to separate, literally and culturally, cotton from the South.

In his two years in office, Wooters remade the CPI with this distancing in mind. First, he moved the research operations from Memphis to the Research

Triangle region of North Carolina, ostensibly to be closer to the mills of the Piedmont where a majority of American cotton cloth was manufactured. Second, he changed the name and structure of CPI itself. The replacement was Cotton Incorporated (CI), a name meant to erase the institutional associations of CPI, to literally remove "producers" (i.e., cotton farmers), from the name. His third drastic change was moving CI from its offices within the National Cotton Council building in Memphis to New York City. This meant that Wooters, and the advertising talent that he recruited, would not have to relocate to the South and could stay in the heart of the advertising world. Wooters could drive his company-owned Mercedes to and from his Connecticut house to the new offices on the Avenue of the Americas, surrounded by corporate headquarters and marketing companies. The move was not inexpensive. NCC bore the $1.3 million dollar relocation cost, which included $72,000 in granite installed in the reception room of the new offices and $125,000 in carpeting and wallpaper.[13] Rumors swirled that Wooters also procured a private airplane and installed his own elevator in the headquarters. (These were untrue, though according to Jacobson and Smith, Wooters "employed, for business lunches, an excellent Chinese chef.")[14]

All these changes and the lavish spending did not go unnoticed by old-school cotton interests in the Deep South. In his first year in office, Wooters gave a long interview to the *Memphis Commercial Appeal* in which he hid nothing about his efforts to separate the fiber from its history and the region where it grew. "He never saw a cotton plant until this summer," opens the story—a line designed to shock Southern readers, readers who had themselves worked in fields, or attended Carnival balls, or dressed their kids in cotton bales to march in the annual Carnival parades. To Memphians and readers across the cotton South, people who had engineered a society to both trumpet cotton's supremacy and replicate in cities and towns the cultural organization of plantation agriculture, Wooters must have come across as an alien, or worse. "One of my mottoes is that cotton isn't dead," he told the paper. "It's just been asleep all these years." Readers must have thought about the frivolity of Carnival when they read Wooters's comment that "the time of playing games is over," and they certainly felt their traditions under attack when Wooters said boldly that CI did not "have a nickel for the Maid of Cotton contest." It wasn't the only change he promised. Wooters boasted about scrapping several traditional NCC projects: the Cotton Fashion Award, the home economics program, and sponsored sewing contests. He made no apologies, bragging, "A lot of guys think I move too fast, but that's my style," and "Any business should reflect the personality of the man running the show." Defending his outsider status, he told Southern readers that his strength was that he did not "play by Memphis rules, or Lubbock, Texas rules or whatever. . . . I know the rules of the game in New York."[15]

Distancing cotton from the South meant more than just moving the headquarters and playing by New York rules. From his posh new digs, Wooters launched a campaign to divorce the "funny looking white stuff" from its history.[16] After all, the problem wasn't producing the crop—there was a surplus supply most years—but converting it from a commodity to a brand. His focus, then, was consumers. Wooters believed the future of cotton was dependent on divorcing products made with the fiber from consumers' notions of the plant, and in his mind, these associations were slavery, poverty, and black oppression. Wooters wanted to rebrand the fiber "to get rid of the image that cotton had of blacks in the field with a hoe."[17]

The move to Manhattan was the first part of a new message to the nation's consumers of fibers: Cotton was a modern product of the city with no connection to the historic connotations of the Southern landscape. Wooters and Cotton Incorporated wanted to make cotton about fabric, not agriculture. The Northerner did not begin with the perspective of most Southerners, who knew what cotton was and imagined selling its strengths. That was the old approach of the Maid of Cotton competition, the Cotton Carnival itself, and the sewing contests. Instead, the New Yorker understood simply how the general clothes-buying public perceived the fabric.

The most important and lasting move Wooters made in his tenure at Cotton Incorporated was the creation of a new logo. The women and men walking the department store aisles shopping for clothes, towels, or fabric would neither know nor care that CI had a fancy office in New York rather than Memphis. So Wooters and his new team had to find a way to make sure that cotton products stood out from the synthetics in a retail setting, but also that cotton would suggest to the shopper a modern fiber with positive appeal.

In 1973 CI paid $50,000 to the San Francisco–based graphic designer Walter Landor to come up with a symbol that would send a new message. The result was the Seal of Cotton.[18] (See figures 1 and 20.) The stylized cotton boll with the script "cotton" underneath sent exactly the message that Wooters intended. It showed the plant itself as a living thing, but one torn from the actual conditions that make it grow. The logo's wording, with the two *t*'s, connected the plant roots upward past the dark burrs to form the soft, blooming cloud of fibers. The image could almost appear animated, showing the motion and vitality of a fruiting boll. But at the same time, the Seal of Cotton was merely representative; obviously, it was not an accurate depiction of the plant. While the logo highlighted the plant's natural attributes, it intentionally decontextualized it from its environmental setting. Cotton bolls ripen on branches, not from twin roots sprouting from the soil, as the icon suggested. The image was biologically nonsensical by design. Stripped from its horticultural reality, it conveyed no message about the crop's past or the labor that went into its growing or processing. It was cotton without context.[19]

This distancing was by design. CI explained this in its *New Cotton Symbol Identification Manual*, which it sent it to board members and marketing partners. The handbook's introduction made the case for the new iconography. This "comprehensive identity system . . . will utilize the type of marketing and communications tool that is employed successfully by countless branded products," a system that has been "long employed by its synthetic competition." "For the first time, cotton, from field to consumer, will be fortified by a modern symbolism that will enhance the fiber, stimulate appeal for cotton products, and help unify the total industry." More than simply positioning the Seal of Cotton as a new branding image, the booklet described the emotions that consumers would associate with the icon. The image portrayed cotton's "naturalness and feel." The seal itself was "soft," accentuating "breathability" and "absorbability." CI's marketers boasted that the new image sent a message of "'honesty,' 'purity,' and 'realness.'"[20]

The *New Cotton Symbol Identification Manual* also previewed how Cotton Incorporated was going to use the logo in advertising. Each of the examples put into practice Wooters's aim to distance the plant from its historical and agricultural contexts. Some concentrated on making cotton seem technically advanced, a natural version of polyester and other synthetics. Under a large brown-and-white logo, the text of one example read "This is the sign of Miracle Fibers. Molecular Genetics. Seed Banks. Computerized Fabrications." It concluded: "Nature and Science. Working for Man." The staccato, fragmented lists of qualities intended to make cotton into a "Natural Wonder," though one created by the combination of the earth and scientists: "This is the sign of The Future. Fuel Saver. Oxygen Producer. Earth Fed. Sun Powered . . . The Natural Wonder" and "This is the sign of Doctors at Work. Entomologists. Agronomists. Biochemists. Geneticists. Agricultural Engineers." But never farmers.

Another ad trumpeted the work of actual human labor—"Spinners, Weavers and Knitters"—but never men and women driving planters or harvesters or spraying chemical fertilizers.

While most of the ads concentrated on one aspect of cotton's new image, the example shown in figure 20 threw all of the ideas into a single, slightly contradictory list of characteristics. "This is the new sign of Cotton. An earth sign. Modern. Uncomplicated. The symbol of purity. This is the new sign of Comfort. Breathability. Intelligent fashion. Planned ecology. Cotton." What "intelligent fashion" meant and how it was related to "planned ecology" were neither explained nor seemingly important to CI marketers. But it sent the right message, that cotton had been reborn as a natural product very separate from the nature that created it.

The logo became the cornerstone of Cotton Incorporated's rebranding. CI made deals with individual companies and mills to ensure that they would include the logo on their product tags. The idea was that consumers should, at the point of purchase, be able to easily identify what comprised the clothing they were considering buying. At a glance, a shopper could see the seal on a tag, rather than having to read the fine print to see which synthetic dominated the cloth. Wooters made a deal with the Arrow shirt company to include the seal on each of their shirts and even personally met with the company's sales staff to teach them how best to sell cotton's qualities.

Despite the early agreements with dress shirt companies, CI's biggest target audience was not a middle-aged man off to work in an office building but jeans-and-T-shirt-wearing teenagers and young adults. Though Wooters had once claimed that "wife power" was his secret weapon in getting more clothing shoppers to buy all-cotton togs, in the late 1970s his strategy soon shifted younger.[21] J. Nicholas Hahn, Wooters's successor at CI, remembered that in those early days research showed that "everyone was wearing polyester double-knit . . . and cotton was going the way of the buggy whip." But among the Baby Boomer generation, cotton was the fabric of choice. So Cotton Incorporated made deals with Levi Strauss and pitched ads at younger buyers. Rather than running from the T-shirt business, CI embraced it. Ads targeted teen buyers in the hopes that cotton would become a fabric choice that lasted throughout their entire lives.[22]

While the logo appeared on more and more store tags, it also became the cornerstone of a four-decade-long print and television advertising campaign that celebrated not a single use for cotton but the fiber itself. These early

FIG. 20. Cotton Incorporated provided board members with a booklet detailing how it would use the new Seal of Cotton. Sample advertisements like this one made broad promises about the nature of the fiber. "New Cotton Symbol Identification Manual," n.d., box 2, "Cotton Incorporated" Folder, George Mullendore Collection, Special Collections, Mississippi State University.

slogans pitched the fiber as classic and traditional on the one hand, but cool and cutting-edge on the other: "Cotton Keeps America Comfortable," "Cotton: It's a Natural Wonder," "Come Home to Cotton," and "The More Cotton, the Better You Feel."[23] Wooters bought air time during popular television events for glitzy spots that conveyed cotton as a modern fiber divorced from its farm roots. *Today Show* host Barbara Walters read live ads for cotton during the wildly popular morning show throughout 1976. Later that year, a staggering 90 percent of American TV households had seen at least one of twenty-eight CI advertisements over the course of the weeks-long live coverage of the Winter Olympic Games in Austria. Cotton Incorporated also flew Wooters and several executives from cotton mills and large retailers to Innsbruck to attend the games. (The move drew criticism from many inside and outside the cotton business who thought that CI was wasting growers' money on needless extravagance.)[24]

It was not until the late 1980s that Cotton Incorporated launched its most far-reaching and long-lasting campaign. On Thanksgiving Day 1989 it aired the first of a long series of television advertisements using the tagline "The Fabric of Our Lives." The catchy jingle sang "The touch, the feel of cotton. The fabric of our lives" and embedded itself in the minds of millions of television watchers in the United States and around the globe. Even into the early twenty-first century, marketing experts pointed to the seal and the "Fabric of Our Lives" campaign as some of the most successful advertising efforts in world history.[25]

The results were remarkable. CI had succeeded in distancing cotton from its history in the minds of millions of consumers. *The New York Times* identified the historical break. In a 1976 article, under a large photograph of two mechanical harvesters rolling through a cotton field white with bolls, it declared, "King Cotton Seeking Throne Lost to Polyester." The paper reported that "King Cotton, dethroned a decade ago by a pretender named polyester," is fighting back with a "sophisticated 'New South' marketing campaign." The *Times* detailed cotton's collapse in the face of the synthetics. Its market share had been 80 percent in 1940 but had fallen to 40 percent in 1970. Engineered fibers claimed 56 percent of the market that year. But by 1976 cotton's fate had turned around. This meant cotton farmers were getting higher prices and planting more acreage. "The story of the cotton renaissance, moreover, is more than simply economic and agricultural," the *Times* explained. "It is almost a primer of the New South."[26]

But cotton's rebirth in the marketplace depended on severing its commercial identity—both literally and symbolically—from the South. Within a decade of the Seal of Cotton's debut, a marketing firm found that 65 percent of Americans recognized the logo—more than any other noncorporate symbol. The fiber's future, it turned out, lay not in Delta fields but in the image crafted far beyond them.[27]

WHILE COTTON'S NEW IMAGE was crafted far from their fields, farmers in the Mississippi Delta were paying close attention to the rebranding. Perhaps the most telling monument to this change was a billboard that sat along a stretch of Highway 61, the storied road that had carried a generation of white and black Mississippians out of the cotton fields of the Delta north into Memphis. The towering sign played on the most famous opening line of the song "Dixie": "I wish I was in the land of cotton." Elvis and others had given the lines newfound fame even in the postwar era. The Delta billboard, however, said simply, "No one's ever sung 'I wish I was in the land of polyester.'" Cotton's resurgence—caused in no small part by Cotton Incorporated's new marketing campaign—captured the attention of Southerners who closely watched the industry changes and felt pride, again, in the plant's place in regional identity.

Cotton growers driving past the billboard seemed fully on board with the changing image of the plant. Local papers were filled with coverage of CI and its campaign. For instance, in the spring of 1971, just months after Wooters's hire and the creation of Cotton Incorporated, the Greenville, Mississippi, *Delta Democrat Times* republished an excerpt from *Rags*, an underground, anti-establishment fashion magazine from Berkeley, California. Calling *Rags* "the sartorial bible of the bell-bottom generation," the Delta paper devoted an entire column to the pro-cotton article. Cotton, the Californian paper had argued, "has been around for a long time. . . . It feels good and does a lot of things. . . . But Americans, in their drive to replace the organic with the fake, have flooded the market since World War II with synthetics." The Berkeley paper even cited Cotton Incorporated's research lab and fabric libraries and encouraged its countercultural readers to write directly to CI's offices "to tell them about prints and weaves or clothes and things you'd like to see made in cotton." The Mississippi author gave little critique or praise of the *Rags* text, as if he was surprised to be agreeing so wholeheartedly with the hippie take on the Southern staple.[28]

More typical coverage of the National Cotton Council in Delta newspapers from the 1970s forward concentrated on research efforts against boll weevils and boll worms. But as word spread about Wooters's spending and his moving the CI office out of Memphis to New York, some cotton planters turned a suspicious eye toward the operation.[29] After all, CI's money came from them, via per-bale payments funneled through the USDA to Cotton Incorporated. Legally, farmers could ask for their money to be refunded, but they had to pay in first. Some did get reimbursed. Knowing this, CI management made sure that Delta farmers knew what it was doing with their payments. Wooters and his staff constantly traveled cotton country to talk about CI's advertising and research efforts.[30] They appeared any place cotton people gathered, from ginners' meetings to seed research presentations.[31] On one 1975 trip, CI's public relations director Libby Clark spoke to small women's groups and to the large Delta Council annual meeting.[32] Media throughout the region covered all of the new CI ad campaigns as closely as they did cotton sales numbers or advances in agricultural technology. Even small papers announced the coming of the "Fabric of Our Lives" campaign, including descriptions of its theme music and the schedule of when the television spots would air so that locals could tune in.[33]

Those Mississippians involved in the industry had no trouble linking the ad campaigns to their bottom lines. From its nadir in 1970 when Wooters took over, cotton sales rebounded over the next two decades. In 1975 the *Clarksdale Press Register* declared, "Cotton is making a comeback in fashion and home textiles."[34] By 1984 the *Greenwood Commonwealth* declared, "Cotton becomes fabric of choice."[35] Articles covered all the CI news, from new cotton-synthetic blends for shirts to fire-retardant batting used in mattresses.[36] The stories highlighted not just industry movement but clothing fashions as well. "The blue jean craze," the *Greenwood Commonwealth* reported in 1977, has moved denim "from the bottom of the fashion line to the top."[37]

The most convincing stories of CI's marketing successes were on the business and farm pages alongside reports of soaring production and profit. In August 1984 the small *Yazoo Herald* concluded that CI's marketing efforts had resulted in "substantial payback." Since its rebirth in 1970, Cotton Incorporated had increased the demand for the fiber, resulting in a staggering $378 million in *additional* cotton sales. Farmers were producing, mills were processing, and consumers were buying more cotton than ever before. The fiber's share of the clothing market was up, the paper reported, across apparel categories from women's clothing to men's dress shirts. "Easy-care cotton" was now competing with polyester and rayon in the high-fashion industry while more fire departments and the military were signing contracts for traditional all-cotton uniforms. The paper even pointed to the Seal of Cotton's impact, which was attached to "millions of identifying tags" on some of the most famous brands in American retail from Sears and JCPenney to Arrow and Cannon.[38]

FOR THE DELTA FARMERS who picked up the *Yazoo Herald* or other local papers and read news of this sales success, it was no surprise. They could see the radical change in the fields outside their windows. The decade when Wooters and his team took over the CPI, renamed it Cotton Incorporated, and launched its rebranding campaign coincided with the Delta's dramatic agricultural changes. As figure 19 reminds us, from 1970 to 1990 the population plummeted by more than 22 percent, while cotton production soared. The number of farms growing any cotton at all fell by an astonishing 72 percent. In just twenty years, fewer white and black Deltans, on many fewer farms, grew 50 percent *more* cotton on about the same number of acres.[39] This new cultural narrative of the crop, told through CI's international campaign and internalized by Mississippians, gave locals a way of understanding the new cotton landscapes they inhabited.

On the farm, economic and technological pressures meant smaller farmers sold out to larger ones, creating consolidation. These larger plantations had more capital and borrowing power and were in a better position to buy costly seeds, harvesters, and other equipment, and to put these technologies to use. By the 1990s, tractors pulled four-row planters that dropped seeds into precisely drilled holes; herbicides replaced people walking the fields to weed with a hoe; mechanical strippers replaced handpicking. Government programs that more closely manipulated overall cotton production numbers on the one hand and encouraged owners of marginal lands to reduce acreage on the other were yet another factor in why larger farms succeeded and small farmers began selling out. The second half of the twentieth century in the Delta was a story of machines and technologies doing the work that had been performed by hands for generations. While in most places in the rural region the landscape looked nearly identical to how it had decades earlier, the *who* and *how* of cotton growing was radically different. The African American population had shrunk and moved away from cabins in the middle of fields.

Small farm owners too were mostly gone, or at least no longer growing cotton.

This new relationship to cotton was of course not just something that played out in the fields. The human costs of these agricultural, technological, and environmental shifts can't be captured by crop statistics or loan records alone, especially when they are so closely tied to the signature social struggles of the era. Before World War II, and even for almost three decades after, many African Americans attempted, through the Cotton Makers' Jubilee and other public cultural and political avenues, to assert their connection to the crop, to make King Cotton's power their power as well. But after World War II, things were different. As historian Greta de Jong insists, many scholars have missed the tight link between the traditional civil rights story and the agricultural one. National victories that ended Jim Crow corresponded with the mechanization of cotton farms, she points out, and this left former tenant farmers in the Delta looking for new paths toward freedom at the same time their labor and economic lives were in upheaval. Thousands of African Americans found themselves unemployed and homeless after they were evicted from cotton plantations, and, perhaps ironically, they became even more dependent on the elite white power structure for access to relief, jobs, and homes. As de Jong put it, "Just when black southerners seemed poised to take their place as equal citizens in their communities, many of their white neighbors wondered whether there was a place for African Americans at all."[40]

By the late 1970s, not only had more immediate and important political and social rights like voting and full integration replaced the cultural importance of cotton, but the agricultural reality also simply meant that fewer and fewer African Americans were involved in any way in farming. Cotton meant less to the entire society, and claiming a connection to it offered black Mississippians a decreasing amount of status.

For white Mississippians, however, the civil rights movement and the changing reality of cotton growing posed a different challenge. First, fewer people were involved with the industry in any capacity, though many farmers and their children who were no longer planting and harvesting the staple were employed selling implements and fertilizers to those who were. In the 1970s it was clear to anyone who looked around the Delta that cotton's old order was no longer in power. While cotton fields still stretched to the horizon in most of the flat, fertile region, life had changed in important ways. To think about these social and political changes from the perspective of a typical white planter is to understand that they saw the world turning upside down. In the towns and small cities of the region, school integration and political rights had changed the entire social order. White Mississippians fled integrated public schools to set up private, segregated academies; many also moved out of the smaller towns altogether.

As these important material changes occurred, many white Mississippians looked to cotton again—as they had for generations—to explain what was going on. While the culture of the plant served white Southerners trying to understand their world since long before the Civil War, it had always been tied closely to its agricultural reality. By the 1970s, with the plant in a different place on the land, white Southerners had to use new ideas about the plant to define themselves. For many of these women and men, the new narrative had already been provided by Cotton Incorporated.

Some scholars have pointed to the ways that ideas about culture, whether historical memory or contemporary representations of their world, are never invented out of whole cloth but built from the explanations offered around them, or "constructed of rhetorical resources."[41] Many white Mississippians—those living on cotton farms, those who had moved away from plantations, and those living in cities often many miles from the nearest blooming plant—embraced "the fabric of our lives" as an explanation of their new situation and the crop's new reality.

For its part, Cotton Incorporated intended rural Southerners—not just department store shoppers—to embrace this new nonagricultural, nonhistorical image of the commodity. Not only did it pay for extension agents from cotton-growing Mississippi counties to travel to North Carolina mills to see the spinning and manufacturing process, it encouraged farmers to understand their product's entire life cycle from field to fabric.[42] CI wanted farmers and their families to think like consumers, not just producers. The booster group continued its involvement in very local events throughout cotton country. It even sent clothing—the latest cotton fashions from New York—directly to Mississippians who were celebrating the plant in some way. When the Delta Cotton Wives put on their 1972 Cotton Fair in Greenwood, hundreds of people crowded onto the grounds of a local mansion along the Yalobusha River to celebrate the crop. "From the rafters to the cellar, cotton was the story in history, arts and crafts, accessories, fashions and home furnishings," reported one newspaper. CI sent men's, women's, and children's outfits, which, according to the paper, "were informally modeled during the day."[43]

CI specifically used its Seal of Cotton to influence how rural Southerners thought of the crop. In direct communications it encouraged farmers to plaster the image "in advertising, on stationery, in promotional items, on products and packaging, and for on-farm needs like vehicles." CI's campaign for "gins, co-ops, farm supply and implement dealers, oil mills, warehouses, and compresses" to embrace the image absolutely thrived.[44] Throughout the 1970s and 1980s, the Seal of Cotton began appearing throughout the rural South, particularly in places that were still (or had been) centers of cotton production. As early as 1973, Cotton Incorporated was distributing T-shirts emblazoned with the image to farmers and others involved in the industry across the rural South. David Jordening, a CI economist based in New York, sent "two cotton logo T-shirts" to Mississippi State Extension Service agronomist George Mullendore after the latter had spent two weeks traveling the East Coast meeting with industry people and politicians.[45] By the 1980s, the shirts were a fairly common sight on farmers and others, but in the 1990s their popularity soared.

Every few years during the 1970s and 1980s, CI commissioned studies of how consumers perceived the Seal of Cotton logo, then wrote glowing press releases to show off the findings. Only three years after the icon's creation, its 18 percent consumer awareness was growing steadily. More than half of all Americans could recognize the Seal by 1979, and it reached a remarkable 75 percent by the mid-1990s. Throughout the Mississippi Delta, small-town newspapers reported on each new survey. The *Greenwood Commonwealth* wrote that "more people now recognize . . . the Seal of Cotton, than at any time since the seal's introduction in 1973."[46] The Clarksdale paper reported a "big jump in awareness" in 1986.[47]

CI's efforts to reach farmers, not just buyers, with the new image of cotton had clearly been successful. The Seal of Cotton and the "Fabric of Our Lives" campaign erased the oppressive and violent association between the crop and its history. White Deltans bought into the campaign; they paid attention to its popularity; they put the logos on their T-shirts and the stickers on their trucks. With a revised script for what cotton meant to the world, many rural Southerners shifted focus to new ways to celebrate the crop and to use its historic landscape to attract visitors and attention.

CHAPTER TEN

Old Times There Are Not Forgotten

IN THE LATE TWENTIETH CENTURY, Cotton Incorporated's logo was everywhere. A new generation of shoppers recognized it on the tags of their clothes, on their television screens, and on shiny magazine pages. The corporate logo and its campaign had convinced millions of people to buy more and more of the fabric of their lives. In cotton country, as well as in the cities and suburbs of the South, people wore Seal of Cotton hats and glued the iconic bumper stickers to their trucks. It had become a symbol of pride for those who wanted to represent some connection to the crop but not get caught up in all its historical weight.

Dukes Wooters and his CI team had been successful divorcing the fiber from its history, but they had done so in fictional worlds of their own creation. The logo and tightly controlled usage occluded the plant's landscape from its public image. With very few exceptions, the CI campaign sold cotton as a natural product that had no specific place in nature. The success depended on that separation.

This chapter returns cotton's cultural narrative to the nonfiction world of Mississippi at the end of the twentieth century, where to talk about the crop, or about the Civil War, or about blues music was to engage with the landscapes of those topics. In fact, state leaders and local tourism officials suddenly had a newfound interest in telling cotton's story, though taking a page from CI's playbook, in many cases they tried to do so without engaging the past, even at self-consciously historic sites.

This chapter describes two events. First, it tells the wild tale of the creation of a living history museum that aimed to be a cotton amusement park set in 1850s Mississippi. The fantasy of that effort stands in stark contrast to the second focus of this chapter, the rise of blues tourism. Unlike the construction of a new museum meant to conjure the past, the museums, hotels, and public sites of blues tourism used the contemporary look of cotton farms in the Delta to make visitors feel like they were stepping back in time to hear a blues crooner at a crossroads juke joint. Like with Cotton Incorporated's rebranding, the cotton museum and the blues sites made outlandish claims to be telling cotton's story while silencing the story of black labor, slavery, tenancy, and violence.

In each case, however, the material reality of what it meant to prepare the land, plant seed, chop the weeds, and pick the bolls ran head first into a narrative that tried to exclude labor from the story. As each of these endeavors demonstrates, it was very hard to tell cotton's history in dirt and brick and fiber and somehow leave out slavery, tenancy, and work itself. The landscapes of cotton that were at the center of these new sites made it impossible to tell a laborless story.

IN 1969 A LOCAL Greenwood official announced a "million dollar plan" to build a kind of Disneyland devoted to cotton. "It could become the biggest single attraction in Mississippi, and famed world wide," reported a Jackson newspaper. Otis Allen, school superintendent for LeFlore County, proposed an ambitious cotton-centric site that included rebuilding a Confederate fort, raising a Union gunboat sunk by the Confederacy, and the creation of a "time museum" with a giant sun dial. But the heart of his planned combination of "[Colonial] Williamsburg and Six Flags," was a living history museum of cotton, with everything that a pre-Civil War plantation entailed. "A giant, permanent exhibition to let the world know all about cotton from what was for many years the cotton capital of the world," reported the paper. The museum would "depict the evolution of cotton farming—from mules and men to machines." Allen did not have in mind the rebuilding of a farm, but a brand-new plantation built to historical specifications. There would be "cotton being cultivated as of old in one plot and with the mechanisms in another." Allen dreamed that "thousands of tourists would come here each year" to see the attraction he dubbed "Cottonlandia." He predicted that the site would net the Delta $20 million annually.[1]

After his initial announcement, two years passed before Allen explained exactly how cotton's story would be told. In 1971 a small Cottonlandia museum opened in an antebellum house in downtown Greenwood near the public library. Volunteers kept it staffed a few hours a week, and locals donated old plows and butter churns to fill out the exhibits. The reality was a long way from what Allen had proposed, but the booster kept working to find funding for his cotton dream.[2] In 1973 the Mississippi state legislature appropriated $2 million to make at least part of Allen's vision a reality. The money was earmarked for construction of the cornerstone of Allen's dream: a nineteenth-century replica plantation to be built on one hundred acres of land donated to the city. Allen and his supporters promised to move the Cottonlandia museum to the site and expand its holdings. Mississippi Governor Bill Waller signed the bill to some fanfare.

The plans for the park, which was now officially named the "Pre-Civil War Living Plantation," included a large house, cotton and corn fields, a river landing area, a school, a blacksmith shop, and six newly constructed slave cabins.[3] When Hank Klibanoff, a journalist from the *Delta Democrat-Times*, pressed Mississippi Parks Commission chair Robert Ashley on just how the new site would interpret cotton's history, Ashley had no answer. Klibanoff—who would later become famous for his coverage of the civil rights movement across the South—pressed Ashley specifically about how African American life would appear in the plantation museum. "The park board, in its master plan for the project, will *consider* presenting the role of the black man in the Delta's history," Ashley wanly replied. Regardless, the *Greenwood Commonwealth* was right to editorialize in May 1973 that what had once seemed like "pipe dreams by Cottonlandia have over-night become likely realities."[4]

Otis Allen was thrilled that the state had funded his dream cotton project and insisted publicly that planners "make the plantation absolutely authentic," which meant representing the institution of slavery in a manner that Allen and the state of Mississippi would dictate.[5] While the state park staff began fine-tuning plans, the Jackson newspaper attempted to generate excitement by promising that when it was complete, visitors would have "the chance to pick some cotton."[6]

This news did not sit well with many in the black community. When the park architect went to a meeting of the Greenwood Voters' League, the city's main civil rights body, and announced that the site would feature "black people . . . performing as slaves on a live plantation," it caused an uproar. The league's leader, David L. Jordan, remembered, "I couldn't believe that they were attempting to rub our faces in the mud again with slavery." Jordan promised that if any white supporters of the park "wanted to see slaves then they could act out the part themselves."[7] The body got word to the governor that it opposed the plan, and soon Waller came out against the building of slave cabins or having African Americans working as slaves on the land, telling reporters that the park could somehow celebrate cotton "without throwing up negative symbols." "There are certain things in the state's background that don't need to be highlighted" in the historic park, the governor said. State NAACP field secretary Emmett Burns agreed with the decision, saying that if slaves were to be depicted at all it should be as Nat Turners, "standing up and fighting." Slaves were not "docile" but "were always protesting slavery in some way."[8] State planners never considered Burns's insurrectionist idea, but in 1974 state park director Bill Banett announced that the plantation would include neither slave quarters nor any reference to slavery at all on the cotton plantation grounds.[9] This promise did not hold true.

A statewide contest to name the project settled on Florewood River Plantation State Park, which opened its gates to visitors on August 15, 1976. Not all of the planned buildings were in place, and the Cottonlandia museum remained in its building downtown, but locals and tourists could finally see the brand-new 1850s-style site. The original three buildings that had been designed as slave quarters sat in a row next to the main house, but when the park opened, staff interpreted the structures as "household quarters, servants quarters, and [a] driver's house."[10]

Despite the ahistorical renaming intended to elide the existence of slavery in antebellum agriculture, cotton itself was at the center of the park's story and space. Visitors began their tours of the hundred-acre complex with a stop in the welcome center and then a short walk to the mansion. Cotton's value to the mythic white planter and his family that lived there was easy to see in the furnishings and housewares. (A few years after its opening, Confederate General Nathan Bedford Forrest's bedroom set became part of the collection and went on permanent display in the main bedroom.) But the house hardly dominated the visitor's experience to Florewood. The landscape itself was the central attraction. Behind the main house and the three small cabins with new names sat a sprawling cotton field.

Any visit to Florewood centered on lessons about cotton production and processing, and the visual representation of that environment was key to the interpretation. Despite the fact that when the park opened in 1976 the fields had been planted with "Stoneville 213," a modern variety of cottonseed developed only miles away at the Stoneville branch of the Mississippi State Experiment Station, farm managers were intent on planting historically appropriate varieties in future years. Making those seeds available meant some reverse breeding, in a sense, to make plants that would grow shorter and whose fibers were grayer than modern types. The farmers in charge of the fields had even procured "Nanking cotton" from the Soviet Union, which was a short-staple version with brown fibers that approximated nineteenth-century American varieties. The first year's plantings were nursed along with modern chemical fertilizers, ginned, and baled on modern equipment, but then wrapped in jute to make it look like pre–Civil War product. Volunteers in period clothes spun and wove the fiber and sold their products in the gift shop.[11]

Buck Galey, the farm manager, told a local paper that he remembered cotton farms from the 1920s, on which he claimed "things had not changed a great deal from eighty years before."[12] Galey's remark hid arguably *the* most important moment of history in the United States: the end of slavery in the very cotton fields he was trying to resurrect. The level of specificity that Galey and his colleagues put into using antebellum-specific equipment, seed type, and fertilizers went out the window when it came to representing the human labor working the crop. At some point after opening, however, local people began playing the roles of enslaved people on the site.

Soon after its opening, regional and national media outlets sent writers to Florewood to review the site, though all these reports focused on cotton and the human actors playing various roles. In a *Memphis Commercial Appeal* article from 1980 the reporter described Dorothy Parker, "an attractive black woman from Greenwood," who was playing the part of a slave, weaving and sewing cotton fabric in an indoor setting. At first Parker would not answer the reporter's questions about how she felt playing an enslaved person, but "after about 10 minutes of cajoling," Parker admitted she sometimes felt self-conscious in the role, but "my doing this doesn't condone the way of life that was practiced back then. . . . It educates people," Parker said. "That's different."[13]

A *National Geographic Traveler* story from 1992 was similarly fixated on cotton but avoided mention of the labor system that underpinned it. At Florewood, the writer promised, "King Cotton is saluted" for tourists, who walk "the world's richest soil" and see "acres of cotton flourish nearby." Visitors who were interested in the human history of the fake plantation could interact with "interpreters in period dress who describe the role that each of their characters played in Florewood's *smoothly functioning* scheme."[14] The magazine piece presented an "authentic" plantation without any signs of slavery, but somehow also with a focus on historically accurate cotton production and processing.

Despite these write-ups in national magazines—or perhaps *because* of them—by almost any measure Florewood River Plantation State Park was not a success. Even by 1981, just five years after opening, a study found that its buildings had been shoddily built, were poorly maintained, and "have deteriorated to the point of presenting a safety hazard to park visitors."[15] Despite local and state efforts to turn the site into a cotton-themed park to draw thousands of visitors a year, Florewood's attendance figures languished throughout the 1980s and 1990s. By the end of the century, the park employed only six people, and its biggest events each year were Civil War reenactments and the annual Christmas displays.[16] Though no visitor numbers became public, one newspaper reported the park was "not frequently used." Without admissions income, and with a dozen buildings made with nineteenth-century construction techniques, operating costs spiraled out of control. In 2003 the park had $25,800 in revenues but a staggering $276,411 in expenditures.[17]

UNLIKE FLOREWOOD'S mansion house, full of furniture from the first grand wizard of the Ku Klux Klan, an hour north sat a house that visitors were actually interested in seeing. This structure too had been built and rebuilt as part of an important local narrative about cotton, labor, and culture. However, rather than a faux antebellum mansion anchoring a fantasy plantation, this was a tiny cabin. And unlike the Florewood setting, made to look like it had been sitting in the same place for a century, this structure had been picked up and moved—several times, actually. At the turn of the twentieth century the cabin rested inside a gallery at the Delta Blues Museum. Tourists from around the world came to Clarksdale, Mississippi, to step inside the home of Muddy Waters.[18]

Born McKinley Morganfield in the southern Delta near Rolling Fork, Waters was raised by his grandmother, Della Grant, on the Stovall plantation about five miles north of Clarksdale. Grant worked as a sharecropper, and as soon as her grandson was old enough to wield a hoe, Waters walked the rows chopping weeds and picking cotton. In his spare time, he learned to sing and play the guitar. His life was a testament to Amiri Baraka's assertion that blues music sprung from whatever "leisure that could be extracted from even the most desolate sharecropper's shack in Mississippi."[19] He liked entertaining others more than cotton work. "I didn't like farming," he told an interviewer later. "I always expected my guitar could beat driving tractors, plowing mules, chopping cotton, drawing water. Sometimes they'd want us to work Saturday, but . . . they'd look for me and I'd be *gone,* playing my guitar in the little town or in some juke joint." In 1941, when Waters was about twenty-seven, Alan Lomax, the famed Library of Congress song collector, visited Stovall and recorded Waters singing a few acoustic blues songs. Neither man's life would ever be the same.[20]

Within a decade of Lomax's recording session, Waters had left the cotton fields, moved to Chicago, and traveled the country performing music for eager white and black audiences. To reduce his blues career to a few superlatives, suffice it to say that Waters was as influential an American performer as nearly anyone, especially if measured in the number of white rock acts that pointed to Muddy as inspiration. The Rolling Stones named themselves after one of his songs; Eric Clapton became his friend and mentee; everyone from Led Zeppelin to ZZ Top to Bob Dylan adapted Waters's songs or recorded versions of them.

But the odd thing about his house sitting in a rural Delta museum is that Waters became the king of the *Chicago* blues. After Lomax's original plantation recordings, Waters made his fame not in Mississippi, or even as a Mississippian, but as an electrified, urban guitar player and singer. After the initial Library of Congress recordings, his music rarely concentrated on rural or agricultural themes. He became famous for "(I'm Your) Hoochie Coochie Man" and "Mannish Boy." And while his early life and exposure to the Delta style of blues certainly impacted his playing and songwriting, he left cotton and farm life behind as explicit themes of his music and embraced sex, love, and masculinity as his central subjects. Even more important to his success than his lyrics were his voice and playing style, which was amplified, often to the point of distortion, reflecting Northern and urban aesthetics. His blues sounded better in Chicago than Mississippi, he claimed: "You know, the country sounds different than in the city, the sound out there be empty." Little of Waters's global influence, or his residency and association with Chicago, seems to matter much to his legacy, however. In fact, the entire blues genre seems impossible to separate from the cottonfield narratives and landscapes from which it was born.[21]

The story of the Waters house makes this point clear. The "cabin" that moved into the Clarksdale blues museum in 2001 was actually the cypress-planked central structure of a larger house whose story represents much of Delta history. On the Stovall plantation before the Civil War, the original building was most likely put together from local trees that were felled, milled, and assembled by enslaved people. After emancipation, the house became part of a growing New South plantation. Col. William Howard Stovall, a Confederate veteran, oversaw the transformation of several hundred acres, and his sons took over the lands as they grew.[22] In 1918 the cabin sat on the edge of the plantation, which at the time contained several hundred acres of cotton land. The Stovalls were a powerful Southern family, running plantations that employed hundreds of African American sharecroppers like Della Grant. William Howard Stovall Jr. was enough of a mover and shaker in the regional cotton scene to be named king of the Memphis Cotton Carnival in 1948. He rode the parade floats and attended the parties, while the African American men and women who worked on his land may have traveled up to participate as float pullers or play stereotypical, demeaning roles on the royal barge or along the parade routes. Or they might have joined the Cotton Makers' Jubilee's segregated celebrations of the crop.[23]

Meanwhile, the cabin sat along the road for more than a century. The various families that lived in it added on to and adapted the structure over the course of the plantation's own expansion. When Muddy Waters moved out and his music began selling throughout the United States and Europe, the cabin became a site for visitors looking to find the "authentic" home of one of the most famous musicians in the world.

Sandra B. Tooze, a Waters biographer, visited the house in the 1990s, and she puts the Waters cabin at the heart of her narrative of the blues singer's life. For researchers and music fans alike, finding Muddy meant looking on the cotton landscapes of Mississippi, not the crowded Chicago neighborhood where Waters spent most of his life. What Tooze found when she visited Mississippi surprised her. Driving through the heart of cotton country, Tooze saw "luxuriant beauty" where she expected to find a landscape raw from a century of cotton farming and human exploitation. "I'd half expected that the harshness of the white man's domination would be reflected in the landscape," she wrote. Instead, "as if to compensate for past injustices . . . nature had burst forth with a profusion of verdant green."[24]

Her description of her visit, though it happened in the late twentieth century, seems to indicate that she thought she would find a Mississippi no different from when Waters had left fifty years prior. "While most of Mississippi's original subtropical forest was leveled long ago to accommodate King Cotton," she explains, some trees still stood, "preventing the stark monotony of a flat, empty vista." When she finds the Waters cabin, "still located on the edge of a cotton field," she claims to feel in touch with the singer and his time. The "weather-wary, crumbling shack resurrected the ghosts of Muddy's early life." Tooze could look at the "bleached timbers" of the old house and imagine "a bereaved three-year old" who "discovered his insatiable appetite for music." At the end of the twentieth century, Muddy Waters's cabin at the Stovall plantation had become a shrine, a destination for the world's blues fans who came on pilgrimages to find the music's holy sites among acres of cotton.[25]

For Tooze and so many other late twentieth-century blues visitors, to understand this music one had to stand on a dirt road next to a cotton field in the Mississippi Delta, not along a busy street on Chicago's South Side. It was "the holy grail" of blues sites.[26] Despite Waters's connection to Chicago—a place he lived longer than he had in any one place in the South—tourists and journalists communed with the blues in these landscapes of rural poverty and cotton agriculture. Tooze claimed that, for Waters, the Stovall plantation "remained his anchor, in both his values and his music," for the rest of his life. "This cabin—this culture—had nurtured a bluesman who would conquer the world."[27]

Yet this connection between the blues and twentieth-century Mississippi cotton fields defied reality in telling ways. Despite tourists' desire to find the blues among Southern cotton fields, many musicians like Waters preferred to stay in the North. When an interviewer of Waters in the 1980s assumed that the singer must go back to Mississippi and Memphis frequently, now that he was a famous musician making real money, he replied, "Nah. No. No. Mississippi is a place I don't hardly ever go."[28] Instead, Waters and his fellow blues musicians played concerts across the country and toured Europe, Africa, and Asia. None of the genre's most successful acts stayed around the Southern cotton fields where the music had been born. Better lives—with economic, political, and social freedoms that were hard to come by in the Delta—could be found in Chicago, New York, or the West.

For blues aficionados, however, the cotton fields of Mississippi were the place to feel the blues. The music itself was a kind of time capsule that trapped historic moments in vinyl, magnetic tape, and digital bytes. No matter how recent the recording or how cosmopolitan the artist, thousands of fans understood the music to be of a place in time and at a spot on a map. Tooze and other blues writers have argued that they could *only* understand Waters and his music in the context of poverty and a falling-down timber shack on the edge of cotton's kingdom, not in a modern city. "When we think about the blues," admitted Waters biographer Robert Gordon, "we often think of cotton fields and summer heat."[29]

It is no wonder, after years of visitors driving up Oakhurst Avenue from Clarksdale to the Stovall land looking for Muddy's house, that one of them stopped and offered to buy the whole thing. In the early 1990s Isaac Tigrett, founder of the chain of music-themed restaurants Hard Rock Café and House of Blues, knocked on Howard Stovall's door and asked if he could have the cabin. Stovall, the grandson of Col. William Stovall, who had owned the plantation when Muddy drove a tractor, was a Yale graduate living in Memphis when Tigrett contacted him. Tigrett and Stovall agreed on a deal: House of Blues would lease the structure for five years, haul it to New Orleans, restore it, and send the house on tour. After five years, the deal was, Stovall would get the cabin back. In return, Tigrett donated $20,000 per year for five years to the Sunflower River Blues Association, which put on an annual blues festival in Clarksdale.[30] Without fanfare—Stovall kept the news of the deal out of the press fearing backlash from blues purists—the cabin was disassembled and hauled off.

After it was trimmed down to the basic structure of its internal board walls, cleaned up, and formed into a modular setup easily loaded on and off a truck, for three years Muddy Waters's cabin became the South's most famous mobile home—an attempt to transport the landscape of cotton, heat, humidity, and rural poverty across the country in the form of a sharecropper's cabin. House of Blues toured the structure to blues festivals and other public events in cities such as Chicago and Los Angeles; the company displayed it at the Rock and Roll Hall of Fame in Cleveland, Ohio, and even set it up for the international crowds at the 1996 Atlanta Olympics.[31] This attempt to transport the zeitgeist of a Delta field around the country did not end with the house. "When the House of Blues opened its new club in Chicago," Mississippi-based blues expert Jim O'Neal recalled, "it placed an order with me for 25 pounds of dirt from Muddy Waters's yard. It was absurd, of course, but I dug it up and sent it."[32]

As blues fans looked for a visceral connection to the landscape of the Delta by visiting the touring house or by seeing a pile of soil on the floor of a Chicago restaurant, many found themselves still drawn to the dirt and cotton of the actual Mississippi Delta.

THE YAZOO-MISSISSIPPI DELTA changed radically in the second half of the twentieth century, but cotton was still everywhere. Agricultural technology, namely, the mechanical cotton picker, advanced pesticides, and computer-guided farming, had made cotton plantations more efficient and highly capitalized. Small farmers and tenants were pushed out or left on their own, or both. Outmigration meant fewer rural farmworkers, and fewer people altogether. Landowners could produce more cotton with fewer human hands working the same number of acres. The third change was cotton's place in Delta society. As the result of the National Cotton Council's successful campaign to rebrand the crop as a modern product of nature separated from its historical roots, locals were celebrating cotton seemingly without any of the crop's painful history. These three changes remade the Delta economy and social organization, but the landscape hardly looked any different at all.

Take, for example, the Delta's historic leader in cotton production, Coahoma County. Despite all the changes in agriculture and who lived and worked where, the area continued to have incredibly productive soil and devastating rates of poverty. But what the experiences of very poor people looked like, especially to an outsider, was different at the end of the twentieth century than at any point prior. With the end of sharecropping, poor Deltans (and their sharecropper cabins) were no longer situated among the cotton fields themselves. Most rural residents lived in the very small towns that previously had been hubs of cotton activity like ginning, warehousing, and marketing. But by the end of the twentieth century, much of that work had moved to regional hubs or been shrunk by technological advances. Poverty became a small-town problem, rather than a diffused reality in scattered plantation cabins. In Clarksdale, for instance, the New World neighborhood, located a short walk from where the Muddy Waters cabin sat inside the Delta Blues Museum, had a poverty rate of 60 percent in 2000. So while the Delta was still poor, and still dominated by cotton agriculture, agro-environmental factors had pushed this poverty out of the farms and into struggling small towns.

This was the world encountered in the 1990s and early 2000s by a new strand of visitors to the Delta: tourists. As the case of Muddy Waters's cabin demonstrates, people from around the world became interested in walking through the landscape of the blues, the place that produced the musicians behind the genre. These visitors saw cotton and poverty—the two forces most important to the creation of the musical form—but it was hardly the combination of conditions that had existed one hundred years prior.

Struggling communities across cotton country turned to the newly professionalizing industry to sell the cotton landscape to visitors who might stay in hotels, eat at restaurants, and pay admission to museums. In the 1990s, not only had industries and communities found interest in tourism, PhD programs in tourism planning and policy emerged, and several peer-reviewed journals made it an academic pursuit. Municipalities hired these experts to rethink the stories being told for potential travelers. The *Greenwood Commonwealth*, for instance, excitedly reported on a boom in agritourism in 2001. "Many visitors grew up on farms and want to relive the experience or share it with their children," the paper reported. "Agriculture also appeals to foreigners." With the Delta's cotton landscape and history, the *Commonwealth* promised, this meant that "the packaging opportunities are limitless."[33]

The tourism industry that emerged in the Yazoo-Mississippi Delta at the turn of the twenty-first century attempted to package blues culture and the cotton environment in a way that would court visitors and their money. Together, the whitewashed history and the dramatic vistas gave municipalities and tourist boards a canvas on which to paint a new picture of blues music. A genre born and refined amid the exploitative labor and racial regimes of these very same cotton fields could be celebrated, locals hoped, with a few twists of the narrative and sleights of hand. Tourists might find the "feel" of an authentic blues experience amid the cotton landscape.

No one captured this early 2000s cultural moment better than the journalists who came to the Delta to see just what blues tourism was all about. In 2001 the *Atlanta Journal-Constitution* sent reporter Jim Auchmutey to suss out the scene. What he found were acres and acres of cotton that made an enticing backdrop to a vacation. The Atlantan met plenty of tourists from outside the South—the North and Europe, mostly—who had come to visit the place where the blues began. As one person he met put it, "The blues is all about a feeling, and you really feel it in a place like this." Tourist boards and local entrepreneurs had made those cotton spaces particularly nostalgic and cleaned up for tourists.[34]

Auchmutey highlighted Clarksdale's Shack Up Inn, "the world's first tourist court made up of shotgun houses." Along with Tallahatchie Flats, a similar lodging setup outside of Greenwood, the Shack Up Inn was a collection of actual sharecropper cabins that had been moved to a single site and rebuilt to include bathrooms with indoor plumbing and electricity. (Wi-Fi was added later.) But the rough-hewn walls and antique signs plastered on them were supposed to lend an air of authenticity, even if that air was now conditioned by window units. "Never mind that John Lee Hooker and most of the other bluesmen who started out on Delta cotton plantations couldn't wait to get out," Auchmutey allowed, but these visitors were choosing to try on a modern imaginary idea of a tenant farmer lifestyle for a night or two. "This place?" the journalist scoffed. "These guys are paying to sleep in a shotgun shack."[35] His unease about the sites did not let up. It was the architecture of poverty, the houses, that the writer could not get past, despite the gussied-up amenities. "Shacks are Chic in Clarksdale, the Crossroads of the Delta Blues," declared his headline.

Though as tourism increased more traditional hotels popped up in Delta towns like Clarksdale, the Shack Up Inn and Tallahatchie Flats were set in very different landscapes from urban lodging. Both were built in plantation settings among the cotton fields. In the case of Shack Up, the setting is out in the country, five miles from the crossroads where bluesman Robert Johnson sold his soul to the devil. The "motel" is on the Hopson plantation, the Coahoma County farm that was the site of the first successful trial of the mechanical cotton harvester in 1944. For a visitor driving out from town toward Shack Up, there would be no doubt that this was cotton land. Not only was the site literally among cotton fields, but old farm equipment littered the driveway to the property. In fact, the gin that for decades whirred away carving seeds from lint served as the Shack Up's lobby and bar.

Similarly, driving out to Tallahatchie Flats involved leaving Greenwood, crossing the Yalobusha River, and immediately encountering flat cotton fields. Large, old plantation houses sat a distance from the road, and just past a one-room AM blues radio station and a church graveyard where Robert Johnson was perhaps buried—there are arguments about this—was the cluster of tenant houses that is Tallahatchie Flats. (If one kept driving only six miles past the Flats driveway along Money Road, they would come upon Bryant Grocery, where Emmitt Till was accused of whistling at Carolyn Bryant, a charge that led to the fourteen-year-old's murder.)

The landscapes around Shack Up and Tallahatchie Flats were certainly evocative, and intentionally so. Visitors who stayed there were seemingly seeking out something both authentic and historic. The Shack Up website trumpeted that very point. "Their corrugated tin roofs and Mississippi cypress walls will conjure visions of a bygone era. Restored only enough to accommodate 21st century expectations (indoor bathrooms, heat, air conditioning, coffee maker with condiments, refrigerators and microwave in all the units), the shacks provide comfort as well as authenticity."[36] It is unclear what time period this authenticity is supposed to evoke, however. The website admits, "(Some people seem to think our shacks were slave shacks, not so), they were sharecropper houses and or tenant houses."[37] It seems that "authentic" post-slavery houses are okay for both the Shack Up and the thousands of guests who have stayed there year after year. This motel, along with so many of the refurbished blues spaces in the Delta, are what John Frow called "a plausible simulation of itself."[38]

From a presentist standpoint this authenticity dance is interesting, though not very fruitful for understanding how landscape and history worked at the turn of the twentieth century. Put simply, it is easy to poke holes in the authenticity of any of these places. Neither those interested in attracting tourists nor the visitors themselves were after the literal lived experience of the people who created or consumed the blues in the past. These spaces do little to interpret, or even memorialize, vast swaths of the past, including political and civil rights history. Places like Tallahatchie Flats offer a fabricated snapshot of a time that never existed. The interpretation is not even nostalgic because no one is arguing that things were better "then," since the portrayal is of a music born of hardship.[39] The revealing rhetorical move in these sites that emerged in the early part of the twenty-first century was the *ease* with which cotton landscapes became marketable blues landscapes. Authentic blues locations could seemingly be built or found wherever cotton was planted.

Florewood Plantation is again a representative case of this process. Though the state of Mississippi shut down the historic site in 2004, it had invested millions of dollars into building and maintaining an "1850s" mansion, gin, and cotton field. But what purpose could the now-decaying site possibly serve if it was no longer a museum? The answer was in the blues. As one local official put it in 2004, "Florewood is for sale and the Blues Commission needs a home."[40]

It seemed that almost no changes would have to be made. Even though Florewood was designed as a pre–Civil War cotton farm, and blues tourists sought the "authentic" experience of the post–World War II explosion of the musical genre, to local officials it seemed close enough. "The blues theme park envisioned by the commission," the *Jackson Clarion-Ledger* reported, "would provide, among other things, a central location for tourists seeking information about the blues and blues sites in the Delta." If it had an aging mansion and cabins lining a cotton field, it seemed, it would pass as "the blues" to tourists.[41]

The state eventually leased the complex to Leflore County for twenty-five years for ten dollars, but the Blues Commission did not move in, and the site shut its doors soon after. Before they let go of the mansion and grounds, however, Mississippi park officials held an auction. The "original Eli Whitney cotton gin" sold for $132,000 and Confederate General Nathan Bedford Forrest's bedroom furniture brought $50,000. All told, the state recouped almost $500,000 before handing over the stripped-down museum to Leflore County.[42]

In 2005 Greenwood tourism groups hired a consultant, Grady Hillman, to propose a plan for how to attract more visitors to the city. Hillman proposed focusing on "heritage tourism," with an emphasis not on antebellum history but on twentieth-century events. He even suggested a remodeling of Florewood to make it a "black history museum with an emphasis on the blues, gospel music and other black cultural contributions." At the same time, the consultant suggested Florewood might keep cotton growing on its fields—as the local paper reported, "an idea not altogether well received." Hillman's plans were never adopted by the city. Other than uses as a county storage site—and the filming location for two Hollywood movie productions—the cotton plantation sat decaying.[43]

The landscape of Florewood changed as well, as the buildings developed leaky roofs, and trees and shrubs moved in. A visitor whom the county allowed inside the gates in 2018 found "natural beauty . . . undisturbed" except for some graffiti on the buildings. "Cypress swamps glow green through trees lining pristine fields," the reporter found, alongside "dense forest [and the] unsullied banks of the Tallahatchie River."[44] By 2018 the only suggestions emerging for use of the park were as a fishing spot, though during the COVID-19 pandemic the county opened the gates to use the Florewood grounds as a vaccination site. Visitors waited fifteen minutes in their cars after getting their arms jabbed while gazing at a run-down replica of an antebellum plantation.[45]

Across town, the Cottonlandia Museum, which in the late twentieth century told a whitewashed version of the Delta's history but sold dozens of cotton-centric products in its gift shop, was rethinking its place in the tourist landscape as well. In 2011 its board voted to change its name to the Museum of the Mississippi Delta and to replace its cotton boll logo with an abstract outline of the state, "to reflect all of the museum's offerings that extended far beyond cotton." In 2019 the museum's executive director, Cheryl Thornhill, explained that the old name gave people the impression that cotton was the sole subject of the museum. Cotton was no longer the center of its interpretation, though the institution had not moved in the blues direction like so many other historical sites in the region. "Many of the more recent museums created in the Mississippi Delta focus on the rich musical heritage of the region," Thornhill said. Her museum, however, "focuses on the entire Delta—the history, science, archaeology, the prehistory, and art."[46]

The remodeling of these formerly cotton-centric spaces like Florewood and Cottonlandia, and the rise of blues tourism sites like Clarksdale's Delta Blues Museum, was not convincing everyone that Mississippi had moved on from the history that gave cotton and the music a home. Leonard Pitts Jr., a syndicated journalist known for his writing on race and culture, visited Mississippi in 2003. The African American writer prefaced his article, which first appeared in the *Miami Herald* but was syndicated across the United States, with a list of all the reasons an African American tourist would not want to visit the state. "I don't like Mississippi," his story began. It was "not just a state where cruel things were done to black people . . . but rather, the meanest and poorest of states where such things were done." To African Americans, Pitts argued, Mississippi was "the one place where, if you have any choice in the matter, any sense in your head, you absolutely, positively do not want to be." His editor, in Pitts's telling, sent him to the Magnolia State with the charge to find ten things that he could recommend to African American tourists.[47]

Pitts's experience in turn-of-the-twenty-first-century Mississippi hit all the tourism marks that the state and regional leaders were suggesting. He stayed in a former slave's room at the Monmouth Plantation in Natchez (though Pitts pointed out that the room now had a whirlpool tub in the bathroom and there were chocolates on the pillow in his canopy bed). He walked the streets of the state capital's Fair Street Historical District. He visited Clarksdale and the Delta Blues Museum, stared into the eyes of the "disturbingly lifelike" Muddy Waters figure, and walked through the shell of the bluesman's rehabbed cabin.[48]

The heart of Pitts's lengthy article about visiting Mississippi, the moment where his critical lens meets the touristy and historic representations of the state, was the moment he laid his eyes on cotton. It was in the Clarksdale blues museum where the writer saw, "off to one side," a cotton bale. It was "bigger than you'd think if you don't know about such things, a heavy cube of white gold." He poked at the fibers bound up in the bale's cover. He was "pleased, and a little surprised" to be able to touch the product whose "cultivation and exploitation . . . gave Mississippi its rhythm and black Mississippi its blues." The sight of a cotton bale, the experiences of touching it and seeing it in the fields, were for Pitts examples of the "rawness" of Mississippi's history. By the end of his article he was selling this aspect of his trip as a strength, as a recommendation for others—even African Americans—to visit the state. He counted "the closeness of history" as one of his "10 good things about Mississippi" and pointed black readers to the "African American Tour Guide," a brochure published by the state's tourism council.

Pitts's side trip to Memphis, "which a Mississippi tourism brochure describes, with somewhat self-conscious irreverence, as 'the biggest city in North Mississippi,'" reveals the extent to which that town's celebration of history and cotton had changed in the years since the Cotton Makers' Jubilee and the Cotton Carnival had shut down. Beale Street, the early twentieth-century heart of black Memphis, the street on which Ransom Venson kept his dental office, had become a Hollywood version of itself. Pitts found it "neon-lit and tourist-ready." African American–owned stores and restaurants had been replaced with a Hard Rock Café at one end and a Starbucks at the other. "Whatever its place in legend, whatever role it once played in the development of the city," Pitts lamented, "Beale Street is now mainly a place for people from out of town." There are places of interpretation for the African American history of the city, of course. The National Civil Rights Museum inhabits the Lorraine Motel only a short walk from Beale's bars and restaurants. Statues and signs mark the places and people who have shaped the city's cultural history as well. Nat D. Williams, Ida B. Wells, and W. C. Handy have signs within a few blocks of each other on the touristy street.

There were few signs of Memphis's century-plus adoration of cotton, however. The parades of Cotton Carnival and Jubilee no longer wound through downtown every spring, and there were no cotton brokers or graders left on Front Street. Thanks to groups as diverse as Monsanto and the Memphis Cotton Wives, the old Cotton Exchange building had become a cotton museum. Tourists could make a donation and go on a self-guided tour through cotton's history in the city. Though the crop was nominally the center of the museum's interpretation, there was relatively little on its agricultural or even marketing aspects. Much of the interpretation focused on culture, with displays devoted to both Carnival and Jubilee, and guitars and other musical memorabilia that told a blues history.

AT THE BEGINNING of the twenty-first century, tourists from all over the world poured into Memphis and the Mississippi Delta to experience the cotton landscape and to commune with its blues history. If they visited during the winter, spring, or summer, many could not tell the soybean fields from the cotton. Little green plants were little green plants. Like the history with which visitors wanted to engage, it was the appearance that mattered, the feeling that they got from the Delta's flat expanse.

In reality, the cotton that formed the backbone of this tourist effort was no longer the king of Mississippi agriculture. In 2002, of the state's 42,186 farms, only 1,596, or 3.7 percent, grew any cotton, though it accounted for 10 percent of the state's agricultural acreage.[49] Those growers netted $444 million from sales of cotton fiber and seed. Cotton was still making money, but it was going to fewer and fewer people, or more precisely the corporations that operated almost all cotton farms. This included almost no black farmers. Though African Americans were 36 percent of the state's population, they were about 10 percent of cotton farmers.[50]

Though fewer and fewer people were involved in the crop's production, the Seal of Cotton T-shirts and blues tourism sites remained popular into the twenty-first century. By then, Cottonlandia's re-created cotton fields, where only twenty years earlier African Americans walked the grounds in imitation antebellum garb and tended to heirloom cotton varieties, were disregarded fields of weeds and the re-created plantation house a few steps away sank slowly into the soft Delta dirt.

Conclusion

Look Away, Dixieland

IN MY FIRST BOOK, *Boll Weevil Blues: Cotton, Myth, and Power in the American South*, I spent two chapters explaining Enterprise, Alabama's monument to the tiny cotton-devouring insect. Rising nearly twenty feet from the middle of a downtown intersection, the top of the statue is a painted cast-iron woman holding above her head a bronze boll weevil. It is an oddity, one that consistently shows up on lists of weird roadside attractions and unexpected historical sites. In 1919 a local merchant lobbied for the statue after several area farmers, worried that the boll weevil would destroy their cotton, had begun growing peanuts instead. The nearby historical marker told half the truth, that those farmers who grew peanuts became rich while those who didn't were destroyed by the boll weevil. The sign calls the pest the "herald of prosperity." In reality, a few years after the statue took its place in downtown Enterprise, those peanut farmers went right back into growing the crop that they had known their whole lives. The return to cotton frustrated one area extension agent so much that he promised them "you will be poor and ignorant and your children will be the same."[1]

What I argue in those chapters was that the boll weevil statue had only limited cultural power in a place that had grown cotton for generations. It became nothing more than a fixture that people drove past on their way through town. More importantly, while the insect pest had one statue, the landscape around Enterprise had dozens of monuments to cotton—not only the fields fruiting white each fall but, as importantly, the pillared mansions and the hulking gins and even new automobiles driven by cotton farmers in good years. Kids sang songs about cotton at school and businesses ran "cotton-pickin'" sales. The argument *for* cotton was embedded in farmers' lives and the world outside their windows. The little bronze boll weevil downtown didn't stand a chance.

Identifying the dissonance between the insect's symbolic meaning and the material importance of cotton started me down the path to this book. The boll weevil monument wasn't a marker of change but a sign of just how deeply cotton's hold had taken root. The landscape itself—its topography, its labor, its cultural overlays—was telling people to stay with cotton. I saw the same disconnect in my classroom, with the Seal of Cotton T-shirts my students wore. Judging by the number of logos on clothing and cars, one might reasonably conclude that the crop was central to Mississippi's economy, or at least its agriculture. But it wasn't. As in Enterprise, there was a gap between cotton's material place on the land and the cultural rhetoric that surrounded it.

As the chapters in this book have shown, the contradictions between cotton's material rise and fall and its cultural persistence evolved together across a range of times and places. When cotton was economically important in the Piedmont and Delta, Southerners who wanted to make a point about race, labor, or politics cozied up to the crop because that's where the power lay. But beyond that familiar story, this book has shown that the physical environment itself mattered to how people like William Henry Gist, Ransom Venson, or Dukes Wooters mobilized cotton for nonagricultural arguments. People projected racist, romantic, and naturalizing ideologies onto the land, yet crucially, the landscapes and cotton pushed back.

One could not stand at the edge of a hundred-foot erosion gully, on land torn apart by cotton-induced soil erosion, and tell a convincing romantic story about the crop's virtue. Nor was it easy to celebrate African American contributions to the cotton industry while million-dollar mechanical harvesters rolled across Delta fields once worked by hand. The environment and the people working it exposed the limits and contradictions of these cultural projections, making landscape an active participant in the South's contested understanding of cotton.

Two counterfactuals play out this point. First, part 1 shows that Rose Hill, long after cotton disappeared and the only visual sign of the crop was the striking, even violent mark that it left on the land, could not have become a Lost Cause tourist site that celebrates secession and Gist if the trees had not covered the gullies. Without the forest, the culture of Union County would be different today. Part 2 highlights how two events changed the material and cultural landscape of Mississippi to allow for a new interpretation of the crop.

From its New York City offices, Cotton Incorporated remade the plant as a brand with an abstracted logo and no connection to history. At the same time, machines replaced people on cotton farms. Without these environmental and agricultural transformations, there would have been no cultural space for sharecropper shack motels, blues museums, and nostalgic celebrations of cotton's past. The new cotton culture was not a simple evolution; it was the product of fundamental changes to both land and labor.

As those counterfactuals suggest, the goal of this book is to reposition the relationship between culture and landscape in history. Through the case of cotton, it reexamines how people's cultural ideas and material landscapes shape one another—a reciprocal relationship at the heart of how environments and cultures are inhabited, imagined, and transformed. It argues not for more environment in cultural histories or more culture in environmental histories, but more analysis of how inseparable the two forces have been.

When we take landscapes seriously not just as settings but as rhetorical and material tools, what becomes possible? What changes is a way to better understand how people used environmental landscapes to empower arguments about nonenvironmental things. This is not just—though it certainly is also this—a call for more histories of the South that take the environment more seriously as a historical force rather than a mere setting. This is not about just thinking about weather or topography during Civil War battles. Rather, my hope is that we have more Southern histories of slavery, war, labor, agriculture, memory, and capitalism that think of landscapes—both in current and historic times—as tools people used to make something else happen. Historians need to look for what was once on the land but is no longer there, and what stories people tell about that process.

ACKNOWLEDGMENTS

In December 2015, Ta-Nehisi Coates and I had a Twitter exchange about book acknowledgments. I can't remember how it started—he and I have both erased all of our tweets since then—but basically he posed a question like "Why isn't anyone honest in their book acknowledgments?" I tweeted back to him that I had been, and I attached a photograph of the acknowledgments from my first book. In it I wrote, "My kids, Walter and Eleanor Giesen, now that I think about it, didn't do too much to help me finish this book. They owe me." Coates retweeted it, saying something along the lines of "I can't believe this guy actually wrote that." Then, hours later, he retweeted it again, still disconcerted, or perplexed, or something short of impressed.

That was a long time ago. And I know that customarily authors acknowledge their families at the end, but given what I wrote the last time, I need to start with my children. While I worked on this book, Walt and Eleanor grew up. They came to understand their parents as real human beings who were doting, to be sure, but sometimes distracted and often irritated. They matured into *fantastic* young adults who ask good questions about research, writing, and history. They also called me out when the frustrations of this project made me grumpy. Other times they prodded me to keep going. They helped me write this book, not because they let me work, but because they pulled me away, back to the present day. I want to say here for posterity that they don't owe me anymore. They've repaid their debts a thousand times over.

Their mother, Anne Marshall, has never owed me anything. She's a fantastic historian, a true partner, and a dedicated mother. She is patient when I talk about federal agriculture policy and tertiary interfluves. She is funny and keeps track of things. She sticks up for people. She makes a great martini. She has cool friends. She's the best and I love her. I dedicate this book to Anne, Walt, and Eleanor.

The History Department at Mississippi State University has been a supportive, rewarding, and fun to place to spend my career. This is in large part due to Alan Marcus, who is exacting, gruff, and critical. He is also thoughtful, sympathetic, and kind. He has made this a great place to work, which is evidenced by the success and camaraderie of the faculty. Kathryn Barbier, Susanna De Stradis, Brenda Harris, Mark Hersey, Alix Hui, Andy Lang, Matt Lavine, Susannah Ural, Pam Wasson, and Chekila Young have been particularly helpful colleagues. Joey Thompson has been a thoughtful and generous sounding board for my ideas about Southern history, music, and writing. Others across the university have in many different ways made MSU an excellent place to research and teach, including Chris Ayers, Megan Bean, Dipangkar Dutta, Brien Henry, Briar Jones, Lis Pankl, Les Potts, Nicole Rader, Eddie Rangel, Michael Seymour, and Don Shaffer. Sheryl Bowen, a great supporter of the College of Arts and Sciences, generously allowed me to stay on her farm for several days while I edited. Whit Waide read an early draft of a proposal and texted me the very helpful insight, "I don't get it." The staff of Mitchell Memorial Library kept the books and documents coming. Jennifer McGillan and David Garraway unearthed ancient A/V equipment so that I could view an archived tape. Various parts of the university have supported research related to this book, including the College of Arts and Sciences and the Institute for the Humanities. The latter sponsored a fellowship that provided incredibly productive hours thinking, writing, and complaining with Julia Osman, Bonnie O'Neill, and Peter Messer.

Teaching at MSU is by far the most satisfying part of the job because our students are unfailingly interesting. I have taught more than three thousand undergrads, but a few stand out (for good reasons), including Javion Anderson, Sophie Bruckmeier, Seth Cannon, Jonathan Franz, Mitchell Grim, Braeden Martin, Jon Mitchel, Matt Rogers, Zoe Simien, Eli Tylicki, Lamarcus Walker, and Jordan Whitten. It's cliché to say that we learn more from our students than we impart, but in the case of my graduate students, it's absolutely true. I owe a special debt to Jason Hauser, Owen Hyman, and Karen Senaga, who taught me how to be a PhD advisor. They were smart, demanding, and fun, and created a structure for collaboration that has lasted long after they left. Madeline Berry, Trevor Cole, Lexi Doutrich, Matt Himel, Charlie Jones, Vasco Lorbner, Kayla McClellan, Kim Neal, Jackie Perkins, Kymara Sneed, and Aaron Thomas have kept that tradition going. Even the G-Lab interlopers, including Bashira Chowdhury, Aiden Daly, Patricia McCourt, Seth Nunley, Ryan Reynolds, and Nate Smith, deserve credit for keeping everyone motivated and moving forward.

Friends and colleagues on and off campus played important roles along the way. I walked former Piedmont cotton fields with Paul Sutter, Al Hester, Thomas Lekan, Dan Richter, and Dan Markewitz, all of whom have helped me better understand history, science, and institutions. I have found an incredibly nurturing intellectual home in the Agricultural History Society thanks to a legion of wonderful people, including Joe Anderson, Wayne Anderson, Shane Hamilton, Cherisse Jones-Branch, Sara Morris, Deb Reid, Sarah Philips, Karen-Beth Scholthof, Drew Swanson, David Vail, Bert Way, and dozens of others. It is a fantastic organization that has had an enormous impact on me.

Others deserve mention for their help, their nagging, or just their being around to talk with about cotton. Edward Blessing at the South Caroliniana Library and the staff at the Memphis Public Library were particularly considerate. I thank *Buildings and Landscapes* and the University of Virginia Press for permission to use revised versions of material previously published. Michelle Jones helped with a specific architectural question. John Walter Strange was encouraging and sharp-eyed on an early chapter draft. Since the start of the pandemic, I have had virtual writing sessions with several people, including Caroline Peyton and Bryant Simon. There is something satisfying in watching good writers struggle in real time. Bryant has long been both a model scholar and steadfast friend, and writing with him on Zoom every week was motivational and fruitful. Even though they moved away—something I will never forgive—Alison Greene and Jason Ward are generous with their friendship and insights about the South. Bart Moffatt and his dog Heidi have accompanied Hooper and me on hundreds of miles of walks; they heard a lot about this book and at times perked an ear to feign interest. Bill Ford, Chuck Holden, Ryan Hooker, Jason Kreag, Bill Link, Chase Newsom, Brant Rumble, Matt Simpson, Mike Tagert, and Kevin Waltman all helped in ways they may not appreciate. Robert Thompson's unrelenting positivity is an inspiration. Steve Hoffius owes me breakfast. Barb Giesen, Katie Giesen, Phil Giesen, Jan Marshall, Virginia Neff, Betty Scalia, Jeff Scalia, Jennie Durham, and Matt Durham are loving and supportive family members without whom I could not have written this book.

Finally, the folks at University of Georgia Press have been a pleasure to work with. Lisa Bayer, Beth Snead, Laura Theobald, and especially Mick Gusinde-Duffy believed in this book from the start and were persistent but never annoying. Copyeditor Lori Rider's keen eye saved me from several embarrassing mistakes. I also thank the two anonymous readers for their feedback, especially Reader Two, who was a smart, funny, and persistent pain. Erin Mauldin began reading drafts of these chapters *years and years* ago and has read the full manuscript more than anyone but me. I know few scholars who are as sharp, *direct*, and helpful.

I am deeply grateful to all who have contributed their time, insight, and generosity to this project.

NOTES

Introduction

1. Elvis Presley, "An American Trilogy," recorded February 16, 1972, single, RCA Victor. The song was originally arranged and recorded by Mickey Newbury a year earlier. The other two song snippets in the trilogy were "Battle Hymn of the Republic" and "All My Trials."

2. This count was not scientific. I tried to keep track each lecture day, which was twice per week. I recorded the number on my lecture notes and kept the running tally. I am certain that some days I missed a logo or two and forgot to count at all on at least one day. While the numbers are therefore rough, they felt right to me at the end of the semester. It was a very popular logo among my students.

3. Stephen Deere, "2 MU Students Apologize for Cotton Ball Incident," *St. Louis Post-Dispatch*, March 6, 2010.

4. "Black Acres Cotton Stalk T-Shirt," Vans.com, accessed February 2, 2023; Ama Nunoo, "Julius Tillery, the Farmer Destigmatizing Cotton Farming Through His Black Cotton," January 6, 2021, https://face2faceafrica.com/article/julius-tillery-the-farmer-destigmatizing-cotton-farming-through-his-black-cotton.

5. U.S. Department of Agriculture, National Agricultural Statistics Service, "2008 Cotton Crop Acreage," 2009 Crop Report, Mississippi Department of Agriculture and Commerce.

6. Cottonlandia was the original proposed name for what became Florewood River Plantation State Park. As explained later in the book, Cottonlandia was also the name of a museum dedicated to the plant in Greenwood, Mississippi.

7. See, for instance, Charles S. Aiken, *The Cotton Plantation South Since the Civil War* (Baltimore: Johns Hopkins University Press, 1998); Edward E. Baptist, *The Half Has Never Been Told: Slavery and the Making of American Capitalism* (New York: Basic Books, 2014); Sven Beckert, *Empire of Cotton: A Global History* (New York: Alfred A. Knopf, 2014); Pete Daniel, *Breaking the Land: The Transformation of Cotton, Tobacco, and Rice Cultures Since 1880* (Urbana: University of Illinois Press, 1985); Gilbert C. Fite, *Cotton Fields No More: Southern Agriculture, 1865–1980* (Lexington: University Press of Kentucky, 1984); Neil Foley, *The White Scourge: Mexicans, Blacks, and Poor Whites in Texas Cotton Culture* (Berkeley:

University of California Press, 1997); Walter Johnson, *River of Dark Dreams: Slavery and Empire in the Cotton Kingdom* (Cambridge, Mass.: Harvard University Press, 2013); Alan L. Olmstead and Paul W. Rhode, "Cotton, Slavery, and the New History of Capitalism," *Explorations in Economic History* 67 (2018): 1–17; Rupert Bayless Vance, *Human Factors in Cotton Culture: A Study in the Social Geography of the American South* (Chapel Hill: University of North Carolina Press, 1929).

8. For discussions that situate cotton within broader treatments of Southern identity and memory, see Grace Elizabeth Hale, *Making Whiteness: The Culture of Segregation in the South, 1890–1940* (New York: Pantheon, 1998); Scott Romine, *The Real South: Southern Narrative in the Age of Cultural Reproduction* (Baton Rouge: Louisiana State University Press, 2008); Tara McPherson, *Reconstructing Dixie: Race, Gender, and Nostalgia in the Imagined South* (Durham, N.C.: Duke University Press, 2003). For an exception that ties cultural meaning more directly to the environment and labor systems, see James C. Giesen, *Boll Weevil Blues: Cotton, Myth, and Power in the American South* (Chicago: University of Chicago Press, 2011).

9. Johnson's *River of Dark Dreams* is somewhat of an exception to this. The most-quoted line from the book makes a strong material claim: the "Cotton Kingdom was built out of sun, water, and soil, animal energy, human labor, and mother wit; grain, flesh, and cotton; pain, hunger, and fatigue; blood, milk, semen, and shit." But as Mark D. Hersey has pointed out, "The particulars of that ecology seem surprisingly unimportant to Johnson." According to his footnotes, Johnson seems not to have consulted decades of major work on the rural and environment history of the South and calls Southern agricultural history a "now sterile field." Johnson, *River of Dark Dreams*, 9, 425n290; Mark D. Hersey, "Slavery and the Landscape of a Dismal Empire," *Ohio Valley History* 13, no. 4 (Winter 2013): 81–82.

10. Paul S. Sutter, "The World with Us: The State of American Environmental History," *Journal of American History* 100, no. 1 (June 2013): 94–119.

11. For a discussion of the important scholarly and institutional developments that gave rise to Southern environmental history, see Mark D. Hersey and James C. Giesen, "The New South and the Natural World," in *Interpreting American History: The New South*, ed. James S. Humphreys (Kent, Ohio: Kent State University Press, 2017), 241–66. Two works, one Southern agricultural and one environmental history, deserve specific mention here because of how they informed the structure and analysis of this book. Philip D. Morgan's *Slave Counterpoint: Black Culture in the Eighteenth-Century Chesapeake and Lowcountry* (Chapel Hill: University of North Carolina Press, 1998) uses the differences in place, and specifically land—its fertility, topography, and workability—to explain the divergent development of two distinct Southern subregions. Morgan demonstrates how different landscapes allowed for, even encouraged, different enslaved labor regimes, social structures, and degrees of autonomy and violence. That attention to how environment shaped

the possibilities of agricultural production and the social systems that surrounded it is foundational to this book's comparative approach, even if Morgan's intention was not an environmental history. Likewise, Mart A. Stewart's *"What Nature Suffers to Groe": Life, Labor, and Landscape on the Georgia Coast, 1680–1920* (Athens: University of Georgia Press, 1996) helped shape this book's approach to landscape as a site of both labor and meaning. His work demonstrated that Southern environmental history could be methodologically broad and analytically ambitious without losing sight of narrative and place.

12. LeCain's clearest statement for New Materialism is *The Matter of History: How Things Create the Past* (Cambridge: Cambridge University Press, 2017). The quotation is from LeCain, "Deep Culture: A Very Brief Brief of the New Materialism," *Agricultural History* 96, nos. 1–2 (May 2022): 226.

13. LeCain, *Matter of History*, 340; LeCain, "Heralding a New Humanism: The Radical Implications of Chakrabarty's 'Four Theses,'" in *Whose Anthropocene? Revisiting Dipesh Chakrabarty's "Four Theses,"* edited by Robert Emmett and Thomas Lekan, *RCC Perspectives: Transformations in Environment and Society* 2 (2016): 19.

14. Hersey points to successful, material-focused environmental histories, such as Mart A. Stewart's work on cattle published three decades prior to the rise of New Materialism. He notes that the best "self-consciously New Materialist studies," like Stewart's work, "have married concrete examples of the ways in which material realities have shaped the past with compelling storytelling." Mark D. Hersey, "Material Stories, Old and New," *Agricultural History* 96, nos. 1–2 (May 2022): 239, 241.

15. Hersey, "Material Stories, Old and New," 239. A different of sort of criticism that emerged from the *Agricultural History* roundtable is Shane Hamilton's point that historians have long understood political and social creations—everything from ideas to taxes—as powerful and real, if not material. Shane Hamilton, "New Materialism and the History of Agribusiness," *Agricultural History* 96, nos. 1–2 (May 2022): 256.

Chapter One. King Making

1. William H. Gist to Thomas Overton Moore, October 5, 1860, reprinted in John G. Nicolay and John Hay, *Abraham Lincoln: A History*, vol. 2 (New York: Century Company, 1890), 306–7; Madison S. Perry to William Henry Gist, November 9, 1860, in Nicolay and Hay, *Abraham Lincoln*, 2:313–14; Troy L. Kickler, "John W. Ellis (1820–1861)," *North Carolina History Project Encyclopedia*, NorthCarolinaHistory.org, accessed July 18, 2025; Thomas O. Moore to William Henry Gist, October 18, 1860, reprinted in Nicolay and Hay, *Abraham Lincoln*, 2:307–10.

2. Timothy Silver, *A New Face on the Countryside: Indians, Colonists, and Slaves in South Atlantic Forests, 1500–1800* (New York: Cambridge University Press, 1990), 186–89.

3. Silver, *New Face*, 171.

4. Angela Lakwete, *Inventing the Cotton Gin: Machine and Myth in Antebellum America* (Baltimore: Johns Hopkins University Press, 2003); Lacy K. Ford, *Origins of Southern Radicalism: The South Carolina Upcountry, 1800–1860* (New York: Oxford University Press, 1988).

5. Mark Megalos, Colby Lambert, Rajan Parajuli, Heather Aldridge, Leslie Boby, and William Hubbard, "Resilient Piedmont Pines: Risk Reduction Guide," Eastern Forestry Notes, North Carolina State Extension Service (2018); Silver, *New Face*, 10. For more on geophysical development of the Piedmont see Silver, *New Face*; Paul S. Sutter, *Let Us Now Praise Famous Gullies: Providence Canyon and the Soils of the South* (Athens: University of Georgia Press, 2015); Daniel D. Richter Jr. and Daniel Markewitz, *Understanding Soil Change: Soil Sustainability over Millennia, Centuries, and Decades* (New York: Cambridge University Press, 2001). Another good source on the cultural and geographic outlines of the Piedmont is John David Smith, "'I Was Raised Poor and Hard as Any Slave': African American Slavery in Piedmont North Carolina," *North Carolina Historical Review* 90, no. 1 (January 2013): 1–25.

6. Silver, *New Face*, 195.

7. Silver, *New Face*, 5–6; Lacy K. Ford, "Self-Sufficiency, Cotton, and Economic Development in the South Carolina Upcountry, 1800–1860," *Journal of Economic History* 45, no. 2 (June 1985): 261–63. For a discussion of early settler agriculture patterns as they relate to prehistoric Native American settlement in the area around Rose Hill, see Michael R. Coughlan and Donald R. Nelson, "Influences of Native American Land Use on the Colonial Euro-American Settlement of the South Carolina Piedmont," *PLoS ONE* 13, no. 3 (2018), e0195036.

8. Ford, "Self-Sufficiency," 262.

9. Richter and Markewitz, *Understanding Soil Change*, 40–41.

10. Richter and Markewitz, *Understanding Soil Change*, 45.

11. For a full explanation of these methods and experimentation, see Lewis Cecil Gray, *History of Agriculture in the Southern United States to 1860*, vol. 2 (New York: P. Smith, 1941), 689–90, 700–704.

12. Daniel Bell, "Interpretive Booklets for Local Historic Sites: Rose Hill State Park, Union, South Carolina as a Model" (MA thesis, University of South Carolina, 1983), 3–23; Allan D. Charles, "Gist, William Henry," *South Carolina Encyclopedia*, scencyclopedia.org, accessed July 18, 2025.

13. Bell, "Interpretive Booklets," 23–30; Charles, "Gist."

14. Daniel Bell's thesis is the best biographical treatment of Gist. See Bell, "Interpretive Booklets," 9–32; Walter Brian Cisco, *States Rights Gist: A South Carolina General of the Civil War* (Shippensburg, Pa.: White Mane Books, 1991), 45.

15. *Agriculture of the United States in 1860: Compiled from the Original Returns of the Eighth Census* (Washington, D.C.: Government Printing Office, 1864).

16. The statistic on cotton land production is rough and obviously varied greatly from one area to the next, which underscores my overall point about the diversity of land use in "the Cotton States." And obviously some of this non-cotton land was used in service of supporting the humans and animals that were focused on the cash crop. Chapter 2 explains that interplantation diversification in detail.

17. David Christy, *Cotton Is King: Or the Culture of Cotton, and Its Relation to Agriculture, Manufacture and Commerce; and Also to the Free Colored People of the United States, and to Those Who Hold That Slavery Is in Itself Sinful*, 2nd ed. (New York: Derby & Jackson, 1856).

18. Christy, *Cotton Is King*, 2nd ed., 6.

19. "Ohio in Africa: Memorial," Ohio General Assembly petition, Library of Congress ([Cincinnati?], 1851), Library of Congress, www.loc.gov/item/11008759/, accessed July 18, 2025.

20. Christy, *Cotton Is King: Or the Culture of Cotton, and Its Relation to Agriculture, Manufacture and Commerce; and Also to the Free Colored People of the United States, and to Those Who Hold That Slavery Is in Itself Sinful*, 1st ed. (Cincinnati: Moore, Wilstach, Keys & Co., 1855), 15–16.

21. Christy, *Cotton Is King*, 1st ed., 17–18.

22. Henry Noble Sherwood, "The Movement in Ohio to Deport the Negro," reprinted in *Quarterly Publication of the Historical and Philosophical Society of Ohio* 7, nos. 2 and 3 (June and September 1912): 56.

23. James Henry Hammond to Thomas Clarkson, March 24, 1845, in Hammond, *Selections from the Letters of the Hon. James H. Hammond of South Carolina* (New York: John F. Trow, 1866), 187. See also Drew Gilpin Faust, *James Henry Hammond and the Old South: A Design for Mastery* (Baton Rouge: Louisiana State University Press, 1985); Eugene D. Genovese, *The Slaveholders' Dilemma: Freedom and Progress in Southern Conservative Thought, 1820–1860* (Columbia: University of South Carolina Press, 1992).

24. Hammond, "Speech on the Admission of Kansas, Under the Lecompton Constitution, Delivered in the Senate of the United States, March 4, 1858," in Hammond, *Selections*, 316–17.

25. Mason I. Lowance, ed., *A House Divided: The Antebellum Slavery Debates in America, 1776–1865* (Princeton, N.J.: Princeton University Press, 2003), 141.

26. Hammond, "Speech on the Admission of Kansas," 321.

27. Hammond, "Speech on the Admission of Kansas," 320.

28. Edward E. Baptist, *The Half Has Never Been Told: Slavery and the Making of American Capitalism* (New York: Basic Books, 2016), 238.

29. Harriet Beecher Stowe, *Uncle Tom's Cabin; or, Life Among the Lowly* (Cleveland: John P. Jewett, 1852).

30. Dickens quoted in "Cotton Is King," *Edgefield (S.C.) Advertiser*, May 20, 1852, 2.

Chapter Two. Enslaved Labor in a Fragile Cotton Ecosystem

1. "Sustainability" here is meant to be only loosely evocative of the environmental sustainability that readers encounter in the twenty-first century. More precisely, I mean sustainability more in the sense of a machine that needs a certain amount of energy and upkeep to keep going, to sustain itself. In the nineteenth-century context, this could mean environmental inputs like fertilizer or farm management like field rotation, but it also included vast amounts of human and animal labor. All of these factors could make a Southern cotton farm, no matter the size, sustainable.

2. See, for instance, "Premium Essay on Hillside Ditching," *Edgefield (S.C.) Advertiser*, January 19, 1853, 5; "An Essay on the Importance of Limes in Soils," *Cheraw (S.C.) Advertiser*, January 10, 1843, 1. On gullies, see Paul S. Sutter, *Let Us Now Praise Famous Gullies: Providence Canyon and the Soils of the South* (Athens: University of Georgia Press, 2015).

3. Edmund Ruffin, "An Address on the Opposite Results of Exhausting and Fertilizing Systems of Agriculture," in *Nature's Management: Writings on Landscape and Reform, 1822–1859*, ed. Jack Temple Kirby (Athens: University of Georgia Press, 2002), 324.

4. Edmund Ruffin, *An Essay on Calcareous Manures* (Petersburg, Va.: J. W. Campbell, 1832).

5. For the best discussion linking Ruffin's writings to historians, see Kirby's introduction to *Nature's Management*. See also David F. Allmendinger, *Ruffin: Family and Reform in the Old South* (New York: Oxford University Press, 1990); Jack Temple Kirby, *Poquosin: A Study of Rural Landscape and Society* (Chapel Hill: University of North Carolina Press, 1995); William M. Mathew, *Edmund Ruffin and the Crisis of Slavery in the Old South: The Failure of Agricultural Reform* (Athens: University of Georgia Press, 1988); Drew A. Swanson, *A Golden Weed: Tobacco and Environment in the Piedmont South* (New Haven, Conn.: Yale University Press, 2014); Sutter, *Let Us Now Praise Famous Gullies.*

6. Avery Craven, *Soil Exhaustion as a Factor in the Agricultural History of Virginia and Maryland, 1606–1860* (1926; repr., Columbia: University of South Carolina

Press, 2006); Sutter, *Let Us Now Praise Famous Gullies*, 142; Gavin Wright, *Old South, New South: Revolutions in the Southern Economy Since the Civil War* (Baton Rouge: Louisiana State University Press, 1986), 17.

7. Mart A. Stewart, "From King Cane to King Cotton: Razing Cane in the Old South," *Environmental History* 12, no. 1 (January 2007): 59–60.

8. Sutter, *Let Us Now Praise Famous Gullies*, 133.

9. See John Majewski, *Modernizing a Slave Economy: The Economic Vision of the Confederate Nation* (Chapel Hill: University of North Carolina Press, 2009); Roger L. Ransom, *The Confederate States of America: What Might Have Been* (New York: W. W. Norton, 2005).

10. Sutter, *Let Us Now Praise Famous Gullies*, 129.

11. Erin Stewart Mauldin, *Unredeemed Land: An Environmental History of Civil War and Emancipation in the Cotton South* (New York: Oxford University Press, 2018), 36.

12. *U.S. Census of Agriculture, 1840* (Washington, D.C.: Government Printing Office, 1841); *U.S. Census of Agriculture, 1860* (Washington, D.C.: Government Printing Office, 1864).

13. See, for example, Mauldin, *Unredeemed Land*; Kirby, *Poquosin*; Majewski, *Modernizing a Slave Economy*; Carville Earle, "The Myth of the Southern Soil Miner: Macrohistory, Agricultural Innovation, and Environmental Change," in *The Ends of the Earth: Perspectives on Modern Environmental History*, ed. Donald Worster (New York: Cambridge University Press, 1988), 175–210; Steven Stoll, *Larding the Lean Earth: Soil and Society in Nineteenth-Century America* (New York: Farrar, Straus & Giroux, 2003).

14. Inefficiency and ignorance had political implications as well. As Mauldin puts it, "Antebellum northerners equated multigenerational farming and intensive continuous cultivation with progress and democracy" (*Unredeemed Land*, 37).

15. Sutter, *Let Us Now Praise Famous Gullies*, 131.

16. Historian Enrico Dal Lago explains that Hammond and Ruffin borrowed from the ethos of industrial capitalism to organize labor on their plantation for greater efficiency. While certainly systems of agricultural organization were important to land reform, the environmental specifics of each plantation must not be overlooked. The impact of organization and the effects of the environment are of course not mutually exclusive. Enrico Dal Lago, *Agrarian Elites: American Slaveholders and Southern Italian Landowners, 1815–1861* (Baton Rouge: Louisiana State University Press, 2005), 160–64. Many other historians have written recently about the relationship between capitalism and slavery. For the best overview, see Christopher Morris, "With 'the Economics-of-Slavery Culture Wars,' It's Déjà Vu All Over Again," *Journal of the Civil War Era* 10, no. 4 (December 2020): 524–57.

17. Dianne D. Glave, *Rooted in the Earth: Reclaiming the African American Environmental Heritage* (Chicago: Chicago Review Press, 2010); Mauldin, *Unredeemed Land.*

18. Lacy K. Ford, "Self-Sufficiency, Cotton, and Economic Development in the South Carolina Upcountry, 1800–1860," *Journal of Economic History* 45, no. 2 (June 1985): 261–67.

19. Ford, "Self-Sufficiency," 265.

20. *Compendium of the Enumeration of the Inhabitants and Statistics of the United States as Obtained at the Sixth Census* (Washington, D.C.: Thomas Allen, 1841), 192.

21. Robert E. Gallman, "Self-Sufficiency in the Cotton Economy of the Antebellum South," *Agricultural History* 44, no. 1 (January 1970): 5–23.

22. 1850 and 1860 U.S. Censuses, via Steven Manson, Jonathan Schroeder, David Van Riper, Tracy Kugler, and Steven Ruggles, *IPUMS National Historical Geographic Information System: Version 15.0* [dataset] (Minneapolis, Minn.: IPUMS, 2020), https://www.nhgis.org/ (hereafter cited as *IPUMS NHGIS*, 2020).

23. 1850 U.S. Federal Census--Agriculture Schedule, Union, South Carolina, Archive Collection Number AD260, roll 2, p. 735, line 22, accessed via Ancestry.com, September 26, 2019; 1850 U.S. Census, Union, South Carolina, roll M432_859, p. 2B, image 254, accessed via Ancestry.com, September 26, 2019.

24. U.S. Census Bureau, Eighth Census of the United States, 1860: Agricultural Schedule, Union County, South Carolina, accessed via Ancestry.com, September 26, 2019.

25. 1860 U.S. Federal Census—Agriculture Schedules; Daniel Bell, "Interpretive Booklets for Local Historic Sites: Rose Hill State Park, Union, South Carolina as a Model" (MA thesis, University of South Carolina, 1983), 101.

26. 1850 U.S. Census, via *IPUM NHGIS*, 2020.

27. Stoll, *Larding the Lean Earth*, 128.

28. Wright, *Old South, New South.* For a similar discussion of the relationship of labor and environmental change, see James C. Giesen, "'The Truth About the Boll Weevil': The Nature of Planter Power in the Mississippi Delta," *Environmental History* 14, no. 4 (2009): 683–704.

29. 1860 U.S. Federal Census, Union, South Carolina, roll M653_1227, p. 189, accessed via Ancestry.com, September 26, 2019; Bell, "Interpretive Booklets," 100.

30. 1850 U.S. Federal Census--Slave Schedules, accessed via Ancestry.com, September 26, 2019; 1860 U.S. Federal Census--Slave Schedules, accessed via Ancestry.com, September 26, 2019.

31. In addition to the environmental history work about soil depletion cited above, some of which has direct repercussions for the history of slavery, the field has made other inroads. See in particular Mauldin, *Unredeemed Land*; David Silkenat,

Scars on the Land: An Environmental History of Slavery in the American South (New York: Oxford University Press, 2022); Glave, *Rooted in the Earth*; Mark Fiege, *The Republic of Nature: An Environmental History of the United States* (Seattle: University of Washington Press, 2012). As Mark D. Hersey has convincingly portrayed, the impact of environmental history on influential mainstream histories of the institution is frustratingly shallow. See Mark D. Hersey, "Slavery and the Landscape of a Dismal Empire," *Ohio Valley History* 13 (Winter 2013): 77–82.

32. Mart A. Stewart, *"What Nature Suffers to Groe": Life, Labor, and Landscape on the Georgia Coast, 1680–1920* (Athens: University of Georgia Press, 1996).

33. "Stories from Ex-Slaves," in *Born in Slavery: Slave Narratives from the Federal Writers' Project, 1936–1938, South Carolina Narratives*, vol. 14, pt. 4 (Washington, D.C.: Library of Congress, American Memory Project), 113, https://memory.loc.gov/ammem/snhtml/. I first came across this interview in Caldwell Sims, ed., *Voices of the Past: Union Countians of the Civil War and Reconstruction Period Describe What It Was Like* (Union, S.C.: Union County Historical Foundation, 1979), 119. Caldwell Sims interviewed Mary Smith in Union, South Carolina, on September 14, 1937, as part of the Federal Writers' Project of the New Deal's Works Progress Administration. Historians have debated the value of these interviews, given the long time that had passed between slavery and the interviews, and many understandably discount their value. Historians have long debated the correct use of the WPA slave interviews, but with so few firsthand accounts of slavery told from the black perspective, they continue to cautiously employ them. Like any primary account that is essentially hearsay, this narrative of Jack's escape most likely contains some errors and embellishments. See C. Vann Woodward, "History from Slave Sources," *American Historical Review* 79 (1974): 470–81; David Thomas Bailey, "A Divided Prism: Two Sources on Black Testimony on Slavery," *Journal of Southern History* 46 (1980): 381–404; Donna J. Spindel, "Assessing Memory: Twentieth-Century Slave Narratives Reconsidered," *Journal of Interdisciplinary History* 27 (1996): 247–61; John W. Blassingame, "Using the Testimony of Ex-Slaves: Approaches and Problems," *Journal of Southern History* 41, no. 4 (1971): 473–92.

34. Indeed, the word "cave" described many different kinds of geomorphologies in the nineteenth century. Most uses of the word in this context invoke the fuller term "cave in" or "cavern," implying land that had recently opened.

35. "Stories from Ex-slaves," 113.

36. "Stories from Ex-slaves," 113.

37. "Stories from Ex-slaves," 113; Rebecca Ginsburg, "Freedom and the Slave Landscape," *Landscape Journal* 26, no. 1 (2007): 36–44; Loren Schweninger and John Hope Franklin, *Runaway Slaves: Rebels on the Plantation* (New York: Oxford University Press, 2000), 100–103.

38. Message No. 1 of Governor William Henry Gist, November 27, 1860, *Senate Journal,* 1860, 14, as quoted in Bell, "Interpretive Booklets," 74.

39. Message No. 1 of Governor Gist, 15.

40. The census estimated his landholdings alone to be worth $800,000. 1860 U.S. Federal Census—Agriculture Schedules.

41. Hammond quoted in Steven A. Channing, *Crisis of Fear: Secession in South Carolina* (New York: Simon & Schuster, 1974), 217, italics added.

42. *Mississippi Free Trader* (Natchez), February 11, 1861, 2.

43. *An Address Setting Forth the Declaration of the Immediate Causes Which Induce and Justify the Secession of Mississippi from the Federal Union and the Ordinance of Secession* (Jackson: Mississippi Book & Job Printing Office, 1861), 5. For Mississippi's secession decree, see "An Ordinance to Dissolve the Union Between the State of Mississippi and Other States United with Her Under the Compact Entitled 'The Constitution of the United States of America,'" January 9, 1861, RG-1, series 475, box 31, State Government Records, Mississippi Department of Archives and History, Jackson.

44. White Southerners had long equated race and heat. As Jason L. Hauser explains, slavery became naturalized by decades of "scientific" thinking and arguments made in the South and around the globe that centered on weather and what the Southern soil could provide as a result. Southerners' "climate," he writes, "not their institution—was peculiar. Peculiar enough, in fact, to split the Union." Jason L. Hauser, "By Degree: A History of Heat in the Subtropical American South" (PhD diss., Mississippi State University, 2017), 185–86, passim.

45. Gist quoted in Bell, "Interpretive Booklets," 127.

46. Lisa Brady, *War upon the Land: Military Strategy and the Transformation of Southern Landscapes During the American Civil War* (Athens: University of Georgia Press, 2012); Judkin Browning and Timothy Silver, *An Environmental History of the Civil War* (Chapel Hill: University of North Carolina Press, 2020).

47. Mauldin, *Unredeemed Land.*

48. Drew Gilpin Faust, *The Creation of Confederate Nationalism: Ideology and Identity in the Civil War South* (Baton Rouge and London: Louisiana State University Press, 1988), 44.

49. Faust, *Creation of Confederate Nationalism*, 44, quotation on 57.

50. Bell, "Interpretive Booklets," 129–30.

51. David Blight, *Race and Reunion: The Civil War in American Memory* (Cambridge, Mass.: Harvard University Press, 2001), 66. Cotton burned across the state at the end of the war. See Megan Kate Nelson, *Ruin Nation: Destruction and the American Civil War* (Athens: University of Georgia Press, 2012), 47, 54.

52. Bell, "Interpretive Booklets," 131–32.

53. *1860 U.S. Census of Agriculture*; Bell, "Interpretive Booklets," 133; Al Hester, "D'Arcy P. Duncan: The 'Wide-Awake Farmer' of Gist's Maverick Tract," unpublished personal research notes, January 11, 2016, in possession of the author.

54. *Newberry (S.C.) Weekly Herald*, October 7, 1874, 2. Some accounts list the cause of death as appendicitis, but Bell calls this diagnosis "apocryphal." Bell, "Interpretive Booklets," 83.

55. *Anderson (S.C.) Intelligencer*, October 15, 1874, 1.

56. "Executrix Sale," *Union Times*, April 26, 1878, 3.

Chapter Three. Freedom on a Broken Land

1. *Testimony Taken by the Joint Select Committee to Inquire into the Condition of Affairs in the Late Insurrectionary States, South Carolina* (Washington, D.C.: Government Printing Office, 1872), 1173–77; Eric Foner, *Reconstruction: America's Unfinished Revolution, 1863–1877* (New York: Harper & Row, 2001), 430–31. See also Kidada E. Williams, *They Left Great Marks on Me: African American Testimonies of Racial Violence from Emancipation to World War I* (New York: New York University Press, 2012); Isabelle Harris, "To Inquire into the Conditions of Affairs in the Late Insurrectionary States: An Institutional History of Congress's 1871 Investigation of Post–Civil War Violence" (undergraduate senior thesis, Columbia University, April 17, 2020).

2. *Testimony Taken by the Joint Select Committee*, 1173–77.

3. *Testimony Taken by the Joint Select Committee*, 1003.

4. *Testimony Taken by the Joint Select Committee*, 1173–77.

5. *Testimony Taken by the Joint Select Committee*, 1128–38; Allan D. Charles, *The Narrative History of Union County, South Carolina* (Spartanburg, S.C.: Reprint Company, 1987), 235; Foner, *Reconstruction*, 431. All of the Vanlew family members are identified as "Vanlue" in the testimony.

6. *Testimony Taken by the Joint Select Committee*, 1613–14.

7. *New York Daily Herald*, December 7, 1871, 3; Harris, "To Inquire," 40.

8. *Testimony Taken by the Joint Select Committee*, 1041.

9. Beckert, *Empire of Cotton*, chap. 10.

10. Bruce quoted in Beckert, *Empire of Cotton*, 270.

11. Beckert, *Empire of Cotton*, 278.

12. David A. Latzko, "Mapping the Short-Run Impact of the Civil War and Emancipation on the South Carolina Economy," *South Carolina Historical Magazine* 116, no. 4 (October 2015): 261.

13. *Unionville Times*, August 17, 1866, as quoted in Charles, *Narrative History of Union County*, 221.

14. For discussion of erosion before the Civil War, see Paul S. Sutter, *Let Us Now Praise Famous Gullies: Providence Canyon and the Soils of the South* (Athens: University of Georgia Press, 2015); Erin Stewart Mauldin, *Unredeemed Land: An Environmental History of Civil War and Emancipation in the Cotton South* (New York: Oxford University Press, 2018).

15. For the postwar transition to sharecropping, see Edward L. Ayers, *Promise of the New South: Life After Reconstruction* (New York: Oxford University Press, 1992); Pete Daniel, *Breaking the Land: The Transformation of Cotton, Tobacco, and Rice Cultures Since 1880* (Urbana: University of Illinois Press, 1985); Mauldin, *Unredeemed Land*; Roger Ransom and Richard Sutch, *One Kind of Freedom: The Economic Consequences of Emancipation*, reprint ed. (New York: Cambridge University Press, 2010); Gavin Wright, *Old South, New South: Revolutions in the Southern Economy since the Civil War* (Baton Rouge: Louisiana State University Press, 1986).

16. Latzko, "Mapping," 265.

17. Latzko, "Mapping," 268.

18. Michael R. Coughlan, Donald R. Nelson, Michael Lonneman, and Ashley E. Block, "Historical Land Use Dynamics in the Highly Degraded Landscape of the Calhoun Critical Zone Observatory," *Land* 6, no. 2 (2017): 32.

19. Al Hester, "D'Arcy P. Duncan: The 'Wide-Awake Farmer' of Gist's Maverick Tract," unpublished personal research notes, January 11, 2016, in possession of the author.

20. See table 1.

21. Mauldin, *Unredeemed Land*, 127.

22. "Management of Soils," *Union Times*, March 18, 1887, 4.

23. Mauldin, *Unredeemed Land*; Sutter, *Let Us Now Praise Famous Gullies*.

24. Sutter, *Let Us Now Praise Famous Gullies*, 112.

25. W. W. Ashe, "The Waste from Soil Erosion in the South," *Yorkville (S.C.) Enquirer*, April 27, 1909.

26. For a complete discussion of the gullying of southeastern soils, see Sutter, *Let Us Now Praise Famous Gullies*; H. A. Ireland, C. F. S. Sharpe, and D. H. Eargle, "Principles of Gully Erosion in the Piedmont of South Carolina," *U.S. Department of Agriculture Technical Bulletin* no. 633 (January 1939).

27. The bulletin was printed in at least two papers. See "How Farms Lose Fertility," *The State* (Columbia, S.C.), February 13, 1913, 7; "How Farms Lose Their Fertility," *The Watchman and Southron* (Sumter, S.C.), March 1, 1913.

28. "Soil Survey of Union County," *Union (S.C.) Times*, October 23, 1914, 1.

29. Anne E. Marshall, "Mildred Lewis Rutherford (1851–1928)," *New Georgia Encyclopedia*, accessed July 29, 2021; Karen L. Cox, *Dixie's Daughters: The United Daughters of the Confederacy and the Preservation of Confederate Culture* (Gainesville:

University Press of Florida, 2019); Elizabeth Gillespie McRae, *Mothers of Massive Resistance: White Women and the Politics of White Supremacy* (New York: Oxford University Press, 2018), 41–52; David W. Blight, *Race and Reunion: The Civil War in American Memory* (Cambridge, Mass.: Harvard University Press, 2001); Caroline E. Janney, *Remembering the Civil War: Reunion and the Limits of Reconciliation* (Chapel Hill: University of North Carolina Press, 2013).

30. Mildred L. Rutherford, *King Cotton: The True History of Cotton and the Cotton Gin* (Athens, Ga., 1922), 20.

31. Rutherford, *King Cotton*, 21.

32. Rutherford, *King Cotton*, 20.

33. Sarah H. Case, "The Historical Ideology of Mildred Lewis Rutherford: A Confederate Historian's New South Creed," *Journal of Southern History* 68, no. 3 (August 2002): 608. On the influence of textbooks, see Fred Arthur Bailey, "The Textbooks of the 'Lost Cause': Censorship and the Creation of Southern State Histories," *Georgia Historical Quarterly* 75, no. 3 (Fall 1991): 507–33.

34. E. T. H. Shaffer, "The Negro Migration—A New South," *Atlantic Monthly*, September 1923, 403–9.

35. Herbert J. Seligmann to Editor of the *Atlantic Monthly*, October 2, 1923, in Scrapbook, E. T. H. Shaffer Papers, South Caroliniana Library, Columbia, South Carolina.

36. The author assumes that Shaffer's visit was in 1936, though he makes no mention of the precise timing. Considering his description of the land and timing of the book publication, that date makes the most sense.

37. Edward Terry Hendrie Shaffer, *Carolina Gardens: The History, Romance and Tradition of Many Gardens of Two States Through More Than Two Centuries* (Chapel Hill: University of North Carolina Press, 1939), 16.

38. Shaffer, *Carolina Gardens*. Quotations are from unknown source quoted in "Edward Terry Hendrie Shaffer Papers, 1900–1963," Manuscript Guide, South Caroliniana Library.

39. E. T. H. Shaffer, "Plantation Masters," *South Atlantic Quarterly* 37, no. 4 (October 1938): 418.

40. Shaffer, *Carolina Gardens*, 246–49.

41. Shaffer, *Carolina Gardens*, 249–50.

42. Shaffer, *Carolina Gardens*, 250–53.

43. Shaffer, *Carolina Gardens*, 250–51.

44. Shaffer, *Carolina Gardens*, 253.

45. Shaffer, *Carolina Gardens*, 250–53.

46. Shaffer, *Carolina Gardens*, 251–53.

47. Shaffer, *Carolina Gardens*, 252. By the time Shaffer visited Rose Hill, the mansion had so lost its place in South Carolinians' consciousness that it did not

even appear in Harriette Kershaw Leiding's well-circulated *Historic Houses of South Carolina* (Philadelphia: J. B. Lippincott, 1921; repr., Spartanburg, S.C.: Reprint Company, 1975).

48. Shaffer, *Carolina Gardens*, 251–53.

49. Sallie Mae Jeter Vinson and Elizabeth Jeter Jones oral history interview by Al Hester, September 25, 2018, Rose Hill Plantation State Historic Site Oral History Project, transcript in possession of author.

50. Shaffer, *Carolina Gardens*, 253.

Chapter Four. Planting the Lost Cause

1. Paul S. Sutter, *Let Us Now Praise Famous Gullies: Providence Canyon and the Soils of the South* (Athens: University of Georgia Press, 2015), 195.

2. Allan D. Charles, *The Narrative History of Union County, South Carolina* (Spartanburg, S.C.: Reprint Company, 1987), 437.

3. Neil M. Maher, "A New Deal Body Politic: Landscape, Labor, and the Civilian Conservation Corps," *Environmental History* 7, no. 3 (July 2002): 437.

4. Charles, *Narrative History of Union County*, 438.

5. Kevin Michael Allen, "Showplace: The Early Interpretation of Rose Hill Plantation, 1943–1960" (typescript, 1999), 7, in C. B. Schulz Manuscript Collection, South Caroliniana Library, University of South Carolina, Columbia; Daniel Bell, "Interpretive Booklets for Local Historic Sites: Rose Hill State Park, Union, South Carolina as a Model" (MA thesis, University of South Carolina, 1983), 8.

6. Al Hester, "The Sumter National Forest and Social Welfare" (MA thesis, University of South Carolina, 1999), 33, 31; see also A. E. Curry, "Emancipation and Erosion: Tenant Farming, Share-Cropping and Soil Erosion on the South Carolina Piedmont, 1860–1925" (MA thesis, Millersville University of Pennsylvania, 2010), 112.

7. Michael R. Coughlan, Donald R. Nelson, Michael Lonneman, and Ashley E. Block, "Historical Land Use Dynamics in the Highly Degraded Landscape of the Calhoun Critical Zone Observatory," *Land* 6, no. 2 (2017): 32.

8. Coughlan et al. "Historical Land Use Dynamics," 32.

9. Zachary S. Brecheisen, Daniel D. Richter, Seulgi Moon, and Patrick N. Halpin, "Quantitative Analysis of Hillshed Geomorphology and Critical Zone Function: Raising the Hillshed to Watershed Status," *Geological Society of America Bulletin*, December 17, 2021, 6.

10. Allen, "Showplace," 5–6.

11. F. A. Silcox to Ellison Smith, March 4, 1939, in South Carolina Parks, Recreation, and Tourism Research Files, Columbia, South Carolina, as quoted in Allen,

"Showplace," 6. Allen attributes Silcox's motivation for writing such a pointed, terse letter to "Yankee arrogance" (6).

12. Allen, "Showplace," 1, 5–7.

13. Elizabeth M. Combs, "Peace Now Resides at Rose Hill—The Home of Secession Governor Gist," *South Carolina Magazine*, December 1968, 17; clipping from *The State* (Columbia, S.C.), September 26, 1948, in folder 5, William Henry Gist Papers, South Caroliniana Library, University of South Carolina, Columbia.

14. "Garden Club at Rose Hill," *Greenville (S.C.) News*, October 20, 1948, 15; "Rose Hill Open to the Public," *The State* (Columbia, S.C.), September 26, 1948, clipping in folder 5, William Henry Gist Papers.

15. Allen, "Showplace," 13–14, 16. One history of the house says that the caretaker in this time was "Aunt Salina Giles" and does not mention Browning. See William Rice Feaster, *History of Union County, South Carolina* (Union, S.C.: Union County Historical Foundation, 1977), 94.

16. Allen, "Showplace," 17; Feaster, *History of Union County*, 94.

17. Feaster, *History of Union County*, 95–96; Bell, "Interpretive Booklets," 78.

18. Bell, "Interpretive Booklets," 54.

19. Combs, "Peace Now Resides at Rose Hill," 17.

20. Feaster, *History of Union County*, 93.

21. South Carolina advertisement, *Woman's Day*, February 1963, 102B. See also South Carolina advertisement, *Woman's Day*, January 1963, 79. It is possible that the Rose Hill mentioned in these advertisements is one of two other restored antebellum mansions of the same name in the Palmetto State. However, Gist's Rose Hill was the only publicly held of the Rose Hills at the time, thus making the state interested in attracting more visitors. Italics added.

22. United States Census Bureau, *1974 Census of Agriculture: Vol. 1, State and County Data* (Washington, D.C.: Government Printing Office, 1974).

Chapter Five. The Limits of Reconciliation and Recovery

1. These details are put together from the author's visits to the site as well as dated photographs. Photos of cemetery in the early 2000s on the Historical Marker Database website, https://www.hmdb.org/m.asp?m=13468, accessed January 13, 2023; Ruth Boughman Bunsed obituary, https://www.findagrave.com/memorial/16131834/ruth-burnsed, accessed January 13, 2023.

2. Everett Leigh photographs of Rose Hill taken in 2014; Al Hester to Daniel Richter, email, February 15, 2018, in possession of author.

3. U.S. Forest Service, Sumter National Forest, Enoree Ranger District, South Carolina, 1999 (map).

4. As tourist scholars have argued, even those parts that are not specifically designed to invoke Confederate imagery are often overwhelmingly "white spaces." William O'Brien argues that "in the South both scenic landscape preservation and design and the provision of recreational resources were enlisted also as tools for delineating and enforcing the values of Jim Crow. Park boundaries, gates, roads, and other features inscribed physical indications of who was entitled to enjoy the scenery and accommodations and who was to be excluded; of who was to be allocated more recreational space, and who would get less—or nothing at all." See William O'Brien, *Landscapes of Exclusion: State Parks and Jim Crow in the American South* (Amherst: University of Massachusetts Press, 2016), 16. See also William D. Bryan, *The Price of Permanence: Nature and Business in the New South* (Athens: University of Georgia Press, 2018), 73.

5. Several important explorations of plantations as sites of public memory and history have been published since 2000. These include David L. Butler, "Whitewashing Plantations: The Commodification of a Slave-Free Antebellum South," *International Journal of Hospitality and Tourism Administration* 2, nos. 3–4 (2008): 163–75; Stephen Small and Jennifer L. Eichstedt, *Representations of Slavery: Race and Ideology in Southern Plantation Museums* (Washington, D.C.: Smithsonian Books, 2002); Jessica Adams, *Wounds of Returning: Race, Memory, and Property on the Post-Slavery Plantation* (Chapel Hill: University of North Carolina Press, 2007); Richard H. Schein, ed., *Landscape and Race in the United States* (New York: Routledge, 2006); Jessica K. Rapson, "Refining Memory: Sugar, Oil and Plantation Tourism on Louisiana's River Road," *Memory Studies* 13, no. 4 (2018): 752–66; Gregory Clark, *Rhetorical Landscapes in America: Variations on a Theme from Kenneth Burke* (Columbia: University of South Carolina Press, 2004).

6. The question of seeing and moving through spaces like museums is one many scholars have grappled with, and again here there is scholarship germane to understanding how the environment mitigated Rose Hill's presentation of history. The French philosopher Henri Lefebvre pioneered an academic understanding of "spatial works" that is useful. He argued that monuments and houses should be understood not as texts but as "textures" that "constitute the strong points, nexuses, or anchors" of a web of significant interactions. Henri Lefebvre, *The Social Production of Space*, trans. Donald Nicholson-Smith (Oxford: Blackwell, 1991), 222, as quoted in Greg Dickinson, Brian L. Ott, and Eric Aoki, "Spaces of Remembering and Forgetting: The Reverent Eye/I at the Plains Indian Museum," *Communication and Critical/Cultural Studies* 3, no. 1 (March 2006): 44n25. A visitor's relationship with the mansion and its grounds was not confined to an interaction with physical structure but with a "shifting hierarchy" of other sensory and intellectual inputs. As Dickinson et al. point out, "The experience of museums

and memorials does not begin at their entrances." These sites "engage visitors . . . on a material level by locating visitors' bodies in particular spaces" ("Spaces of Remembering and Forgetting," 29).

This is perhaps an obvious point, but sites of public memory like Rose Hill sit within natural landscapes that are usually not considered part of the memory experience. Communication scholars have written about the "experiential landscapes" around museums, though the work is rarely about the specific natural environment of the site. Dickinson et al., for example, have written about the effect of nationalistic ideas about the landscape of the American West on a visitor's understanding of the Plains Indian Museum; other scholars have examined the Birmingham, Alabama, Civil Rights Museum's urban siting. For examples of studies of Southern museums and sites that demonstrate unintended interpretations, see Victoria J. Gallagher, "Memory and Reconciliation in the Birmingham Civil Rights Institute," *Rhetoric and Public Affairs* 2, no. 2 (1999): 303–20.

7. Ashley Carse, "'Like a Work of Nature': Revisiting the Panama Canal's Environmental History at Gatun Lake," *Environmental History* 21 (April 2016): 231–39.

8. Kenneth E. Foote, *Shadowed Ground: America's Landscapes of Violence and Tragedy* (Austin: University of Texas Press, 1997), 176–78. There is also scholarship that embraces how material decay—the falling down of a house, or a rotting farm implement sitting in a field, for example—can change visitors' interactions with a space or item and affect how a site contains and reflects memories as the decline happens. However, there is little about how ecological transition like at Rose Hill hid the human imprint and thereby lost the memories that it contained. The work that gets closest to what I'm describing here is Caitlin DeSilvey, *Curated Decay: Heritage Beyond Saving* (Minneapolis: University of Minnesota Press, 2017).

9. Dickinson et al. describe how "experiential landscapes" like state parks are designed to "direct particular ways of looking" ("Spaces of Remembering and Forgetting," 30).

10. Jennifer Price, review of *Landscape and Memory*, by Simon Schama, *Environmental History* 1, no. 4 (October 1996): 77.

11. Paul S. Sutter, *Let Us Now Praise Famous Gullies: Providence Canyon and the Soils of the South* (Athens: University of Georgia Press, 2015), 192.

12. Allan D. Charles, *The Narrative History of Union County, South Carolina* (Spartanburg, S.C.: Reprint Company, 1987), 438.

13. Thomas D. Clark, *The Greening of the South: The Recovery of Land and Forest* (Lexington: University of Kentucky Press, 1984), 10.

14. Wikipedia, "Sumter National Forest," *last modified June 28, 2025*, https://en.wikipedia.org/wiki/Sumter_National_Forest.

15. Daniel D. Richter and Sharon A. Billings, "Ansichten der Calzone: Views from the Calhoun Critical Zone Observatory," in *Critical Zones: The Science and Politics of Landing on Earth*, ed. Bruno Latour and Peter Weibel (Cambridge, Mass.: MIT Press, 2020), 140.

16. Louis J. Metz, "The Calhoun Experimental Forest," United States Forest Service, June 1958, 1–8; Richter and Billings, "Ansichten der Calzone," 3.

17. There have been dozens of major publications from the Calhoun Critical Zone Observatory in addition to those cited in this book. For a full list, see Critical Zone Network website at criticalzone.org.

18. Daniel D. Richter, Allan R. Bacon, Sharon A. Billings, Dan Binkley, Marilyn Buford, Mac Callaham et al., "Evolution of Soil, Ecosystem, and Critical Zone Research at the USDA FS Calhoun Experimental Forest: Past, Present, and Future," *Soil Science Society of America Journal* 81, no. 5 (2017): 406; Michael R. Coughlan, Donald R. Nelson, Michael Lonneman, and Ashley E. Block, "Historical Dynamics of Land Use Transition in the Highly Degraded Landscape of the Calhoun Critical Zone Observatory," *Land* 6, no. 2 (May 2017): 32.

19. Critical zone science is the study of the layer of earth from bedrock to atmosphere, including "integrated studies of water with soil, rock, air, and biotic resources in the near-surface terrestrial environment." In the United States, critical zone scientists are drawn from backgrounds in ecology, hydrology, geology, biogeochemistry, and a host of related disciplines. The Calhoun Critical Zone Observatory includes the area of present-day Rose Hill State Park. H. Lin, "Earth's Critical Zone and Hydropedology: Concepts, Characteristics, and Advances," *Hydrology and Earth System Sciences* 14 (2010): 25–45; Daniel D. Richter, Allan R. Bacon, Sharon A. Billings, Dan Binkley, Marilyn Buford, Mac Callaham et al., "Evolution of Soil, Ecosystem, and Critical Zone Research at the USDA FS Calhoun Experimental Forest," in *USDA Forest Service Experimental Forests and Ranges: Research for the Long Term*, ed. Deborah C. Hayes, Susan L. Stout, Ralph H. Crawford, and Anne P. Hoover (New York: Springer, 2014), 428.

20. Daniel D. Richter, "Past Critique but Much Praise for Restoration Ecology: Four Decades On," *Restoration Ecology* 31, no. 4 (2023): 2. On Odum, see also Albert G. Way, *Conserving Southern Longleaf: Herbert Stoddard and the Rise of Ecological Land Management* (Athens: University of Georgia Press, 2011), 210–11.

21. Richter, "Past Critique," 2.

22. E. Barstow, director, and Daniel D. Richter, co-producer, *The Education of Bruno Latour: On the Anthropocene*, video (Durham, N.C.: Franklin Humanities Institute at Duke University, 2015).

23. Barstow and Richter, *Education of Bruno Latour*. Historians of science and the environment have long pointed out the extent to which scientists are influenced by social factors. As Linda Nash put it, science "was not a neutral tool of analysis

that revealed an objective nature but a historical product already shot through with certain assumptions and perspectives, many of which served to further existing relations of power." Linda Nash, "Furthering the Environmental Turn," *Journal of American History* 100, no. 1 (2013): 132.

24. Union County Community Remembrance Project, https://www.unioncountycrp.com, accessed January 22, 2023.

25. The town that served as the seat of Union County was known as Unionville until sometime in the early twentieth century, when it became Union.

26. "Historical Markers Dedicated in Union County, South Carolina," Equal Justice Initiative, June 26, 2021, https://eji.org/news/historical-markers-dedicated-in-union-county-south-carolina/, accessed January 22, 2023.

27. "Historical Markers Dedicated in Union County, South Carolina."

28. Al Hester, "Learning from Failure: Agricultural Sites as Environmental Sites of Conscience," National Council on Public History's Agriculture and Public History Working Group, April 2018, https://ncph.org/phc/agriculture-and-public-history-2018-working-group/al-hester/#_ftnref1.

29. "Rose Hill Plantation: Memorial to a 'Land-Killing Past?'," https://scsps-rmi.maps.arcgis.com/apps/Cascade/index.html?appid=daf17a20dd4b4c9eb379bdcf1070ac1c, accessed January 23, 2023.

30. "Historical Markers and War Memorials in Union County, South Carolina," Historical Marker Database, https://www.hmdb.org/results.asp?Search=County&State=South%20Carolina&County=Union%20County, accessed January 24, 2023.

31. Hester, "Learning from Failure."

32. Amy E. Potter, Stephen P. Hanna, Derek H. Alderman, Perry L. Carter, Candace Forbes Bright, and David L. Butler, *Remembering Enslavement: Reassembling the Southern Plantation Museum* (Athens: University of Georgia Press, 2022), 295.

Part 2. Memphis and the Yazoo-Mississippi Delta

1. On the development of the Delta and Memphis's relationship to this cotton-centric hinterland, see James C. Cobb, *The Most Southern Place on Earth: The Mississippi Delta and the Roots of Regional Identity* (New York: Oxford University Press, 1992); Mikko Saikku, *This Delta, This Land: An Environmental History of the Yazoo-Mississippi Floodplain* (Athens: University of Georgia Press, 2011); James C. Giesen, *Boll Weevil Blues: Cotton, Myth, and Power in the American South* (Chicago: University of Chicago Press, 2011), chaps. 3–4; John C. Willis, *Forgotten Time: The Yazoo-Mississippi Delta After the Civil War* (Charlottesville: University Press of Virginia, 2000); Robert L. Brandfon, *Cotton Kingdom of the New South:*

A History of the Yazoo Mississippi Delta from Reconstruction to the Twentieth Century (Cambridge, Mass.: Harvard University Press, 1967).

2. John M. Barry, *Rising Tide: The Great Mississippi Flood of 1927 and How It Changed America* (New York: Simon & Schuster, 1997), 97.

3. David Cohn, *Where I Was Born and Raised* (New York: Houghton Mifflin, 1948), 26. Cobb also uses this quotation as the title of his introduction to *Most Southern Place on Earth*, 4, 6. The Yazoo-Mississippi Delta is not actually a river delta at all but the confluence between the two rivers. Also, geographers and Arkansans may quibble with my use of "Delta" to refer only to the Mississippi portion. The term often refers to the entire floodplain of the rivers, which includes land west of the Mississippi River in Arkansas and Louisiana. However, when I use "Delta" I refer strictly to the Yazoo-Mississippi Delta, which lies entirely in the state of Mississippi.

4. Cobb, *Most Southern Place on Earth*, 8.

5. Giesen, *Boll Weevil Blues*, 49.

6. 1860 U.S. Census, via *IPUM NHGIS*, 2020.

7. Cobb, *Most Southern Place on Earth*, chap. 1; Saikku, *This Delta, This Land*, chap. 4; Giesen, *Boll Weevil Blues*, chap. 3.

8. Giesen, *Boll Weevil Blues*, 49–54.

9. Cobb, *Most Southern Place on Earth*, 99.

10. Cobb, *Most Southern Place on Earth*, 99; Giesen, *Boll Weevil Blues*, 73–75.

11. David L. Cohn, *The Mississippi Delta and the World: The Memoirs of David L. Cohn*, ed. James C. Cobb (Baton Rouge: Louisiana State University Press, 1995), 61–63; Cohn, *Where I Was Born and Raised*, 41.

12. Cohn, *Where I Was Born and Raised*, 41.

13. Anne O'Hare McCormick, "The South: A Fabric of Cotton," *New York Times*, June 1, 1930.

14. For more on how Delta planters understood the boll weevil as a labor problem, see James C. Giesen, "'The Truth About the Boll Weevil': The Nature of Planter Power in the Mississippi Delta," *Environmental History* 14, no. 4 (2009): 683–704.

15. U.S. Censuses of 1850, 1930, 1950, via *IPUM NHGIS*, 2020.

Chapter Six. Pageantry and Power in Cotton's Metropolis

1. "Glittering Barge, Pop Tunes, Rock 'n' Roll and Cheering Thousands Open Carnival," *Memphis Commercial Appeal*, May 16, 1956, 1; "Colonel Memphis Primping for Role as Carnival Host," *Memphis Commercial Appeal*, May 13, 1956, 1.

2. "22nd Cotton Carnival Opens Tomorrow with 'Spectacular,'" *Memphis Commercial Appeal*, May 14, 1956; "Barge Docks Tonight to Open Carnival,"

Memphis Commercial Appeal, May 15, 1956, 2; "Magnificent Royal Barge, Spectacular River Show to Open Carnival Tonight," *Memphis Commercial Appeal*, May 15, 1956, 1.

3. Elvis returned to Memphis later that month to buy his first house, a one-story ranch in an all-white upper-class neighborhood less than two miles from where Mallory lived with her parents. Karal Ann Marling, "Elvis Presley's Graceland, or the Aesthetic of Rock 'n' Roll Heaven," *American Art* 7, no. 4 (Autumn 1993): 82.

4. Paul Molloy, "Teenagers Writhe, Groan as Presley Sings, Swivels," *Memphis Commercial Appeal*, May 16, 1956, 21.

5. Peter Guralnick, *Last Train to Memphis: The Rise of Elvis Presley* (Boston: Little, Brown, 1994), 277.

6. Guralnick, *Last Train to Memphis*, 277–79, quotation on 279.

7. William Cronon, *Nature's Metropolis: Chicago and the Great West* (New York: W. W. Norton, 1992).

8. Jeanne M. Whayne, "Cotton's Metropolis: Memphis and Plantation Development in the Trans-Mississippi West, 1840–1920," in *Comparing Apples, Oranges, and Cotton: Environmental Histories of the Global Plantation*, ed. Frank Uekötter (Frankfurt: Rachel Carson Center, 2014), 49–84.

9. David Cohn, *Where I Was Born and Raised* (New York: Houghton Mifflin, 1948), 12.

10. Whayne, "Cotton's Metropolis," 61.

11. John McLeod Keating and O. F. Vedder, *History of the City of Memphis and Shelby County, Tennessee: With Illustrations and Biographical Sketches of Some of Its Prominent Citizens* (Syracuse, N.Y.: D. Mason, 1888), 422.

12. John E. Harkins, *Metropolis of the American Nile*, 2nd ed. (Oxford, Miss.: Guild Bindery Press, 1991), 95.

13. Sven Beckert, *Empire of Cotton: A Global History* (New York: Alfred A. Knopf, 2014), 319.

14. James L. Watkins, *King Cotton: A Historical and Statistical Review, 1790 to 1908* (New York: James L. Watkins & Sons, 1908), 266.

15. Harkins, *Metropolis of the American Nile*, 95.

16. William D. Miller, "Rural Ideals in Memphis Life at the Turn of the Century," *West Tennessee Historical Society Papers* 4 (1950): 41.

17. Kathleen Christine Berkeley, "'Like a Plague of Locust': Immigration and Social Change in Memphis, Tennessee, 1850–1880" (PhD diss., University of California, Los Angeles, 1980), 72n65; Robert Emmett McLean, "Cotton Carnival and Cotton Makers Jubilee: Memphis Society in Black and White" (PhD diss., George Mason University, 1994).

18. Arthur A. Halle, *Authentic History and Growth of the Memphis Cotton Carnival Association* (Memphis, 1952), 5–6, 12, in Arthur A. Halle Papers, Memphis

Public Library (hereafter Halle Papers). Carnival was held in March the first year, but the following year it was permanently moved to the first week in May.

19. Halle, *Authentic History*, 7.

20. McLean, "Cotton Carnival," 39–41.

21. Beverly G. Bond and Janann Sherman, *Memphis: In Black and White* (Charleston, S.C.: Arcadia, 2003), 108–9; Cynthia Jones Sadler, "The Pageantry of Segregation: The Socio-Cultural Impact of the Cotton Makers' Jubilee," *West Tennessee Historical Society Papers* 65 (2011): 90–92.

22. Sadler, "Pageantry of Segregation," 90.

23. Sadler, "Pageantry of Segregation," 88; the "unsurpassed loveliness" part of Sadler's quotation is from "350,000 View King Cotton's 'Dream of Fair Women,'" *Memphis Commercial Appeal*, May 12, 1935.

24. Photograph, 1941, album 2, Halle Papers.

25. "The Children's Parade," undated typescript, box 2, folder 6, Halle Papers.

26. Memphis Cotton Carnival Program, 1964, box 3, folder 9, Halle Papers.

27. Halle, *Authentic History*, 7. See also D. Clayton Brown, *King Cotton in Modern America: A Cultural, Political, and Economic History Since 1945* (Oxford: University Press of Mississippi, 2011), 204.

28. McLean, "Cotton Carnival," vii.

29. Halle, *Authentic History*, 14.

30. "Carnival Boosters to Tour Mississippi," *Memphis Commercial Appeal*, May 6, 1956.

31. "Plantation Estates Tell Shelby History," *Memphis Commercial Appeal*, May 11, 1947, clipping in box 8, folder 1, Halle Papers.

32. McLean, "Cotton Carnival," 50.

33. Clark Porteous, "1948 Memphis Cotton Carnival," box 2, folder 6, Halle Papers.

34. McLean, "Cotton Carnival," 50; "Plantation Tour," album 3, Halle Papers. Photograph also appears in Sadler, "Pageantry of Segregation," 91.

35. "Visitors Get Taste of Life on Plantation," *Memphis Press Scimitar*, May 17, 1940, as quoted in McLean, "Cotton Carnival," 50; ticket, Memphis Cotton Carnival Pilgrimage, May 12–13, 1947, box 2, folder 12, Halle Papers.

36. Mrs. C. B. Outzen to Director of Memphis Cotton Carnival, n.d. [February 1960], box 2, folder 14, Halle Papers.

37. "1958 'Cotton Wonderland' Children's Parade," box 1, folder 2, Halle Papers.

38. Memphis Cotton Carnival Program, 1934, box 3, folder 1, Halle Papers.

39. See, for instance, Memphis Cotton Carnival Program, 1964, box 3, folder 9, Halle Papers.

40. Memphis Cotton Carnival Program, 1964, box 3, folder 9, Halle Papers; Roger Biles, *Memphis: In the Great Depression* (Knoxville: University of Tennessee Press, 1986), 67.

Chapter Seven. A Jubilee for Cotton Labor

1. Michael K. Honey, *Sharecropper's Troubadour: John L. Handcox, the Southern Tenant Farmers' Union, and the African American Song Tradition* (New York: Palgrave Macmillan, 2013), 42.

2. Honey, *Sharecropper's Troubadour*, 91; John L. Handcox, "King Cotton," quoted in Robert Emmett McLean, "Cotton Carnival and Cotton Makers Jubilee: Memphis Society in Black and White" (PhD diss., George Mason University, 1994), 44.

3. Cynthia Jones Sadler, "The Pageantry of Segregation: The Socio-Cultural Impact of the Cotton Makers' Jubilee," *West Tennessee Historical Society Papers* 65 (2011): 88.

4. Lewis Nolan, "Carnival, Jubilee Royalty Hobnob for First Time," *Memphis Commercial Appeal*, April 30, 1977, G5.

5. "The Cotton-Makers Jubilee Initiation and Aims," in Souvenir Program of the Memphis Cotton Makers Jubilee, 1937, in Dr. R. Q. and Ethyl H. Venson Cotton Makers' Jubilee Collection, box 1, Memphis Public Library (hereafter Venson Collection).

6. McLean, "Cotton Carnival," 50.

7. Charles L. Hughes, "'You Pay One Hell of a Price to Be Black': Rufus Thomas and the Racial Politics of Memphis Music," in *An Unseen Light: Black Struggles for Freedom in Memphis, Tennessee*, ed. Aram Goudsouzian and Charles W. McKinney Jr. (Lexington: University Press of Kentucky, 2018), 233, italics added.

8. Leviticus 25:8–38 (New Revised Standard Version).

9. *Oxford English Dictionary*, "Jubilee," online ed. (last updated December 2020). For a full accounting of the political meanings of "jubilee" in the African American community, see Bennett Parten, "Blow Ye Trumpet, Blow: The Idea of Jubilee in Slavery and Freedom," *Journal of the Civil War Era* 10, no. 3 (September 2020): 298–318.

10. Souvenir Program of the Memphis Cotton Makers Jubilee, 1938, box 1, Venson Collection.

11. "The Cotton-Makers Jubilee Initiation and Aims," in Souvenir Program of the Memphis Cotton Makers Jubilee, 1937, box 1, Venson Collection.

12. "Cotton-Makers Jubilee Initiation and Aims."

13. "The Cotton-Makers Jubilee: A Historical Sketch," in Souvenir Program of the Memphis Cotton Makers Jubilee, 1940, box 1, Venson Collection.

14. Souvenir Program of the Memphis Cotton Makers Jubilee, 1939, box 1, Venson Collection.

15. "Cotton-Makers Jubilee Initiation and Aims." Souvenir Program of the Memphis Cotton Makers Jubilee, 1937, box 1, Venson Collection.

16. Souvenir Program of the Memphis Cotton Makers Jubilee, 1941, box 1, Venson Collection. All quotations in this passage come from this program.

17. Souvenir Program of the Memphis Cotton Makers Jubilee, 1947, box 1, Venson Collection; Souvenir Program of the Memphis Cotton Makers Jubilee, 1939, box 1, Venson Collection.

18. Charley Patton, "Down the Dirt Road Blues," recorded June 14, 1929, Paramount 12854, 78 rpm.

19. Gloria Brown Melton, "Blacks in Memphis Tennessee, 1920–1955: A Historical Study" (PhD diss., Washington State University, 1982), 283n4.

20. Venson obituary, *Memphis Commercial Appeal*, August 6, 1970, 37.

21. *Nashville Banner*, May 10, 1946, 23.

22. Mention of Williams's degrees is not verified but appears in a few sources including Bernie Hayes, *The Death of Black Radio: The Story of America's Black Radio Personalities* (New York: iUniverse, 2005), 6.

23. *Nashville Banner*, May 10, 1946, 23.

24. Hughes, "'You Pay One Hell of a Price,'" 235.

25. Nat D. Williams, "Historical Resume," in Souvenir Program of the Memphis Cotton Makers Jubilee, 1949, box 1, Venson Collection.

26. "Plantation mentality" is a term at the heart of Laurie B. Green, *Battling the Plantation Mentality: Memphis and the Black Freedom Struggle* (Chapel Hill: University of North Carolina Press, 2007). The opening anecdote of Green's book describes an African American union organizer who rebuffs a factory owner for giving workers not a drinking fountain for water but "one of them country buckets I already done left in Mississippi!" (1).

27. Honey, *Southern Labor and Black Civil Rights*, 203.

28. McLean, "Cotton Carnival," 10.

29. Memphis Cotton Carnival Program, 1964, box 3, Halle Papers.

30. Sadler, "Pageantry of Segregation," 99.

31. Shirletta Jeanette Kinchen, "'We Want What People Generally Refer to as Black Power': Youth and Student Activism and the Impact of the Black Power Movement in Memphis, Tennessee, 1965–1975" (PhD diss., University of Memphis, 2011), 28–33.

32. Kinchen, "'We Want,'" 33–38.

33. Kinchen, "'We Want,'" 38; "Why Students Picket Cotton Jubilee," *Tri-State Defender*, May 14, 1960; Report of Executive Secretary, Memphis Branch of the NAACP, April 10–May 2, 1961, in box 1, folder 1, Maxine A. Smith NAACP Collection, Memphis Public Library (hereafter Smith NAACP Collection).

34. "Negroes in Memphis Assail 'King Cotton,'" *Chattanooga Times*, May 16, 1960.

35. "Why Students Picket Cotton Jubilee."

36. "NAACP Against the Jubilee," *Memphis Press-Scimitar*, May 3, 1961, 14. The chapter called for a continuation of its boycott and started a letter-writing campaign to black-owned businesses that took out advertisements in the Jubilee program. Report of Executive Secretary, Memphis Branch of the NAACP, May 3–June 6, 1961, box 1, folder 1, Smith NAACP Collection.

37. "Cotton Makers Jubilee Set for May 8 thru 12," *Memphis Press-Scimitar*, April 25 1961, 13.

38. "Cotton Makers Jubilee Set."

39. Souvenir Program of the Memphis Cotton Makers Jubilee, 1961, box 1, Venson Collection. All quotations in this passage come from this program.

40. "Opposition Fails to Spoil Jubilee Fun," *Memphis Press-Scimitar*, May 13, 1961, 3.

41. "Opposition Fails."

42. "NAACP Against the Jubilee," *Memphis Press-Scimitar*, May 3, 1961, 14; Report of Executive Secretary, Memphis Branch of the NAACP, April 10–May 2, 1961, box 1, folder 1, Smith NAACP Collection; *Memphis Commercial Appeal*, May 13, 1961.

43. Souvenir Program of the Memphis Cotton Makers Jubilee, 1963, box 1, Venson Collection.

44. Souvenir Program of the Memphis Cotton Makers Jubilee, 1966, box 1, Venson Collection; Souvenir Program of the Memphis Cotton Makers Jubilee, 1967, box 1, Venson Collection.

45. Souvenir Program of the Memphis Cotton Makers Jubilee, 1966, box 1, Venson Collection.

46. *Memphis Commercial Appeal*, October 19, 1963.

47. See John Dittmer, *Local People: The Struggle for Civil Rights in Mississippi* (Urbana: University of Illinois Press, 1995); Charles M. Payne, *I've Got the Light of Freedom: The Organizing Tradition and the Mississippi Freedom Struggle* (Berkeley: University of California Press, 2007); Françoise N. Hamlin, *Crossroads at Clarksdale: The Black Freedom Struggle in the Mississippi Delta After World War II* (Chapel Hill: University of North Carolina Press, 2012); Goudsouzian and McKinney, *Unseen Light*; Honey, *Southern Labor and Black Civil Rights.*

48. *Memphis Commercial Appeal*, April 6, 1968, 13, 17.

49. *Memphis Commercial Appeal*, April 12, 1968.

50. *Memphis Commercial Appeal*, August 10, 1968.

51. *Memphis Commercial Appeal*, September 7, 1968.

52. Souvenir Program of the Memphis Cotton Makers Jubilee, 1969, box 1, Venson Collection.

53. Souvenir Program of the Memphis Cotton Makers Jubilee, 1969, box 1, Venson Collection; Souvenir Program of the Memphis Cotton Makers Jubilee, 1970, box 1, Venson Collection.

54. McLean, "Cotton Carnival," 127.

55. McLean, "Cotton Carnival," ix, x; "Jubilee Looks Back on 40-Year History," *Memphis Press-Scimitar*, May 2, 1977, 17.

56. *Memphis Commercial Appeal*, April 30, 1977; "Jubilee Looks Back."

57. McLean, "Cotton Carnival," ix, x.

58. *Memphis Commercial Appeal*, April 30, 1977; "Jubilee Looks Back"; *Memphis Commercial Appeal*, January 21, 1998.

Chapter Eight. Pickers and Polyester on a New Delta Landscape

1. *Memphis Commercial Appeal*, May 20, 1956, section II, 8.

2. "South's Top Party Ends on Gala Note as Barge Departs," *Memphis Commercial Appeal*, May 20, 1956, 1.

3. "Oscar Carr Dies at Clarksdale," *Jackson (Miss.) Clarion-Ledger*, June 12, 1973, 2.

4. James C. Cobb, *The Most Southern Place on Earth: The Mississippi Delta and the Roots of Regional Identity* (New York: Oxford University Press, 1992), 97.

5. For the boll weevil example, see James C. Giesen, *Boll Weevil Blues: Cotton, Myth, and Power in the American South* (Chicago: University of Chicago Press, 2011).

6. Brian S. Williams, "Cotton, Chemicals, and the Political Ecologies of Racial Capital" (PhD diss., University of Georgia, 2018).

7. Walter Sillers Sr. to P. M. Burrill, December 31, 1907, folder 19A, Walter Sillers Sr. Papers, Delta State University Archives.

8. Cornelius Bostick, oral history transcript, DPLC Papers, series 16: Oral History, folder 5; R. M. (Dick) Holman, oral history transcript, series 16: Oral History, folder 27, Delta and Pine Land Company Records, Special Collections, Mississippi State University.

9. H. H. Hopson Jr., "Mechanization of a Delta Cotton Plantation as applied to Hopson Planting Company, Clarksdale, Mississippi, by the management" (October 1944), 11, in Special Collections, Mississippi State University.

10. E. A. Boeger and E. A. Goldenweiser, *A Study of the Tenant Systems of Farming in the Yazoo-Mississippi Delta*, U.S. Department of Agriculture Bulletin no. 337 (Washington, D.C.: Government Printing Office, 1916), 3; Robert L. Brandfon, *Cotton Kingdom of the New South: A History of the Yazoo-Mississippi Delta from Reconstruction to the Twentieth Century* (Cambridge, Mass.: Harvard University Press, 1967), 56.

11. Sally Palmer Thomason, *Delta Rainbow: The Irrepressible Betty Bobo Pearson* (Jackson: University Press of Mississippi, 2015), 112.

12. Oscar Clark Carr Jr., recorded interview by Dennis J. O'Brien, May 5–6, 1969, Robert F. Kennedy Oral History Project of the John F. Kennedy Library;

Ellen B. Meacham, *Delta Epiphany: Robert F. Kennedy in Mississippi* (Jackson: University Press of Mississippi, 2018); Minion K. C. Morrison, *Aaron Henry of Mississippi: Inside Agitator* (Fayetteville: University of Arkansas Press, 2015); Greta de Jong, *You Can't Eat Freedom: Southerners and Social Justice After the Civil Rights Movement* (Chapel Hill: University of North Carolina Press, 2016), 61.

13. Donald Holley, *The Second Great Emancipation: The Mechanical Cotton Picker, Black Migration and How They Shaped the Modern South* (Fayetteville: University of Arkansas Press, 2000), 52–53.

14. Gerard Helferich, *High Cotton: Four Seasons in the Mississippi Delta* (Berkeley, Calif.: Counterpoint, 2008), 174 (both quotations). Historians and economists have written a great deal about the causes and effects of the African American exodus from Southern cotton farms in this period. Many point to the arrival of the mechanical cotton harvester as the most important factor to push laborers out of the fields. Others have argued that the machine merely picked up the slack created by workers who had already left, pulled to industrial jobs in Southern and Northern cities. Like much econometric scholarship, these studies are effective at tracing the relationship between economic value and other hard numbers like crop price, population, and wages. They have a more difficult time tracing the causes and effects that reside in human hearts and brains. Indeed, much of this work ignores or diminishes the voices of those who moved or stayed behind. However, the historical record is full of people saying exactly why they left, or why they stayed, or why they were glad that others were gone. The unsatisfying but certainly true explanation is that there were as many reasons for leaving or staying as there were people making those decisions. And there were certainly enough reasons to leave Mississippi in the mid-twentieth century.

15. Holley, *Second Great Emancipation*, 94.

16. Hopson, "Mechanization."

17. Holley, *Second Great Emancipation*, 102–3.

18. Charles Patrick Joseph Mooney, *The Mid-South and Its Builders: Being the Story of the Development and a Forecast of the Future of the Richest Agricultural Region in the World* (Memphis: Mid-South Biographic and Historical Association, 1920), 385.

19. Hopson, "Mechanization," 4, 6.

20. Hopson, "Mechanization," 9. For more of the Hopson Brothers' self-promotion of their modernization, see Earl Lamm, "4000-Acre Hopson Plantation Viewed as Ideal Mechanized Setup," *National Petroleum News* 37, no. 22 (May 30, 1945): 26–34.

21. de Jong, *You Can't Eat Freedom*, 2.

22. Holley, *Second Great Emancipation*, 190.

23. Holley, *Second Great Emancipation*, 150.

24. James R. Supak, Carl G. Anderson, and William D. Maxfield, "Trends in Cotton Production: History, Culture, Mechanization and Economics," in *Weeds of Cotton: Characterization and Control* (Memphis: Cotton Foundation, 1992), 30–31.

25. Vann R. Newkirk II, "The Great Land Robbery," *Atlantic*, September 2019; Pete Daniel, *Dispossession: Discrimination Against African American Farmers in the Age of Civil Rights* (Chapel Hill: University of North Carolina Press, 2013); de Jong, *You Can't Eat Freedom*.

26. "King Oscar Urges All Out Promotion," *Memphis Commercial Appeal*, May 20, 1956.

27. "King Oscar Urges All Out Promotion"; Francoise Nicole Hamlin, *Crossroads at Clarksdale: The Black Freedom Struggle in the Mississippi Delta After World War II* (Chapel Hill: University of North Carolina Press, 2012), 215.

28. "King Oscar Urges All Out Promotion."

29. Advertisement, *Memphis Commercial Appeal*, May 20, 1956, 15; Goldsmiths advertisement, *Memphis Commercial Appeal*, May 19, 1956, 19.

30. David L. Cohn, *The Life and Times of King Cotton* (Boston: Houghton Mifflin, 1956), 265.

31. Cohn, *Life and Times*, 264.

32. Industrial uses made up 25 percent and exports accounted for 7 percent of U.S. cotton use that year. Maurice R. Cooper and Frank Lowenstein, "Cotton," *1954 USDA Yearbook of Agriculture* (Washington, D.C.: Government Printing Office, 1954), 446–53.

33. Timothy Curtis Jacobson and George David Smith, *Cotton's Renaissance: A Study in Market Innovation* (New York: Cambridge University Press, 2001), 122.

34. "King Oscar Urges All Out Promotion."

35. Charter of Incorporation and By-Laws of the National Cotton Council of America, n.d., and Minutes, National Cotton Council of America, First Annual Meeting, January 24, 1939, Cully Cobb/Ruralist Press Papers, box 11, Special Collections, Mississippi State University.

36. Cooper and Lowenstein, "Cotton," 453.

37. Walter M. Scott, "What Cotton Has; What It Needs," *1950–51 USDA Yearbook of Agriculture* (Washington, D.C.: Government Printing Office, 1950), 387.

38. "Local Grandmother Wins Sewing Contest at Fair," *Times* (Shreveport, La.), October 25, 1956, 20.

39. Jacobson and Smith, *Cotton's Renaissance*, 114, 121.

40. Karen Ruoff Kramer, "Jeans," *Historical Materialism* 14, no. 4 (2006): 289–94.

41. For a fascinating and convincing argument about gender, power, and dress in the civil rights movement, see Tanisha C. Ford, "SNCC Women, Denim, and the

Politics of Dress," *Journal of Southern History* 79, no. 3 (August 2013): 625–58. See also C. Regan, "Role of Denim and Jeans in the Fashion Industry," in *Denim: Manufacture, Finishing and Applications*, ed. Roshan Paul (Amsterdam: Textile Institute, 2015), 191–217.

42. Scott, "What Cotton Has," 387.

43. Jacobson and Smith, *Cotton's Renaissance*, 123, 124.

Chapter Nine. The Fabric of Our Lives

1. Timothy Curtis Jacobson and George David Smith, *Cotton's Renaissance: A Study in Market Innovation* (New York: Cambridge University Press, 2001), 123–27.

2. Albert R. Russell, *The First 40 Years: The National Cotton Council, 1939–1979* (Memphis: National Cotton Council), 78.

3. Jacobson and Smith, *Cotton's Renaissance*, 129.

4. The last-minute compromise that convinced many holdouts to vote for the new plan was that it allowed for growers to take back their contributions after the fact if they chose to. This would become a significant lever for cotton farmers to fight against the NCC and CPI in the decades to come. Jacobson and Smith, *Cotton's Renaissance*, 132–37.

5. "Cotton Leaders Told of Research, Future Plans," *Jackson (Miss.) Clarion-Ledger*, September 3, 1970, 6; *Bridgeport (Conn.) Post*, July 14, 1968, 15; *Hartford Courant*, July 15, 1968, 14.

6. *Bridgeport (Conn.) Post*, November 23, 1969, 46, January 11, 1970, 27.

7. Jacobson and Smith, *Cotton's Renaissance*, 147.

8. *Memphis Commercial Appeal*, May 13, 1970, 32.

9. *San Angelo (Tex.) Standard-Times*, May 16, 1970, 6.

10. Jacobson and Smith, *Cotton's Renaissance*, 149.

11. Quotations from "Cotton Leaders Told of Research"; see also "State Cotton Men Get Report on Dollar-a-Bale Promotion," *Kosciusko (Miss.) Star-Herald*, September 3, 1970, 33.

12. Jacobson and Smith, *Cotton's Renaissance*, 151.

13. Martha Angle and Robert Walters, "Cotton's King: Why Is J. Dukes Wooters Subsidized?" *Twin Falls* (Id.) *Times-News*, November 24, 1978, 4.

14. Jacobson and Smith, *Cotton's Renaissance*, 154.

15. Barney DuBois, "Plain Talk, Fast Action Prod Cotton," *Memphis Commercial Appeal*, October 6, 1970.

16. Jacobson and Smith, *Cotton's Renaissance*, 155–56.

17. Jacobson and Smith, *Cotton's Renaissance*, 154.

18. Jacobson and Smith, *Cotton's Renaissance*, 162–63.

19. I owe an anonymous reader of a draft of this manuscript for the term "biologically nonsensical."

20. Cotton Incorporated, "New Cotton Symbol Identification Manual," n.d., box 2, "Cotton Incorporated" Folder, George Mullendore Collection, Special Collections, Mississippi State University (hereafter Mullendore Collection). All quotations in this passage are from this document.

21. "Wives Aid Efforts to Keep King Cotton on His Throne," *Memphis Commercial Appeal*, February 1, 1951, 3.

22. Stuart Elliott, "Promoting Cotton as a Piece of the Nation's Social Fabric," *New York Times*, July 21, 1992, 47; Jacobson and Smith, *Cotton's Renaissance*, 176.

23. "This Is Cotton Incorporated" (n.d.), in box 2, Mullendore Collection; Jacobson and Smith, *Cotton's Renaissance*, 176, 178.

24. Untitled transcript of slide show about Cotton Incorporated (June 1976), 8–9, box 2, "Cotton Incorporated" Folder, Mullendore Collection.

25. Cotton Incorporated History Timeline, https://www.cottoninc.com/about-cotton/history/company-timeline/, accessed September 2022; Jeffrey P. Silberman, "Building a 21st Century Fibre Company: A New Model," *Textiles Magazine* 31, no. 1 (April 2004): 21–22.

26. Wayne King, "King Cotton Is Seeking Throne Lost to Polyester," *New York Times*, September 27, 1976, 51, 53.

27. *Greenwood (Miss.) Commonwealth*, June 3, 1984, 46.

28. *Greenville (Miss.) Delta Democrat-Times*, April 11, 1971, 5.

29. "Beltwide Cotton Sessions to Stress Farm Profits," *Memphis Commercial Appeal*, January 10, 1971.

30. See, for instance, "Delta Women Make Plan for Promotion of Cotton," *Greenwood (Miss.) Commonwealth*, April 1, 1975, 3; "Cotton Inc. Report Given at Seminar," *Jackson (Miss.) Clarion-Ledger*, January 18, 1976, 41.

31. "Ginners May Draw 2,000," *Memphis Commercial Appeal*, February 27, 1977, 22.

32. "Plans Outlined," Greenville (Miss.) *Delta Democrat-Times*, April 3, 1975, 8.

33. "Cotton Producers Ready New Promotion Campaign," *Scott County Times* (Forest, Miss.), November 22, 1989, 10. See also *Greenwood (Miss.) Commonwealth*, November 19, 1989, 25.

34. "Cotton Is Making a Comeback in Fashion and Home Textiles," *Clarksdale (Miss.) Press Register*, October 8, 1975, 3.

35. "Cotton Becomes Fabric of Choice," *Greenwood (Miss.) Commonwealth*, June 3, 1984, 46.

36. *Clarksdale (Miss.) Press Register*, January 4, 1975, 7; *Memphis Commercial Appeal*, February 9, 1975, 40.

37. "Delta Cotton Wives Get Fashion Preview," *Greenwood (Miss.) Commonwealth*, October 30, 1977, 19.

38. "Cotton Inc. Seeks More Money for Promotion," *Yazoo (Miss.) Herald*, August 29, 1984, 22.

39. U.S. Censuses of Population, 1970, 1980, 1990; U.S. Censuses of Agriculture, 1969, 1974, 1978, 1982, 1987, 1992, 1997, 2002. I follow James C. Cobb's definition of the core eight Delta counties: Bolivar, Coahoma, Humphreys, Issaquena, Leflore, Quitman, Sharkey, and Sunflower (*Most Southern Place on Earth*, 335).

40. de Jong, *You Can't Eat Freedom*, 1–3, quotation on 4.

41. Greg Dickinson, Carole Blair, and Brian L. Ott, "Introduction: Rhetoric/Memory/Place," in *Places of Public Memory: The Rhetoric of Museums and Memorials*, ed. Greg Dickinson, Carole Blair, and Brian L. Ott (Tuscaloosa: University of Alabama Press, 2010), 13.

42. "Where Does All That Cotton Go After It Is Baled?," Greenville (Miss.) *Delta Democrat-Times*, November 3, 1976, 18.

43. Jane Biggers, "Cotton Reigns Supreme at Tallahatchie Home," *Jackson (Miss.) Clarion-Ledger*, November 17, 1972.

44. Cotton Incorporated, "New Cotton Symbol Identification Manual," n.d., Mullendore Collection.

45. David L. Jordening to Dr. George Mullendore, August 24, 1976, Mullendore Collection.

46. "Awareness of Cotton's Seal Continues to Grow," *Greenwood (Miss.) Commonwealth*, June 3, 1984, 46.

47. "Cotton's Trademark Turns Twenty!," *Clarksdale (Miss.) Press Register*, February 20, 1993, 38.

Chapter Ten. Old Times There Are Not Forgotten

1. "Million Dollar Plan Told," *Greenwood (Miss.) Commonwealth*, May 27, 1969, 1; "Tourism Possibilities Explained to Rotarians," *Jackson (Miss.) Clarion-Ledger*, May 28, 1969, 7; Carl McIntire, "Cottonlandia Plans," *Jackson (Miss.) Clarion-Ledger*, March 17, 1971, 75.

2. "Cottonlandia Seeks Gifts for Museum," *Greenwood (Miss.) Commonwealth*, July 27, 1971, 1.

3. Jimmy Thompson, "Suggestions Made for New Park," *Greenwood (Miss.) Commonwealth*, July 5, 1973, 1.

4. Hank Klibanoff, "New Park Goes to Leflore," *Greenville (Miss.) Delta Democrat-Times*, May 29, 1973, 8; "Editorial," *Greenwood (Miss.) Commonwealth*, May 30, 1973, 4, italics added.

5. Thompson, "Suggestions Made for New Park."

6. "Park Visitor Increase Seen," *Jackson (Miss.) Clarion-Ledger*, March 10, 1974, H5.

7. David L. Jordan with Robert L. Jenkins, *David L. Jordan: From the Mississippi Cotton Fields to the State Senate, A Memoir* (Jackson: University Press of Mississippi, 2014).

8. "Burns Backs Waller View," *Greenville (Miss.) Delta Democrat-Times*, July 28, 1974, 5.

9. "Plans for Farm Move Forward," *Greenville (Miss.) Delta Democrat-Times*, July 23, 1974, 8.

10. "Florewood Plantation: Past Pages," *Greenwood (Miss.) Commonwealth*, August 15, 1976, 39.

11. "Exotic Cotton Plants Are Planned," *Greenwood (Miss.) Commonwealth*, August 15, 1976, 52.

12. "Manpower, Mulepower at Farm," *Greenwood (Miss.) Commonwealth*, August 15, 1976, 40.

13. Ron Russell, "Sidetreks/Cotton Heritage Root of Pride in Greenwood," *Memphis Commercial Appeal*, September 19, 1980, 26.

14. William Schemmel, "In the Land of Cotton," *National Geographic Traveler*, September/October 1992, 106, italics added.

15. Wilbur Douglas Webb, "Florewood River Plantation State Park: Inspection and Maintenance Recommendations" (MA thesis, Mississippi State University, 1985), iv.

16. Susan Montgomery, "Florewood as Blues Park?," *Greenwood (Miss.) Commonwealth*, May 13, 2004, 1, 6.

17. "4 State Parks, Historic Site, May Be Closed, Sold, or Leased," *Jackson (Miss.) Clarion-Ledger*, June 1, 2004, 6.

18. Shelley Ritter email to author, November 7, 2022. Ritter was executive director of the Delta Blues Museum in Clarksdale, Mississippi.

19. LeRoi Jones (later Amiri Baraka), *Blues People: Negro Music in White America* (New York: William Morrow, 1963), 61.

20. Robert Palmer, "Muddy Waters: The Delta Son Never Sets," *Rolling Stone*, October 5, 1978.

21. Palmer, "Muddy Waters."

22. "W. H. Stovall," in *The Mid-South and Its Builders*, ed. C. P. J. Mooney (Memphis: Mid-South Biographic and Historical Association, 1920), 626.

23. Memphis Cotton Carnival Program, 1964, 11, box 3, Halle Papers.

24. Sandra B. Tooze, *Muddy Waters: The Mojo Man* (Toronto: ECW Press, 1997), 15.

25. Tooze, *Muddy Waters*, 15.

26. Dave Ferman, "A Birthplace to the Blues," *Fort Worth Star-Telegram*, June 24, 1990, section 6, p. 1.

27. Tooze, *Muddy Waters*, 15–16.

28. Waters interview in O'Neal and Singel, *Voice of the Blues*, 169.

29. Robert Gordon, *Can't Be Satisfied: The Life and Times of Muddy Waters* (Boston: Little, Brown, 2002), xvi.

30. *Memphis Commercial Appeal*, May 15, 1996, 4; *Biloxi Sun Herald*, May 17, 1996, 16.

31. *Jackson (Miss.) Clarion-Ledger*, April 9, 2001, 13.

32. Jim O'Neal quoted in O'Neal and Singel, *Voice of the Blues*, 157.

33. "Agriculture Ripe with Tourism Potential," *Greenwood (Miss.) Commonwealth*, August 1, 2001, 4.

34. Jim Auchmutey, "Welcome to the Hotel Mississippi: Shacks Are Chic in Clarksdale, the Crossroads of the Delta Blues," *Atlanta Journal Constitution*, July 29, 2001, K1.

35. Auchmutey, "Welcome to the Hotel Mississippi," *Atlanta Journal Constitution*, July 29, 2001, K1.

36. "The Ritz We Ain't," https://www.shackupinn.com/ourstory, accessed January 25, 2023.

37. "FAQ," https://www.shackupinn.com/faq, accessed January 25, 2023.

38. John Frow, "Tourism and the Semiotics of Nostalgia," *October* 57 (1991): 131.

39. Jennifer Ryan, "Beale Street Blues? Tourism, Musical Labor, and the Fetishization of Poverty in Blues Discourse," *Ethnomusicology* 55, no. 3 (2011): 473–503; Victoria J. Gallagher, "Remembering Together: Rhetorical Integration and the Case of the Martin Luther King, Jr. Memorial," *Southern Communication Journal* 60 (1995): 109; Brian Foster, *I Don't Like the Blues: Race, Place, and the Backbeat of Black Life* (Chapel Hill: University of North Carolina Press, 2020); Stephen A. King, *I'm Feeling the Blues Right Now: Blues Tourism in the Mississippi Delta* (Jackson: University Press of Mississippi, 2011); David Grazian, *Blue Chicago: The Search for Authenticity in Urban Blues Clubs* (Chicago: University of Chicago Press, 2005).

40. "Leflore County Looking at Buying Florewood," *Jackson (Miss.) Clarion-Ledger*, August 4, 2004, 10.

41. "Leflore County."

42. "Leflore County."

43. "What's Next for Florewood Park?," *Greenwood (Miss.) Commonwealth*, June 24, 2018, A1, A8.

44. "What's Next?"

45. "Vaccinations Moving to Florewood," *Greenwood (Miss.) Commonwealth*, January 28, 2021.

46. "Museum of the Mississippi Delta to Host Anniversary Party," *Greenwood (Miss.) Commonwealth*, November 9, 2019, C1.

47. Leonard Pitts Jr., "Mississippi Turning?," *Miami Herald*, February 16, 2003, J1, J7.

48. Pitts, "Mississippi Turning?," J7. All remaining quotations from Pitts are found on this page.

49. U.S. Department of Agriculture, National Agricultural Statistics Service, *2002 Census of Agriculture*, vol. 1: *Geographic Area Series* (Washington, D.C.: Government Printing Office, 2004).

50. U.S. Census Bureau, Census 2000 Summary File, https://www2.census.gov/census_2000/census2000/sumfile1.html.

Conclusion. Look Away, Dixieland

1. James C. Giesen, *Boll Weevil Blues: Cotton, Myth, and Power in the American South* (Chicago: University of Chicago Press, 2011), chaps. 5 and 6, quotation on 133.

INDEX

ENVIRONMENTAL HISTORY AND THE AMERICAN SOUTH

Lynn A. Nelson, *Pharsalia: An Environmental Biography of a Southern Plantation, 1780–1880*

Jack E. Davis, *An Everglades Providence: Marjory Stoneman Douglas and the American Environmental Century*

Shepard Krech III, *Spirits of the Air: Birds and American Indians in the South*

Paul S. Sutter and Christopher J. Manganiello, eds., *Environmental History and the American South: A Reader*

Claire Strom, *Making Catfish Bait Out of Government Boys: The Fight Against Cattle Ticks and the Transformation of the Yeoman South*

Christine Keiner, *The Oyster Question: Scientists, Watermen, and the Maryland Chesapeake Bay Since 1880*

Mark D. Hersey, *My Work Is That of Conservation: An Environmental Biography of George Washington Carver*

Kathryn Newfont, *Blue Ridge Commons: Environmental Activism and Forest History in Western North Carolina*

Albert G. Way, *Conserving Southern Longleaf: Herbert Stoddard and the Rise of Ecological Land Management*

Lisa M. Brady, *War upon the Land: Military Strategy and the Transformation of Southern Landscapes During the American Civil War*

Drew A. Swanson, *Remaking Wormsloe Plantation: The Environmental History of a Lowcountry Landscape*

Paul S. Sutter, *Let Us Now Praise Famous Gullies: Providence Canyon and the Soils of the South*

Monica R. Gisolfi, *The Takeover: Chicken Farming and the Roots of American Agribusiness*

William D. Bryan, *The Price of Permanence: Nature and Business in the New South*

Paul S. Sutter and Paul M. Pressly, eds., *Coastal Nature, Coastal Culture: Environmental Histories of the Georgia Coast*

Andrew C. Baker, *Bulldozer Revolutions: A Rural History of the Metropolitan South*

Drew A. Swanson, *Beyond the Mountains: Commodifying Appalachian Environments*

Thomas Blake Earle and D. Andrew Johnson, eds., *Atlantic Environments and the American South*

Chris Wilhelm, *From Swamp to Wetland: The Creation of Everglades National Park*

Christopher C. Sellers, *Race and the Greening of Atlanta: Inequality, Democracy, and Environmental Politics in an Ascendant Metropolis*

Gregory S. Wilson, *Poison Powder: The Kepone Disaster in Virginia and Its Legacy*

Caroline Rose Peyton, *Radioactive Dixie: A Nuclear History of the American South*

James C. Giesen, *The Land of Cotton: Culture, Landscape, and the Fabric of Southern History*